P9-AFV-094

DATE DUE

MY 21 '93			
OC 9 '93			
OC 21 '94			
MY 19 '95			
JY 27 '95			
MY 17 '96			
OC 2 '99			
AP 8 00			
JE 6 00			
MY 23 02			
AG 5			

Demco, Inc. 38-293

VISIONS OF A FLYING MACHINE

SMITHSONIAN HISTORY OF AVIATION SERIES

Dominick A. Pisano, Series Editor

On December 17, 1903, on a windy beach in North Carolina, aviation became a reality. The development of aviation over the course of little more than three-quarters of a century stands as an awe-inspiring accomplishment, in both a civilian and a military context. The airplane has brought whole continents together; at the same time it has been a lethal instrument of war.

The Smithsonian History of Aviation Series is intended to contribute to the over-all understanding of the history of aviation—its science and technology as well as the social, cultural, and political environment in which it developed and matured. Some publications help fill the many gaps that still exist in the literature of flight; others add new information and interpretation to current knowledge. While the series appeals to a broad audience of general readers and specialists in the field, its hallmark is strong scholarly content.

The series is international in scope and includes works in three major categories: Smithsonian Studies in Aviation History, works that provide new and original knowledge; Smithsonian Classics of Aviation History, carefully selected out-of-print works that are considered essential scholarship; and Smithsonian Contributions to Aviation History, previously unpublished documents, reports, symposia, and other materials.

VISIONS OF A
FLYING
MACHINE

The Wright Brothers and the Process

of Invention

Peter L. Jakab

Smithsonian Institution Press   Washington and London

Riverside Community College
Library
4800 Magnolia Avenue
MAY '92   Riverside, California 92506

```
TL670.5 .J35 1990
Jakab, Peter L.
Visions of a flying machine
: the Wright brothers and
the process of invention
```

Copyright © 1990 by the Smithsonian Institution
All rights reserved
Editor: Debra Bertram
Designer: Janice Wheeler

Library of Congress Cataloging-in-Publication Data
Jakab, Peter L.
    Visions of a flying machine : the Wright brothers and the process
of invention / Peter L. Jakab.
        p.   cm.—(Smithsonian history of aviation series)
    Includes bibliographical references.
    ISBN 0-87474-456-3
    1. Airplanes—History.   2. Wright, Orville, 1871–1948.   3. Wright,
Wilbur, 1867–1912.   I. Title.   II. Series.
TL670.5.J35   1990
629.13′092′2—dc20   89-39643

British Library Cataloging-in-Publication Data available

For permission to reproduce individual illustrations appearing
in this book, please correspond directly with the owners of
the works, as listed in the photo credits at the back
of the book. The Smithsonian Institution Press does not retain
reproduction rights for these illustrations individually or
maintain a file of addresses for photo sources.

⊗ The paper used in this publication meets the minimum
requirements of the American National Standard for Permanence
of Paper for Printed Library Materials Z39.48–1984.

Manufactured in the United States of America

5   4   3   2   1   94   93   92   91   90

To
László Jakab
and
Alice Alvinczy Jakab

Two Americans who made the journey

Isn't it astonishing that all these secrets have been preserved for so many years just so that we could discover
them!!

Orville Wright

June 7, 1903

Contents

Foreword

Eighty-five years after the invention of the airplane, Wilbur and Orville Wright have lost none of their power to fascinate and intrigue us. A veritable ocean of ink has been spilled in attempts to tell their story. Arthur G. Renstrom's classic bibliography, *Wilbur and Orville Wright: A Bibliography*, published by the Library of Congress in 1968, lists thousands of closely packed entries on 176 double-column pages. And that was only the beginning. An unabated flood of biographies, children's books, technical articles, and scholarly monographs on the subject continues to flow from the presses.

Just when it seems that there is little more to be usefully said about the two brothers from Dayton, along comes someone like Peter Jakab to surprise and delight us with fresh insights. The book that you hold in your hands differs from many earlier studies of the invention of the airplane that brush lightly over the key technical issues of the story. It takes us straight to the heart of the Wright achievement, focusing on the technology and offering a clear and concise statement of precisely *what* the Wrights accomplished and *how* they did it.

At its core, this is a book about the process of invention. The author begins by defining the problem of the flying machine as it was understood when the Wrights entered the field in 1899. He then proceeds to describe how the brothers identified and resolved the range of technical puzzles that had baffled the best-trained engineers and scientists for over a century.

Step by step, he walks us down the path of invention blazed by the Wright brothers. Along the way, we come to understand and appreciate the fundamental nature of the Wright genius—their ability to conceive solutions to the most difficult technical problems as concrete mental images. Simply put, the Wrights had an extraordinary gift for visualizing abstraction.

Nowhere is the value of this ability more apparent than in the story of the wind tunnel experiments of 1901. The Wrights had reached a frustrating impasse. They knew that there was an error in one or more of the experimentally derived coefficients employed in the equations used to design their flying machines. But which of the long-accepted coefficients was incorrect, and to what extent?

To solve the problem, the Wrights designed a pair of wind tunnel balances that functioned as mechanical analogs of the equations for lift and drag. In a few short weeks of concentrated effort, they were able to measure the minute fluctuations in pressure dancing over their tiny wings in such a way as to isolate the coefficients and correct the error. In the process, they also identified the most efficient airfoil among all of those tested. Other authors have *told* us that the wind tunnel experiments were important. Peter Jakab explains why they were important and what the experiments tell us about the Wrights' thought processes.

This is a book about the invention of the airplane, but it offers important insight into a much broader range of questions. In focusing our attention on the nature of Wilbur and Orville Wrights' achievement, the author sheds new light on the fundamental nature of the inventive process. The result is a book of lasting interest and value to all students of innovation in technology and science.

Tom D. Crouch

Acknowledgments

The first book of every young scholar has a long trail of people in its wake that helped to train the author and to shape his or her thinking. This one is no exception. To the lengthy list of teachers, advisors, colleagues, family, and friends who have assisted me in one way or another through graduate school and my beginning years as a professional historian, I express a resounding thank you.

A number of individuals deserve special mention. Tom D. Crouch, the recognized authority on early aeronautics and the Wright brothers, has always been ready to drop everything in his busy schedule to share his vast expertise on the subject and his experience as an author. Our many phone conversations and luncheon discussions over the past several years have contributed in countless ways to my understanding of the Wright achievement and of the brothers as human beings, as well as to my development as a writer. Few students enjoy as productive and rewarding a relationship with a senior scholar as this one has been. My research effort on the Wright brothers has yielded not only a book, but a valued friend and colleague.

Great appreciation goes to Howard S. Wolko, special advisor for technology in the aeronautics department at the Smithsonian Institution's National Air and Space Museum, who honed my understanding of how an airplane flies and helped me through the complexities of the Wright brothers' wind tunnel experiments. John D. Anderson, special advisor for aerodynamics in the aeronautics department, also extended many helpful and enthusiastic comments concerning the science of flight as it related to the Wrights.

Two other National Air and Space Museum staff members, Von D.

Hardesty and Dominick A. Pisano, offered numerous useful comments and suggestions and showed unwavering personal support of my work. They too have become trusted and valued friends and colleagues over the course of the project.

Rick and Sue Young, fellow Wright scholars and builders of a reproduction 1902 Wright glider, shared many important insights into the design and construction of Wright aircraft, as well as what it's like to climb on board a Wright flying machine and challenge the sand dunes at Kitty Hawk firsthand. I am also in debt to craftsmen Karl Heinzel, Richard Horigan, and Reed Ferguson of the National Air and Space Museum's aircraft restoration facility, who provided an opportunity to examine the disassembled original 1903 Wright Flyer during its 1985 restoration.

Gratitude is extended to Professor Virginia Yans-McLaughlin of Rutgers University and Professor John H. Morrow, Jr., of the University of Georgia for their careful reading of the manuscript and their constructive comments. Thanks also goes to Barbara Brennan of the National Air and Space Museum exhibits department for her preparation of the graphs and the diagrams.

Two others deserve mention for their role in bringing this book to fruition. They are James Sharp, for never letting me take the labor of scholarship too seriously, and George Sirgiovanni, for always lending a sympathetic ear during periods of frustration.

My final word of acknowledgment might be described as a sign of the times. Shane S. Truffer, computer specialist in the office automation department at the National Air and Space Museum, retrieved and reconstructed the first half of the manuscript after it was badly scrambled by a computer virus. Words cannot express the sinking feeling an author endures when he sees fragments of Chapter 2 in Chapter 4, bits of Chapter 4 in Chapter 1, sections of the manuscript in the computer operating system, etc., and then realizes that all his backup disks are also infected. I will be forever grateful to Shane for taking a week of his valuable time to put my jumbled words back into some sort of readable order.

Peter L. Jakab

Introduction

One of the most significant and well-known artifacts in the history of technology is the Wright brothers' 1903 Flyer, the first powered airplane to fly successfully. The original aircraft hangs gracefully in the central exhibit gallery of the Smithsonian Institution's National Air and Space Museum. Lying prone in the pilot's position is a likeness of Orville Wright, dressed in a business suit, a stiff collar, and a cap, the brothers' typical attire on the ground or in the air. When sunlight fills the spacious display hall illuminating the aircraft's translucent, fabric-covered structure, the airplane takes on a majestic quality that is synonymous with flight. Suspended in the air, this human-made assemblage of wood, fabric, and metal is completely within its element. It is a sight that fails to stir only the most jaded of onlookers.

As millions of visitors file past this treasured relic each year, what leaves the greatest impression on them is that this is the actual machine with which the Wrights inaugurated the aerial age. Through the original artifact it is possible, to a degree, to transcend time and identify with the Wright achievement in a very direct way. The Flyer is a visible, tangible symbol of the monumental inventive effort that has immortalized the Wright name.

Why do certain museum objects attain this level of popular, emotional appeal? Part of the answer lies in the cultural images we bring to them. With regard to the history of invention, there is a tendency to focus on the triumphant moment of success, the so-called eureka moment, when, in a flash of insight or with a groundbreaking creative act, a new discovery or invention is born. Often the laborious, less romantic aspects of the inventive process are supplanted by simplified, dramatic renditions of heroic accomplishment. Images of larger-than-life figures such as Thomas Edison "inventing" the electric light with the dramatic illumination of an incandescent lamp for over thirteen hours on October 21, 1879, or Alexander Graham Bell inaugurating the telephone with his famous phrase, "Watson, come here! I want you," on March 10, 1876, are as much a part of America's cultural heritage as the art of Whistler and the poetry of Frost.

These romanticized versions of events tend to enhance the intrinsic significance of the objects connected with them. The artifacts often assume a cultural importance that is distinct from what they represent technologically or historically. The Wright Flyer certainly has taken on this characteristic. The remarkable degree of public interest, and often veneration, attributed to this object reflects its powerful symbolism as a testament to human ingenuity in general, apart from the specific technological contributions to aeronautics it embodies. Few other artifacts on display at the Smithsonian Institution engender such an immediate and universal response of awe and excitement as this one.

Despite this great interest and familiarity with the Wright Flyer, the true nature of its development and the men who created it is not widely known or understood. The accomplishments of people such as the Wrights, Edison, and Bell have made their names instantly recognizable. Yet the long, difficult paths that led to their world-changing technological milestones are often overshadowed by their subsequent notoriety. The average general history text devotes little to the history of invention beyond enumerating important technological firsts and providing brief biographical details about the extraordinary individuals responsible for them. These sketchy popular treatments are typically reinforced by melodramatic Hollywood productions depicting great inventors as heroic figures leading the world triumphantly into a new age with the fruits of their genius. The complex and plodding course of study and experimentation that invariably characterized their creative endeavors is rarely presented.

Of all the names on the roster of great American inventors, perhaps none are shrouded in more of these false impressions than Wilbur and Orville Wright. They have attained a level of popular appeal that compares with Abraham Lincoln and a degree of recognition that rivals George Washington. Their inventive work has been divorced from its technological and scientific context and likened by some to the achievements of intellectual giants such as Einstein. They have been plucked out of the nineteenth-century midwestern American setting in which they lived and worked and delivered to us as a pair of clever and beneficent bicycle mechanics who made the airplane their gift to the world.

Part of the reason why the Wrights have attained such a lofty popular standing stems from an enduring question regarding their aeronautical achievement. How were these two men, working essentially alone, with little formal scientific or technical training, able to solve a problem so complex and demanding as heavier-than-air flight in only a few short years, when it had defied better-known experimenters for centuries? On the surface, the fact that the Wrights did invent a successful airplane quickly and with little assistance would suggest that genius had to have been at work. Popular accounts that have done little more than glowingly highlight the brothers' steps to mechanical flight understandably have led to an uninformed, superficial assessment of them as inventive supermen. If, however, the subject is addressed in a more substantive, analytical way, avoiding the celebratory aspect of the story, it is possible to grasp a meaningful understanding of the brothers' accomplishment. The technology they created can be explained clearly and thoroughly.

The following investigation of the invention of the airplane steps back from the enormity of the Wright achievement and analyzes objectively their approach and techniques. It takes the reader through their research and experiments step by step, illustrating how Wilbur and Orville worked through each major problem. If close attention is paid to their methodology, it becomes quite apparent that there were a number of specific personality traits, innate skills, and particular research techniques present in the Wrights' approach that came together in a unique way and largely explain why these two men invented the airplane. In short, the Wrights had a definable method that in very direct terms led them to the secrets of flight.

Addressing the fundamental question of why Wilbur and Orville Wright were the inventors of the airplane from the perspective of their methodology offers both a credible explanation of their contributions to aeronautics and a legitimate foundation for their stature as great inventors. The Wright brothers do indeed deserve much of their towering popular reputation. But their genius should be understood in terms of the approach they evolved and employed to create the technology of flight, not just the singular act of getting a machine into the air.

Despite the sea of ink that has been spilled in attempts to portray the Wrights and their achievement, a thorough, analytical explanation of how they invented the airplane has never been wholly achieved. Many books on the subject—and there are several fine ones—attempt to present a biography of Wilbur and Orville as well as provide a complete account of their work. Typically, in an effort to accomplish both of these admittedly demanding tasks, previous authors do neither exhaustively. In spite of this drawback, there are a number of well-written, informative books on the subject. Among the most worthwhile full treatments of the life and work of the Wright brothers are Harry Combs, *Kill Devil Hill: Discovering the Secret of the Wright Brothers*; Fred Howard, *Wilbur and Orville: A Biography of the Wright Brothers*; and Fred C. Kelly, *The Wright Brothers*.

The best work on the subject to date is Tom D. Crouch's *The Bishop's Boys: A Life of Wilbur and Orville Wright*. This is the first true biography of the Wrights in the sense that the roots of their personalities and their approaches to life and work are thoroughly addressed. This is also the first treatment of Wilbur and Orville in which a rich portrait of the brothers emerges distinct from their persona as the inventors of the airplane. Crouch does a fine job with the technology as well. However, his heavily biographical style makes it difficult for him to explain thoroughly the complex inventive effort of the Wrights.

Where this study breaks new ground is in its approach. It is not a biography. It specifically addresses Wright technology within a fresh conceptual framework. By examining the brothers' achievement from the perspective of their creative method, the aeronautical work of the Wrights is more clearly explained and can be better evaluated in the larger context of the history of invention. What they accomplished can now be compared more readily with the work of other aeronautical experimenters, as well as with the achievements of nineteenth-century inventors in other fields.

An analysis of inventive method presents special problems for the historian. Traditional forms of literary documentation do not always convey the essence of creativity completely. So many of an inventor's actions and design choices are intuitive and not written down. Quite often it is apparent from examining a series of actions taken by an inventor what he or she was thinking when making a particular conceptual breakthrough or creating a piece of hardware, but it is not possible to document these thought processes directly with a letter or a notebook entry. Sketches, drawings, and photographs, as well as actual artifacts, can help the historian piece together an accurate sequence of events. Relying too heavily on this form of interpretative judgment, of course, runs the risk of putting thoughts in the inventor's head that never existed. Nonetheless, if used carefully in conjunction with literary documentation, conclusions based on this kind of indirect evidence are valid. In many cases, it is the only means of rendering an account of a critical period in the creation of an invention.

Despite the abundant collection of correspondence, diaries, and notebooks left by the Wright brothers, a number of the more important decisions they made during the course of their aeronautical work were not recorded clearly or completely. In certain instances, I have expressed what I believe took place based on the alternative forms of evidence pointed to above. At times, the particular way in which the Wrights thought through a problem becomes apparent by analyzing the specific steps the brothers took, which are documented, even though they do not reveal explicitly what they were thinking. Scrutinizing the design of the aircraft, which is shown in photographs and drawings, and examining the actual airplane have provided other entrées into the brothers' thought processes. Pairing this type of evidence with the Wrights' explicit statements regarding their inventive effort widens the base of information upon which to interpret and explain their work.

My insights into the Wrights' invention of the airplane have stemmed from yet another means of inquiry. It was possible to recreate some of the brothers' experiences, based on accurate reproductions of various examples of Wright technology, in an effort to confirm information that is only alluded to or commented upon sparingly in their papers. Personal experience using a reproduction of the Wrights' wind tunnel and interviews with individuals who have built and experimented with reproduction Wright aircraft and engines have helped to clarify several aspects of the brothers' thought process that they themselves only vaguely express. Care has to be exercised when drawing conclusions from artifacts that are not in fact historical, only built from historical

sources. But, again, if used only to support or supplement more traditional evidence, this technique can provide information otherwise lost
or unavailable to the historian.

1

Why Wilbur and Orville?

The inventive method that undergirded the Wright brothers' aeronautical research and experimentation was comprised of many elements. Some were techniques readily adopted from common engineering practice, others were innate abilities of a less tangible nature. The blending of these standard approaches to technical investigation and the Wrights' own unique talents resulted in the impressive flow of creativity that produced the world's first airplane.

In general, the Wright brothers' approach to mechanical flight reflected a strict engineering perspective. They did not develop their aircraft using uninformed trial-and-error methods like so many of their contemporaries, nor did they tackle the problem as theoretical scientists.[1] The distinctions are important to understanding the Wrights' inventive process. Wilbur and Orville did not set out to discover the theoretical principles of flight in the same sense that Newton or Einstein sought to explain physical phenomena in nature. The Wrights' work focused explicitly on determining the design features required to make an airplane fly. Among their considerations, for example, were the shape of the airfoil; the size and layout of the wing platform; and the type and the location of stabilizing surfaces, structural design, materials, and control mechanisms. While they certainly took advantage of established scientific tenets and formulas pertaining to the forces involved in heavier-than-air flight, they did not develop any that were fundamentally new. They investigated the relationships between such things as lift and drag, flight loads and structure, and stability and control in order to find the best combination of design features for the size and form of aircraft they believed would fly. The goal was less to under-

1. Wilbur (left) and Orville Wright pose for the camera on the back porch of their Dayton home in June of 1909.

stand *why* in principle these forces behaved as they did than to learn *how* in actual practice they acted with respect to one another, and in turn to use this information to construct a successful flying machine. This was engineering in its most basic form and the supporting foundation for all other aspects of the Wrights' inventive method.[2]

The keen engineering technique that characterized their work was not the product of professional training in engineering. In fact, neither Wilbur nor Orville received their high school diplomas. Because of a sudden family move back to Dayton, Ohio, in June of 1884, Wilbur was unable to complete all the final requirements of his senior year curriculum at an Indiana high school. Despite being nearly finished, Wilbur never bothered to complete his formal course of study. Orville chose not to follow the prescribed curriculum in his junior year, opting for a series of advanced college preparatory courses instead. As a result, he was not going to qualify for his high school degree at the end of his senior year and decided to forgo attending school at all for that term. Like his brother, Orville evinced little concern over missing out on his degree.

Despite their lack of interest in formal credentials, the Wrights were committed to broad learning and were excellent students. They made good use of the extensive family library and supplemented their formal schooling with a great deal of private study. They excelled in mathematics and science, and were both well read in the humanities and fine writers. Years later, Orville reflected upon the environment he and his siblings grew up in:

We were lucky enough to grow up in an environment where there was always much encouragement to children to pursue intellectual interests; to investigate whatever aroused curiosity. In a different kind of environment, our curiosity might have been nipped long before it could have borne fruit.[3]

The Wrights are often described as high school dropouts. While this is true, such a characterization belies their extensive self-education and their strong intellect.[4]

An important beginning step of the Wrights' engineering approach to human flight was to become acquainted with the work of previous experimenters. By the time the brothers began their study of flight at the close of the nineteenth century, a growing community of aeronautical experimenters had emerged. As the field slowly organized, publication and dissemination of aeronautical research grew more widespread.[5] Through contact with several key individuals and sources of information, the brothers were able to digest the work of generations of experimenters. Familiarization with these prior developments aided the Wrights in defining the basic obstacles to human flight and outlining their initial approach to the problem. Their literature search enabled them to take advantage of already established principles and to avoid dead-end paths pursued by others.

Merged with this basic engineering perspective and its associated practices were a number of conceptual capabilities and approaches present in the Wrights' method that in large measure explain why they were able to invent the airplane. Among the most important was their capacity for developing conceptual models of a problem that could then be transformed into practical hardware. Both brothers were adept at moving back and forth between the abstract and the concrete. This is seen most notably in the wind tunnel experiments they performed. The test instruments the Wrights designed and built to gather aerodynamic data on lifting surfaces mirrored the conceptual and mathematical models they developed to represent the physical forces generating lift and drag on a wing. These devices were mechanical analogs of the equations the Wrights used to calculate the size and the projected performance of their flying machines. As such, the information yielded by these instruments could be incorporated directly into the design of their aircraft. The brothers' ability to turn abstract concepts into workable machinery reveals itself in several other crucial areas as well, such as in their development of an effective control system and their design of an efficient aerial propeller.

Another feature of the Wright brothers' creative thought process that figured prominently in their advance toward powered flight was the great extent to which they used graphic mental imagery to conceptualize basic structures and mechanisms, even aerodynamic theory. In recent years, historians have pointed increasingly to the role of nonverbal thought in engineering and invention.[6] A great many of the objects surrounding us were designed in part by mental visualizations. Even though there may be fundamental mathematical relationships or articulated scientific principles that underlie the creation of a new machine or structure, there is invariably a distinct facet of the design that is aesthetic in nature, an aspect that results from the maker's intuitive sense of what will or will not work, or what "looks" right or wrong.

This aesthetic element is not limited merely to the object's appearance. The more important contribution centers on the technical feasibility and the physical arrangement of components that leads to the design's success or failure. Especially creative and productive inventors and engineers quite often have an acutely developed ability to think pictorially and spatially in addition to facility in the use of verbal forms of thought. They can visualize an object in their mind, turn it over, form new images of it, incorporate old forms from other designs, and, finally, arrive at a much-improved device or something totally original that will accomplish new goals. This part of the creative process cannot be reduced to unambiguous verbal descriptions. The designer literally has a vision of what the object or structure should look like and how it will work and, in conjunction with verbal forms of knowledge, produces a tangible article based upon what has already been seen in the mind's eye.

Individuals who are adept at this mental manipulation of images are often the ones who conceptualize useful and practical combinations of component parts, or modifications to individual devices, that result in original inventions or more sophisticated technological systems. They and the fruits of their creativity stand out because they are able to see a workable arrangement of the essential elements of a proposed invention or existing device in ways that have eluded others.

Samuel F. B. Morse, for example, built his successful electromagnetic telegraph in 1837 after all the basic scientific principles and technical components necessary for transmitting intelligence electronically were in place. His unique accomplishment was the first working, practical arrangement of these critical elements. He had no greater understanding of the scientific principles involved than other contemporary experimenters in the field, nor was he more skillful. In fact, Morse was rather inept mechanically and turned out to be a poor telegraph operator. What he did possess was an ability to visually conceptualize a workable interrelationship of the basic elements of the telegraph. His capacity to puzzle through the problem using concrete mental imagery was central to his making the primary breakthroughs that opened the door to instantaneous long-distance communication.[7]

Design is a process that is characterized by numerous evolving combinations of alternative forms. Spatial thinking and mental manipulation of graphic images are clearly at the heart of this activity. Examples such as Morse and the telegraph demonstrate that, frequently, truly groundbreaking technological innovations are not based solely on articulated scientific or engineering principles, mathematical calculations, or other forms of knowledge that can be expressed verbally. Wilbur and Orville's facility for nonverbal thought was among the most prevalent and salient aspects of their inventive method.

The brothers' emphasis on continuity of design was another key to their success. Their path to practical flight moved through an evolving series of gliders and powered machines of a single basic design, each incorporating what was learned from the previous craft. Haphazard, mercurial approaches to flight research were common among their contemporaries, and rarely productive.[8] The Wrights' aeronautical work, on the other hand, was a coherent program of experimental development that finally led to success.

The Wrights' persistent attention to the overall goal of a completely successful flying machine during every phase of the work was also an important aspect of their inventive method. Each experimental glider and powered airplane they built, as well as every individual element of each aircraft, was seen and valued in terms of the ultimate aim of building a practical aircraft. The Wrights' approach was distinct among aeronautical experimenters in that they believed no specific component to be more important than any other. They recognized that every aspect of a workable flying machine must be designed to coordinate with every other. No matter how advanced the wing, without an adequate control system, an aircraft will not fly. No matter how effective the control system, without a sound structural design to carry the flight loads, an aircraft will not fly. And so on. Wilbur and Orville understood that an airplane is not a single device, but a series of discrete mechanical and structural entities that, when working in proper unison, resulted in a machine capable of flight. Moreover, realizing that the pilot is a part of this system, they devoted as much attention to learning to fly their aircraft as they did in designing and building them.

The Wright brothers are frequently described as having been good mechanics.[9] Their talents in this regard, however, went well beyond such a mundane characterization. They had a particularly acute sense of materials, knowing instinctively which worked best and how to manipulate them, and a highly developed, sensuous affinity for machines. They possessed an uncommon intuitive ability to see how various mechanical components and assemblies worked and how they fit together. With a sort of tactile ease, they could modify technological devices to improve their operation or turn them into something new.

A telling example of their mechanical aptitude dates from the late 1880s, when as young men the Wrights improved a printing press Orville was using to turn out a small local newspaper he had started. To make even copies they needed to devise a way of putting the exact amount of pressure required on the type each time. After rummaging around the Wright barn, Orville stumbled upon an old family buggy with a folding top. The mechanism that supported the top stretched it just enough to put it in proper position. This was precisely what was needed for the press. With Wilbur's help, the buggy frame was mated to the press bed. Even though some of Wilbur's suggestions for improving the press appeared to violate basic mechanical principles, the system worked perfectly. Some time later, a visiting foreman from the pressroom of a Denver newspaper came by to see the homemade press. After a thorough inspection he remarked, "'Well, it works, but I certainly don't see how it does the work.'"[10] This kind of mechanical ingenuity appeared time and time again in the Wrights' work and was another critical component of their inventive effort.

The Wrights' ability to draw upon their experience with other technologies also proved valuable to their invention of the airplane. They excelled at deriving significant connections between seemingly unrelated technologies. On numerous occasions, concepts and even basic hardware garnered from other fields were incorporated into their aeronautical work. Their familiarity with bicycles is a conspicuous example.

The Wrights are commonly described as bicycle mechanics turned airplane builders, yet the highly influential role bicycles played in their inventive work is rarely emphasized. More than a few late nineteenth-century prognosticators suggested that the ultimate resolution to the flying problem would rest with bicycle makers. One such forecaster, James Means, editor of the widely read aviation journal *The Aeronautical Annual*, published an article in the 1896 edition pointing to the links between bicycles and airplanes. "Wheeling is just like flying," he wrote. "To learn to wheel one must learn to balance; to learn to fly one must learn to balance."[11]

Bicycles had existed in various forms since the early nineteenth century. But they had no significant impact in the United States until the mid-1870s, when the famous high-wheel, or *ordinary*, bicycle was introduced from England by a Boston merchant named Albert A. Pope. In 1878, he contracted the Weed Sewing Machine Company of Hartford, Connecticut, to produce an American-made version of the British ordinary. Within a decade, Pope had produced a quarter of a million high-wheelers.[12]

In 1887, the bicycle craze in America began in earnest with the introduction, again from England, of the safety bicycle. The safety, with its

2. The Wright brothers' bicycle shop at 1127 West Third Street in Dayton.

two wheels of equal size, a sturdy frame, and a chain-driven transmission system, did not require quite the degree of athletic ability to ride as the ordinary. It therefore made the freedom of wheeling accessible to a much wider market. At the height of the 1890s bicycle boom, the industry was comprised of over three hundred companies and was producing more than a million bicycles per year.[13]

Like so many other Americans, Wilbur and Orville were quite taken by this new form of locomotion. In the spring of 1892, Orville bought a brand-new Columbia safety for the then-considerable sum of 160 dollars. A short time later, Wilbur purchased a used Eagle for half that price. The brothers quickly became avid cyclists. Orville demonstrated his prowess with many successful performances in local races. Their skill at riding, matched with an already established local reputation as skillful mechanics, prompted the brothers to go into the bicycle business before the year was out. They opened their first shop in December of 1892.[14]

The Wrights were not the only bicycle makers in their hometown of Dayton, Ohio. By the mid-nineties, there were no fewer than fourteen shops in the city doing a brisk business in response to the safety-bicycle craze that was sweeping America, and the Wrights' shop was by no means the biggest. Initially they only sold and repaired bicycles. But by 1895, with competition growing stiff, they decided to begin manufacturing their own line. By this time there were four other shops within two blocks of the Wrights'. The brothers' inaugural model was called the Van Cleve, in honor of their pioneering ancestors, who had been among Dayton's first settlers in the late eighteenth century.[15]

While the major bicycle manufacturers were employing mass-production techniques adopted from the firearm and sewing-machine industries, the Wrights remained small scale and continued to produce handmade originals. At a time when manufacturing was becoming increasingly mechanized and rapidly rushing toward the twentieth century, the Wrights stayed firmly within the classic artisan tradition of handcrafted, carefully finished individual pieces.[16] This kind of attention to detail and craftsmanship would be a hallmark of their flying machines. Every component of their aircraft was designed and built with great care and served a specific and essential function. It is a bit ironic that an invention that has been so influential in the twentieth century was the product of men whose approach was so firmly anchored in the nineteenth century.

Bicycles possess a number of significant conceptual links to the airplane, strongly suggesting that it was not coincidental that the invention of mechanical flight emanated from the minds of experimenters knowledgeable of these two-wheeled vehicles. One of the primary breakthroughs the Wrights made was the realization that a positive means of controlling, or balancing, an aircraft must be devised before any significant progress on the flying machine could be made. The bicycle is an unstable vehicle, but despite this characteristic it can still be balanced and kept under control. The Wrights' transference of this important concept to the airplane is clear, and it was central to the design of their aircraft. Their understanding of the operating principles of the bicycle prevented them from being hampered by the erroneous, though widely held, notion that control and instability were incompatible.

This was just one of several connections between bicycles and airplanes that the Wrights astutely saw. The engineering demands of light-weight, but strong, structures important in bicycle design would be even more crucial with aircraft. Their adaptation of the chain-drive-and-sprocket transmission system of the safety bicycle to link the engine and the propellers on their later powered airplanes is unmistakable. Even concerns regarding wind resistance and aerodynamic shape that are fundamental to aircraft design were addressed by bicycle makers. Of course, of the thousands of bicycle mechanics in America at this time, only two invented the airplane. Clearly there were many other elements critical to the Wrights' success with flight. A familiarity with bicycles, however, was certainly one of the important ingredients in the mix of factors leading to their achievement.

Beyond these approaches to technical investigation and their innate talents, the Wrights possessed a number of character traits and personal experiences that had a bearing on their being the inventors of the airplane.

Much has been made of the collaborative aspect of the Wrights' work.[17] So intertwined were their ideas and their contributions to the airplane, it has become difficult to distinguish them as individual personalities. From a historical perspective, they have become a single entity. This image was in part fostered by the brothers themselves. In April of 1912, only a few weeks before his sudden death from typhoid, Wilbur wrote,

From the time we were little children my brother Orville and myself lived together, played together, worked together and, in fact, thought together. We usually owned all of our toys in common, talked over our thoughts and aspirations so that nearly everything that was done in our lives has been the result of conversations, suggestions and discussions between us.[18]

This close interaction was a genuine and essential component of the Wrights' inventive work. It is unlikely that either Wilbur or Orville would have achieved alone what they did as a team. Even so, Wilbur's later reflection upon his relationship with his brother is a little overly romantic. As children their relationship was much like any pair of siblings four years apart, interested and caring but somewhat distant.[19]

As they approached adulthood, not much changed. Following a debilitating skating accident sometime in late 1885 or early 1886, Wilbur became extremely withdrawn. For several years he spent nearly all of his time reading and caring for his mother, who was dying of tuberculosis. He cut himself off from almost everyone and everything. One of Wilbur and Orville's older brothers, Reuchlin, wrote to their sister Katharine with growing concern: "What does Will do? He ought to do something. Is he still cook and chambermaid?"[20]

It was not until 1888, when Wilbur assisted Orville with the improvements to his printing press, that he began to emerge from his self-imposed confinement. After helping his younger brother redesign the press, he contributed articles and editorial assistance to the short-lived neighborhood newspaper. It was at this point that the brothers began to interact in the cooperative way that was so important to their later success with flight. There would be several more collaborative efforts on local newspapers over the next few years. Then, in 1892, they opened their first bicycle shop, firmly establishing the teamwork and close relationship that would be such a significant factor in the creation of the airplane.

In the summer of that year, a dispute erupted between the brothers that offers an interesting insight into their working relationship. The disagreement arose over the division of the proceeds garnered from the construction of a press for another local printing firm and from a rush printing job that had interrupted progress on the press. Initially it was decided that the profits from the jobs were to be divided evenly. But later on Orville felt that he was doing the lion's share of the work and believed the original agreement to be unfair.

What is telling about the incident is how the conflict was resolved. The family set up a mock "court," and the "complainant" and the "defendant" each wrote up formal depositions stating their positions. Wilbur argued for the "court" to determine a fair and equitable distribution of the earnings from both jobs, to order Orville to "apologize for his insulting conduct," and to request him "to keep his mouth shut in the future, lest he should again be guilty of befouling the spotless and innocent character of others." The results of the proceedings are unknown, but the affair reveals something about the way the brothers approached interpersonal conflicts between them, and how they dealt with others in general. As the brothers conducted their aeronautical work, there were many differences of opinion that produced heated discussions. But they never let these disputes interfere with their progress, always settling them in a constructive manner. In fact, these arguments

3. The brothers' father, Bishop Milton Wright,
1828–1917.

often helped to forge a collaborative answer to a difficult problem.[21]

In addition to the closeness between the brothers, their relationships with their father, Milton, and their sister, Katharine, also played an important role in their inventive success. Wilbur and Orville were two of seven children born to Milton Wright and Susan Koerner Wright, married in Indiana in 1859. Their first child, a son named Reuchlin, was born in 1861. The following year, Susan gave birth to another son, Lorin. Wilbur was next, born on April 16, 1867, near Millville, Indiana. After giving birth to a set of twins that died in infancy, Susan delivered

4. The Wrights' younger sister, Katharine, at the time of her graduation from Oberlin College in 1898. After receiving her degree, she taught classics at Steele High School in Dayton.

another healthy son, Orville, on August 19, 1871, in Dayton. The Wrights' last child, a daughter named Katharine, was born three years to the day after Orville, in 1874.[22]

By the time Wilbur and Orville began to think seriously about flight, only they, Milton, and Katharine still lived in the family home at 7 Hawthorn Street in Dayton. The older children had moved out and started families of their own. In 1889, Wilbur and Orville's mother, Susan, succumbed to tuberculosis. Katharine had taken over the responsibility of caring for the family when her mother became ill, and

5. The Wright family home at 7 Hawthorn Street, Dayton, Ohio.

she formally adopted that role after her death. The remaining four Wright family members became an extremely tightknit group. They shared everything with one another and provided a network of support that enabled them to weather all manner of crises. When any one of them was away, they corresponded almost daily, even if the absence was only for a few days.[23]

This supportive home life provided Wilbur and Orville with a belief in themselves that gave them the confidence to reject the theories of well-known and experienced aeronautical researchers when they felt their own ideas were correct.[24] The path to invention is littered with stumbling blocks and confusing dead ends. It takes a powerful belief in oneself to work through immensely perplexing problems and stand firm on personal conclusions, even if they run contrary to accepted wisdom. On a number of occasions, the Wrights were so confounded by the complexity of the aerodynamic and design problems they faced that they nearly gave up. At one point during their early glider experiments, Orville wrote home to Katharine,

We tried it with tail in front, behind, and every other way. When we got through, Will was so mixed up he couldn't even theorize. It has been with considerable effort that I have succeeded in keeping him in the flying business at all.[25]

Often it was the emotional anchor provided by their strong family ties that helped the Wrights persevere when things looked bleak. On a more pragmatic level, their father and Katharine assisted the brothers by looking after the bicycle shop while they were away experimenting with their aircraft and helping them prepare for the trips. If the role of Wilbur and Orville's home life is considered, it would not be entirely inaccurate to credit these *four* Wright family members with giving humans their wings.

Strong personal self-confidence was particularly important with respect to inventing the airplane because the brothers had to solve so many of the fundamental problems almost from scratch. After they familiarized themselves with the work of the major aeronautical experimenters prior to their own entrance into the field, the Wrights realized how little real progress had been made toward the resolution of the problem of mechanical flight. Once they began their work in earnest, it became apparent to them that they were quite on their own. They invented the airplane in a much truer sense than Edison the electric light or Morse the telegraph. The majority of the critical elements in the airplane were original to the Wrights, whereas with the electric light and the telegraph, the inventors achieved final success based on a much sounder, better-developed foundation of prior research. Without a deep reservoir of self-confidence, the Wright brothers would likely have been unable to conquer the many daunting challenges presented by the problem of human flight.

Another significant factor in their success was timing. One of the most striking things about the brothers' invention of the airplane was the relative speed with which they defined the problems, devised solutions, and took to the air. It took the Wrights only six years to progress from their first experimental kite to a fully practical powered airplane. Their phenomenal pace was largely a result of the creative approaches, the innate abilities, and the personal circumstances thus far described. But it was also partly attributable to their tackling the problem at a propitious moment.

When Wilbur and Orville emerged on the aeronautical scene in the late 1890s, a crucial phase of the prehistory of flight had drawn to a close. By that time, flying machines were no longer merely the domain of dreamers and visionaries. During the last half of the nineteenth century, mechanical flight had gained legitimacy as a worthwhile field of scientific and engineering research. A community of professional engineers and researchers interested in flight had evolved and were collectively amassing a body of aeronautical knowledge and technical data that provided the first definitive steps toward solving the problem of mechanical flight. This research was also being disseminated through publications and through gatherings of interested experimenters, further expanding and strengthening the reputation of aeronautics as a serious area of endeavor.[26]

As the century wound down, this building momentum slowed. Greater advancement had been made in the years since 1860 than in the preceding millennium. But despite all the promise shown during the last decades of the nineteenth century, final success remained elusive. Major barriers still existed, and the progress of the leading experimenters had reached a plateau. Many had come to the logical conclusion of their work, some had simply given up, and others had lost their lives in accidents.[27]

Despite this lull, the phase of aeronautical development just prior to the Wrights' entry into the field had yielded much productive research and had laid a foundation of critical inquiry that would be invaluable to the next generation of experimenters. The status of the invention of the airplane was still much like searching for a needle in a haystack, but now at least it was known in which haystack to look.

It was at this point that Wilbur and Orville began serious study of flight. The experience of their predecessors did more to reveal fundamental questions than to provide answers, but wading through the failures and the misunderstandings of others aided the brothers in focusing quickly on the basic problems that needed to be addressed. Much of what the Wrights accomplished was highly original, but the findings of the late nineteenth century definitely gave them several useful pieces to the puzzle, as well as saving them from many unfruitful avenues of research. If the brothers had been a generation older, it is not at all certain that they would have avoided the stumbling blocks of those who were working in the second half of the nineteenth century. The Wrights were especially talented to be sure, but there is no reason to believe their genius operated in a vacuum, and that they would have invented the airplane no matter when they took up the problem.

As we trace the Wrights' inventive work, it will become apparent that each advance was grounded in one or more of the principal elements of their methodology outlined in this chapter. It will become clear that the invention of the airplane was the product of a complex interaction of the Wrights' engineering techniques, creative abilities, and personality traits. It was the combination of these factors that distinguished them from their peers and led them to success. The term *genius* is often loosely applied to the Wright achievement. But if its use has any real meaning, it has more to do with these general aspects of the brothers' approach to invention than with their specific creation of the airplane. The following analysis of the brothers' inventive work from the perspective of their methodology therefore provides the clearest insight into how they produced the world's first airplane and yields the most enlightening answer to the question: Why Wilbur and Orville?

2

Aeronautics before the Airplane

The desire to fly is an ancient one, indeed. The famous myth of Daedalus and Icarus, kites in ancient China, medieval birdmen donning makeshift wings and leaping from towers, and the renowned work of Leonardo da Vinci are just a few of the more notable examples that reflect the long-standing human aspiration to emulate the birds. By the close of the eighteenth century, the thrilling sensation of flight could be experienced in free balloons. These initial ascents into the air were followed in the nineteenth century by a rapidly increasing number of attempts to build heavier-than-air flying machines. With their first successful airplane flights in 1903, the Wright brothers concluded a quest for wings that had spanned centuries.[1]

In light of this long preoccupation with flight, it is surprising to note that little technical progress was made in aeronautics prior to the nineteenth century. The reason for this, in large measure, lies in the complexity of the airplane. Although on the surface it would seem a simple matter to fashion a pair of homemade wings and launch oneself skyward, in fact, a practical flying machine presented enormous conceptual and technical challenges.

The first obvious requirement of a successful airplane is a lifting surface of some kind. The development of a suitable wing involves not only determining the size and planform of the surface, but also the shape of the wing profile, known as the airfoil. An additional aerodynamic surface or device that acts in conjunction with the wing to maintain stability in flight is also needed. Beyond these rudimentary aerodynamic elements, an airplane must have an effective means of control. Mechanical flight presents special structural demands as well. Unlike a stationary structure or most other forms of land or water transportation, building a lightweight airframe without sacrificing strength is a primary concern of aircraft design. Further, there is, of course, the question of propulsion. This includes not only the development of a light yet powerful engine, but also an efficient propeller and transmission system to convert horsepower into thrust to move the craft through the air.

Each of these basic aspects of the airplane presented its own set of complicated challenges. To resolve the problems associated with any one of these general elements was an extremely involved undertaking. Creating a successful airplane, however, necessitated finding solutions to all of them. So complex an array of tasks demanded a sustained and concerted effort. Isolated attempts at imitating winged creatures would not be enough. Organized programs of research through which individual contributions could be shared and incorporated into a usable corpus of aeronautical knowledge were required.

The refusal of trained scientists to take a serious interest in flight was one of the major reasons why such programs did not materialize more quickly than they did. Few considered the airplane a realistic possibility. For a long period, the absence of leadership from the scientific community relegated the dream of flight to the realm of absurd impracticality. Those professional scientists who had expressed formal interest in the airplane found themselves in a lamentable situation. The feeling of frustration is evident from the following comment, which appeared in the fifth annual report of the Aeronautical Society of Great Britain in 1870:

Now let us consider the nature of the mud in which we are stuck. The cause of our standstill, briefly stated, seems to be this: men do not consider the subject of 'aerostation' or 'aviation' to be a real science, but bring forward wild, impracticable, unmechanical, and unmathematical schemes, wasting the time of the Society, and causing us to be looked upon as a laughing stock by an incredulous and skeptical public.[2]

Without broader acceptance of aeronautics as a legitimate field of investigation, the necessary community of theorists, technicians, and experimenters that could identify the basic questions and develop viable avenues for research would be slow to evolve. It was only in the nineteenth century that such a set of circumstances came about, and that is why the origins of the practical airplane are comparatively recent. The

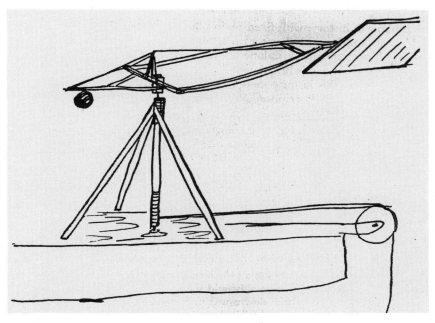

6. Sir George Cayley's first whirling-arm apparatus, used in 1804 to collect aerodynamic data on model wing surfaces.

Wright brothers' invention of the airplane was a highly original achievement; however, the first concrete advances made in aeronautics during the preceding century provided an important beginning foundation for their work.[3]

The critical turning point in the history of aviation was marked by the career of an English baronet from Yorkshire, Sir George Cayley. Working throughout the first half of the nineteenth century, Cayley was the first to mount a well-conceived, systematic program of aeronautical research grounded in scientific method. He was among the first to study bird flight beyond casual observance. He took note of the curvature of birds' wings and measured their weight, body surface, and velocity. Cayley was also the first to apply a whirling-arm apparatus to aeronautical experimentation. He attached a one-square-foot wing to one end of a horizontally rotating arm and a series of weights to the other. He then observed how much weight was lifted as the wing moved through the air at various speeds and angles. The inventor of

7. Cayley's silver disk, struck in 1799, showing his conception of the rudimentary elements of the airplane.

the whirling arm, Benjamin Robins, and other predecessors of Cayley
had originally used the device to measure the effects of air resistance
on projectiles and windmill sails.[4]

Cayley recognized that publishing his theories and findings was just
as important as performing the research. In a groundbreaking three-
part article that appeared in *Nicholson's Journal of Natural Philosophy,
Chemistry and the Arts* in 1809 and 1810 entitled "On Aerial Navigation," Cayley laid out the basic foundations of aerodynamics and flight
control. "The whole problem," he wrote, "is confined within these
limits—to make a surface support a given weight by the application of
power to the resistance of air."[5] It is evident from this article that Cayley had a sound understanding of the essential principles of flight. As
the first to grasp and articulate these ideas, Cayley stands as a pivotal
figure.

Although he never achieved his goal of powered flight, nor lived to
see the Wrights do it, Cayley set down several fundamental concepts
that, in general terms, define the airplane in its present-day form. He
conceived the airplane to be a machine with fixed wings, a fuselage,
and a tail, with separate systems to provide lift, propulsion, and control.
While this may seem self-evident and simplistic to the modern ob-

8. The obverse of the Cayley disk, showing a basic aerodynamic force diagram illustrating the lift and drag forces on a wing surface.

server, it was a major intellectual leap over all that had come before. Cayley commemorated his important breakthrough by striking a silver disk in 1799 with an image of the airplane as he conceived it. On the obverse, he inscribed an aerodynamic force-diagram showing the lift and drag vectors with respect to a lifting surface, further illustrating how clearly he understood the basic requirements for flight. But Cayley did more than theorize. He built and flew the world's first successful model glider in 1804 and, later, two full-size gliders capable of brief flights with a pilot on board. He made the all-important first steps away from the fanciful notions of flying machines that had dominated aeronautical thinking for centuries toward serious, experimentally based research that was directly linked to the success of Wilbur and Orville Wright in December of 1903. For these seminal steps toward the invention of mechanical flight, Cayley is identified as the Father of Aerial Navigation.[6]

Immediately following Cayley's initial breakthroughs during the first decades of the nineteenth century, a number of experimenters took up the study of flight. But they made few significant technical contributions. The absence of an organized drive focused on the goal of creating a successful airplane continued to thwart progress. The disparate mid-

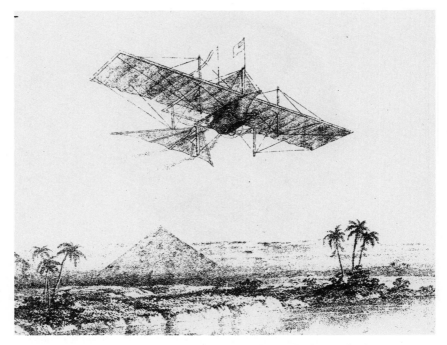

9. The *Aerial Steam Carriage*, designed by William Henson and John Stringfellow in 1842. Its forward-looking appearance influenced many subsequent experimenters.

century experimenters did advance aeronautics, however, by popularizing it and by beginning to attract professional engineers and other serious researchers to the field. The most noted practitioners of this variety were the Englishmen William Henson and John Stringfellow. Contemporaries of Cayley at the end of his career, they designed several aircraft based on the fixed-wing configuration. Although never built, the most famous and influential of these was the *Aerial Steam Carriage*, designed in 1842. It was quite modern in appearance with its fixed single wing, enclosed fuselage, and steam engine driving two propellers. Images of the aircraft were circulated widely, usually portraying it sailing gracefully over European cities or over faraway places such as China and the Pyramids.[7] Even though Henson and Stringfellow were minor figures in the history of aeronautics from a technical point of view, the *Aerial Steam Carriage* offered a compelling idea of what an airplane should look like for many future experimenters.

They and people like them were an important link between the pioneering Cayley and the community of dedicated, serious researchers who rapidly advanced the field of aeronautics after 1860.

The emergence in this period of an organized community of experimenters interested in aeronautics was in part due to a slowly growing belief that human flight was technically feasible. Equally important was the rise of professional engineering. As the Industrial Revolution displaced the artisan and traditional methods of handcrafting, a new and different group of technologists arose. While self-trained mechanics in the mold of Edison continued to make contributions to industrial development, more and more, modern technology emanated from an expanding pool of trained engineers.

In time, these engineers began to see themselves as an identifiable professional group. They possessed an ever-increasing body of esoteric knowledge based on specialized training, and they began applying their methods successfully to a wide variety of complex technical problems. With increasing ease, this new brand of professional technologist conquered the difficult challenges of the day. As a result, an ethos arose among engineers concerning their responsibility for solving society's difficult technical problems and benefiting all humankind. To legitimize their profession, they sought to create an institutional and organizational structure that would parallel that of scientists. Developments included the standardization of training and other basic qualifications, the establishment of professional societies, and, perhaps most importantly, the founding of journals in which research could be published and disseminated, thereby expanding the base of general engineering knowledge.[8]

The initial steps taken by Cayley and others and the emergence of the modern engineer were the critical factors that set the stage for significant progress toward a practical airplane in the last decades of the nineteenth century. The airplane now became just one more in a series of complex technical challenges through which engineers could demonstrate their prowess. They approached it in the same manner as any other mechanical problem, often finding elements of their previous professional experience directly applicable to aeronautics. For example, Octave Chanute, an accomplished American civil engineer, was able to transfer structural features of bridges to the construction of biplane-wing designs. By 1860, the development of a professional methodology that could be applied universally to technical problems made the resolution of mechanical flight seem as reasonable as that of any other challenge encountered by engineers. The final decades of the nineteenth century saw the emergence of a readily identifiable community of aeronautical pioneers coming out of this maturing engineering tradition.[9]

As this last important phase of pre-Wright aeronautics progressed, flight research became increasingly more active and better organized. Clear lines of experimentation arose, three in particular. Some experimenters believed that enough was known of aerodynamics for a full-size, piloted aircraft to be built and flown with little preparatory work. Another group of researchers suggested that the best approach was to start with models. Still others chose to experiment with full-size gliders before making the move to powered aircraft.[10]

Practitioners following the first avenue saw the development of a powerful, lightweight aeronautical engine as the only remaining significant barrier to human flight. The most prominent member of this group was Sir Hiram Maxim, an expatriated American living in England who had earlier achieved fame as the inventor of the machine gun. "Without doubt the motor is the chief thing to be considered," Maxim asserted in 1892. "Scientists have long said, Give us a motor and we will very soon give you a successful flying machine."[11]

In the early 1890s, Maxim built and conducted trials with a huge, four-ton biplane fitted with two very efficient steam engines, each delivering 180 horsepower, driving an eighteen-foot propeller. The aircraft, however, amounted to little more than a complex engine test-rig. It rode on an elaborate track equipped with guardrails to prevent it from rising more than a few inches. On the last of its trials, on July 31, 1894, after traveling six hundred feet down the track and reaching a speed of forty-two miles per hour, the airplane rose slightly, broke from the guardrails, and crashed. Maxim had indeed shown that, with enough power, a winged craft could be coaxed into the air for a brief hop. But his airplane was devoid of all the other elements necessary for practical flight and contributed little to the eventual resolution of the problem. Maxim did go on to perform some modest wind tunnel tests on curved airfoil surfaces in 1896, but this work did not lead anywhere.[12]

Another prominent experimenter who chose to build full-size, powered airplanes with little preliminary work with models or gliders was

10. Hiram Maxim's four-ton, behemoth flying machine resting on its track in 1894.

Clément Ader, a distinguished French electrical engineer who was a pioneer in the development of the telephone. Shortly before Maxim began his experiments with full-size aircraft, Ader attempted to fly a batlike, steam-powered machine called the *Éole*. Like Maxim's airplane, the sole remarkable feature of the *Éole* was its powerful, lightweight steam engine. Also like Maxim, Ader had given little serious thought to controlling his aircraft if it should somehow get off the ground. There was no elevator. Control was derived entirely from a complicated crank-and-worm-gear arrangement that moved the wings fore and aft. It required some twenty or thirty turns of the crank to make any aerodynamic effect, hardly an efficient means of control.[13]

In October of 1890, Ader staggered through the air at an altitude of eight inches for 165 feet with the *Éole*.[14] Similar to Maxim's later effort, Ader did no more than get his aircraft aloft with brute power. This was hardly flying. The work of Maxim and Ader demonstrated that the aerodynamic problems were far from resolved, or even completely understood, and that it would take a great deal more than the development of a suitable power plant before humans would be able to fly.

A second major approach to aeronautical research pursued by nineteenth-century experimenters was the study of flight using model

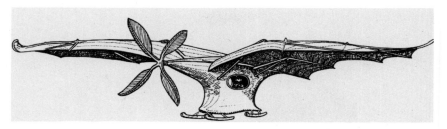

11. Clément Ader's *Éole*, 1890.

aircraft. Cayley first demonstrated the value of models with his classic glider of 1804. With its fixed wing and adjustable cruciform tail for stability, Cayley's 1804 glider can be considered the progenitor of all successful heavier-than-air flying machines.[15] For testing certain ideas, models had the obvious advantage over complex, full-size aircraft because of their relative simplicity, low cost, and rapid construction. If a comparatively large model could be made to fly, it was reasoned, it would only be necessary to scale the model up to a size capable of carrying a human being.

This seemingly logical, but erroneous, assumption led more than a few experimenters down a dead-end path. In fact, it led to the most heralded aeronautical failure of the era. After building and flying a series of successful, large steam-and-gasoline-powered models, Samuel P. Langley, eminent astronomer and secretary of the Smithsonian Institution, attempted in late 1903 to fly an enlarged, man-carrying version of his model design, the *Great Aerodrome*. Two highly publicized trials of the airplane resulted in disaster and made Langley the subject of vicious ridicule for the remaining three years of his life.[16] Such failures notwithstanding, the model aircraft approach made a far greater contribution to the growing corpus of aeronautical knowledge than that which resulted from the avenue taken by Maxim and Ader.

Of the many researchers who built models throughout the nineteenth century, by far the most influential was Alphonse Pénaud, a French marine engineer who had been confined to a wheelchair at a young age because of a debilitating hip disease. He introduced the use of twisted strands of rubber to power small models, a development that has no doubt helped stimulate childhood interest in aviation in every generation since.[17]

12. One of Samuel P. Langley's large, steam-powered models making a successful flight on May 6, 1896.

Pénaud's most significant contribution to aeronautics was his seminal work on *inherent stability*. This term describes the characteristic of an aircraft to return to equilibrium when disturbed by an outside force, such as a gust of wind. In 1871 he built and publicly flew a small, rubber-powered monoplane glider he called the *Planophore*. It maintained lateral inherent stability by incorporating dihedral angle (an upward cant of the wing tips) and longitudinal inherent stability by positioning the horizontal tail surface at a slight positive angle with respect to the wing. (Why this provides inherent stability will be addressed at length in Chapter 4, when the Wrights' design ideas regarding stability are discussed.) The *Planophore* was an important link between Cayley and the modern airplane. With it, Pénaud correctly theorized and demonstrated the fundamentally important concept of aircraft stability that Cayley exhibited, but did not fully understand, in his original 1799 con-

13. Langley's man-carrying *Great Aerodrome* collapsing upon itself immediately after takeoff on December 8, 1903, just nine days before the Wright brothers flew successfully at Kitty Hawk.

ception of the airplane and later gliders.

Frustrated and in ill health, Pénaud tragically took his own life in 1880 at the youthful age of thirty.[18] But besides having been the dominant figure in aeronautics during the 1870s, he inspired those who later contributed the most to the invention of the airplane, including the Wright brothers. Wilbur and Orville credited him as one of their most important predecessors.

The third and most fruitful approach taken to flight research in the late nineteenth century was the building and flying of full-size, man-carrying gliders. Experimenters taking this path believed in a gradual,

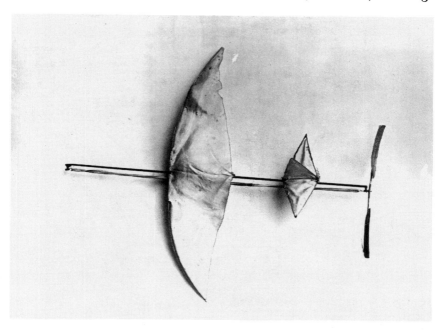

14. Alphonse Pénaud's 1871 rubber-band-powered model glider, the *Planophore*.

evolutionary path to powered flight. Careful study of aerodynamics would be followed by brief exploratory flights with simple hang gliders. Having gained a feel for handling a craft in the air, the next step would be a more sophisticated, powered glider, which in turn would be developed into a true airplane capable of sustained, controlled flight.

Here again, as with so many aspects of nineteenth-century flight research, George Cayley played a pioneering role. He built and tested a full-size glider in 1849 called the *Boy Carrier*. Although it flew only a few yards, it was the first time in history that a human being was carried aloft in a heavier-than-air craft. A second machine, known as the *Coachman Carrier*, also made a short flight in 1853. It was so named because Cayley's coachman was the reluctant pilot. After coming to a less than smooth landing, he is said to have emerged from the glider with the following admonition for his employer: "'Please, Sir George, I wish to give notice. I was hired to drive, and not to fly.'"[19] Although Cayley's gliding efforts did not produce any startling results, his aircraft

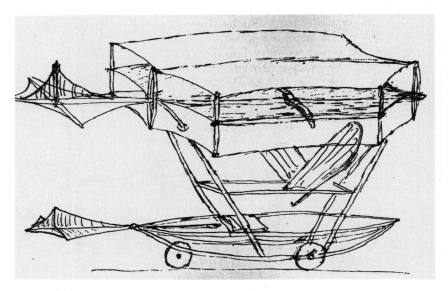

15. Cayley's 1849 *Boy Carrier* glider.

were based on his many years of aeronautical study. Unlike brave but reckless tower jumpers, who merely attempted to emulate birds with crudely fashioned wings, Cayley established a methodology for flight research that consisted of a thorough examination of aerodynamics followed by the construction of aircraft to test the results of that research. Virtually all experimenters who were making genuine progress in aeronautics toward the end of the nineteenth century worked in this way.[20]

Several experimenters made brief flights in unpowered aircraft during the second half of the nineteenth century, but without question the most famous and influential of all glider pioneers was Otto Lilienthal.[21] Born in the small village of Anklam, Pomerania, in 1848, he was trained in the highly regarded German technical education system. Following a stint in the military during the Franco-Prussian War, he went on to build a reputation as a talented engineer. By 1880 he was operating his own manufacturing plant near Berlin, producing small steam engines and marine foghorns, among other things.

Boyhood interest in flight evolved into serious study of aeronautics in 1879, when Lilienthal began a series of aerodynamic experiments

16. Otto Lilienthal, 1848–1896.

using a whirling arm and other techniques. Since childhood, he and his brother Gustav had been fascinated by bird flight, spending many hours observing the storks that populated the meadows surrounding Anklam. Careful examination convinced Lilienthal that the bird wing was a suitable model for human flight. The experiments he began in 1879 focused on revealing the dynamics of bird flight and determining the efficiency of various wing shapes and sizes.

A decade of imaginative research and experimentation by Lilienthal produced the best and most complete body of aerodynamic data of the day. He also established definitively the widely held belief that a curved wing section produces optimum lift.[22] Using his data and tables, an experimenter could easily calculate the size wing required to support a given weight at a particular velocity. This, of course, is a basic step necessary in the design of any airplane. Lilienthal published his important aerodynamic research in *Der Vogelflug als Grundlage der Fliegekunst* (Birdflight as the Basis of Aviation) in 1889, and in several

17. Lilienthal gliding in one of his standard monoplanes, using weight shifting to balance the craft.

other articles.[23] His work in this area became the established starting point for all serious turn-of-the-century aeronautical experimenters.

Lilienthal followed up his impressive program of data collection with the construction and the testing of a series of elegant, full-size gliders. Between 1891 and 1896 he made close to two thousand brief flights in sixteen different glider designs, which were based on his aerodynamic investigations. Most were monoplanes with stabilizing tail surfaces mounted at the rear. Lilienthal also tried a few biplane and folding-wing designs, but the original monoplane glider, or *Normal-Segelapparat* (standard sailing machine) as he called it, produced the best results. Upon seeing an assembled Lilienthal glider, Robert Wood, a Boston-based news correspondent, commented enthusiastically, "'Here was a flying machine, not constructed by a crank, . . . but by an engineer of ability. . . . a machine not made to look at, but to fly with.'"[24]

The gliders had split willow frames covered with cotton-twill fabric sealed with collodion to make the surface as airtight as possible. *Collodion* is a viscous solution of nitrated cellulose in a mixture of alcohol and ether that dries to form a tough elastic film. The wings ranged in area from ten to twenty square meters and could be folded to the rear for easier transport and storage. Control was derived by shifting body weight. The pilot cradled himself vertically in a harness suspended below an elliptical opening between the wings. Swinging his legs from side to side and fore and aft, the pilot could adjust the center of gravity and thereby maintain equilibrium. Lilienthal did most of his gliding from a manmade hill he had constructed near his home at Gross-Lichterfelde and from the hills surrounding the small village of Rhinow, about fifty miles from Berlin. His best efforts with these gliders covered over one thousand feet and were twelve to fifteen seconds in duration.

In the summer of 1896, Lilienthal's aeronautical experiments came to an abrupt end. On August 9, while soaring in one of his standard monoplane gliders, a strong gust of wind caused the craft to nose up sharply, stall, and crash from an altitude of fifty feet. Lilienthal suffered a broken spine and died the following day in a Berlin hospital.

It is, of course, hard to say what Lilienthal would have accomplished had he not been killed, but in all likelihood he had reached the limit of his contribution to solving the problem of mechanical flight. Although he made great strides in aerodynamics and design, he remained committed to two dead-end ideas that would have precluded further advancement.

The first of these was his method of control. Lilienthal's technique of shifting body weight as a means of maintaining equilibrium did place him ahead of other experimenters insofar as he recognized the need for a control system and gave attention to developing one. But, as revealed in his fatal crash, the control response of his method was very limited. Even more significant, weight shifting as a means of control placed a severe restriction on the aircraft's size. Because control was achieved by altering the aircraft's center of gravity as a result of repositioning the pilot's body weight, the weight of the aircraft had to be kept comparatively low. This presented a great problem in the design of a powered airplane. Any aircraft capable of lifting an engine and pilot, let alone any sort of a payload, would be of a size so large that weight shifting would be totally ineffectual.

The second pitfall that would have hindered any further advance toward the airplane by Lilienthal was his continued preference for flapping wing-tips as a means of propulsion long after the propeller had become widely accepted as the most practical method for generating thrust. Before his death, Lilienthal did build two powered aircraft. Both were equipped with a carbonic-acid gas motor driving flapping wing tips. Neither was successful, and they demonstrated an uncharacteristically short-sighted approach on Lilienthal's part to this area of flight research.

Despite Lilienthal's limited vision with regard to matters of control and propulsion, the enormity of his contribution to the ultimate creation of a successful powered airplane is undeniable. His accomplishments both in aerodynamics and in practical design were the most significant breakthroughs since Cayley's work. He approached the problem of flight in strict engineering fashion, focusing on deriving a set of experimental aerodynamic data and design specifications that would enable him to build a flying machine. He was less concerned with why his gliders flew from a theoretical point of view than with learning what design characteristics would enhance their performance. The aerodynamic data resulting from this methodology formed the basis for much later aeronautical research, including that of the Wright brothers. They also adopted his engineering approach, as well as his practice of gaining actual flying experience in full-size gliders. Like Lilienthal, the Wrights were concerned only with what they needed to know to make an airplane fly, not with the scientific principles that lay behind what they were doing. Wilbur would later refer to Lilienthal as "the greatest of precursors."

Equally important, Lilienthal demonstrated unquestionably that gliding flight was possible. No one before him had gained any appreciable amount of actual flying experience with aircraft based on carefully collected, sound aeronautical data. Granted, he was flying for only seconds at a time, but he was truly flying. His tentative trips through the air made headlines everywhere. He was hailed as the Flying Man, the Winged Prussian, and the German Darius Green.[25] Inspirational photographs showing him soaring gracefully over hillsides appeared in newspapers and magazines the world over, making him quite a sensation in an age when, for most, human flight still seemed a distant possibility at best. Lilienthal's notoriety and this visible proof that a human being could actually fly contributed as much to spurring other experimenters forward as did his groundbreaking aerodynamic research.

While the three approaches to flight research focused upon here were by no means the only ones pursued, they defined the general direction in which aeronautical experimentation was moving in the second half of the nineteenth century. Professionals and technicians of reputation were advancing aeronautics through the application of rapidly maturing engineering principles and techniques. Also, basic groundwork in the critical areas of aerodynamics, propulsion, and control was falling into place.

Yet, despite the comparative strides made in this period, by the late 1890s, the momentum building toward the invention of a successful powered airplane had wound down. The most promising experimenters had for the most part either given up, reached the logical conclusion of their ideas, or died in accidents. (Percy Pilcher, a Scottish glider pioneer who followed in Lilienthal's path, was killed in 1899 in an accident remarkably similar to that which had taken the life of his better-known German predecessor.)[26] It was true that people like Lilienthal and Pénaud had built upon the seminal work of Cayley in a productive way, and that the less fruitful efforts of experimenters such as Maxim, Ader, and Langley had also helped assess the obstacles to mechanical flight. But, as the century drew to a close, humans were still far from enjoying the freedom of movement displayed teasingly by nature's winged creatures. At this point, an experimenter(s) was needed who could assimilate this rich body of nineteenth-century flight research and make the necessary conceptual leaps that would provide a genuine understanding of and a resolution to the complex set of problems constituting the barrier to human flight.

The Wright brothers, of course, fulfilled this role. They entered the field at a time when aeronautics had moved beyond blind, daring attempts to get into the air by would-be birdmen but was still lacking a clear definition of the many remaining obstacles to mechanical flight. With uncommon insight and engineering acumen, the Wrights raised the field of aeronautics to an entirely new level and brought the invention of a practical airplane to fruition. They were able to analyze critically what had preceded them, reduce the remaining problems to their most basic elements, and design methods and devices for the practical resolution of these problems. The incredible facility with which they were able to cut through to the heart of a problem and arrive at workable solutions enabled the Wrights to move well ahead of even the most productive of their contemporaries with amazing speed. Yet, as original and revolutionary as the Wrights' accomplishments were, it is important to recognize that a foundation of basic knowledge and experience had been set down during the nineteenth century by a growing community of dedicated and talented experimenters. Without a thorough immersion in the body of work performed by their predecessors, the unproductive as well as the more successful, it is highly unlikely that the Wright airplane would have emerged in the form it did, when it did. The Wrights' genius lay as much in their insightful analysis and adaptation of what had come before them as it did in their own innate creativity.

3

"You Must Mount a Machine"

The first experience the Wright brothers had with flight dates to an often-recounted story about a rubber-band-powered toy helicopter given to them by their father in 1878. The earliest form of the device dates to the fourteenth century; the version Milton Wright gave to his sons was developed by Alphonse Pénaud in the 1870s. The brothers were predictably intrigued by the little flying machine, and they later made several copies of it in varying sizes. After a period of playing and experimenting with these toy helicopters, the brothers behaved like most young boys and went on to other diversions. Unlike Otto Lilienthal and his brother Gustav, who maintained an avid interest in bird flight and flying machines all their lives, the Wrights were not driven by a consistent curiosity about flight. The brothers, Orville in particular, did a fair amount of kite flying for sport during their youth and took an interest in any news stories on flying that came their way, but they did not consider aeronautics seriously until they were in their late twenties.[1]

The Wright brothers' youth coincided with the height of the Industrial Revolution in the United States. The thirty years after the end of the Civil War witnessed the introduction of such technological marvels as a transatlantic telegraph line, the electric light, the telephone, the sewing machine, the phonograph, and the internal combustion engine, to name only a few. One of the dominant themes of the nation's gala centennial celebration in Philadelphia in 1876 was the inherent virtue of technology and its critical role in the American democratic experiment and prosperity.[2] It was an exciting era in the history of technology in America and, not surprisingly, more than a few would-be Edisons and Bells became infatuated with mechanics and applied science during this period.

One area of technology that had witnessed tremendous change during the nineteenth century was transportation. The railroad and the steamship dominated the century. In addition, the safety bicycle was adding a hitherto unknown individual freedom of mobility, and the automobile was traversing its first tentative miles. By century's end, travel by airplane had emerged as one obvious mode of transportation yet to be realized.

During the 1890s, the field of aeronautics had become quite active. A number of individuals had made headlines with attempts to fly full-size aircraft. Samuel Langley was making flights of significant duration with several large steam-and-gasoline-powered models he called Aerodromes. Otto Lilienthal was stretching hesitant leaps into the air into rides of a few hundred feet or more with his graceful wood-and-fabric hang gliders. The notion of human flight was becoming less and less ridiculous all the time.[3]

Although the bicycle trade furnished the Wrights with an adequate and enjoyable living, it did not provide the mental rigor their fertile, active minds craved. In 1894, Wilbur wrote his father expressing a desire to attend college, admitting that he did not feel he was particularly well suited for, nor very interested in, a commercial career. "Intellectual effort is a pleasure to me and I think I would be better fitted for reasonable success in some of the professions than in business," Wilbur wrote.[4] Despite his father's willingness to help with the costs, Wilbur decided not to follow up on his college plans. Still, the yearning to tackle something more engaging remained. Both Wilbur and Orville were becoming a bit restless, and they began to contemplate a new outlet for their inquisitiveness.

As the world knows, they chose the airplane. In large measure, circumstance turned their attention skyward. The emphasis on technological innovation in late nineteenth-century America, the freshness of the challenge of flight, and the promising advances that had been made recently in the field were all important factors in leading the Wrights to aeronautics. It was an exciting, wide-open area that provided the type of rich possibilities for investigation sought by the Wrights. Wilbur in particular had a sense that life was passing him by during this period. He was convinced that he was capable of bigger things than running a modest bike shop. Their pursuit of aeronautics was far more a case of fulfilling these needs than a response to a long-held commitment to flight.

Precisely when Wilbur and Orville began to consider joining those actively working on the problem of mechanical flight is somewhat hard to pin down. Traditional accounts, including the brothers' own version, cite the death of Otto Lilienthal in August of 1896 as the event that finally prompted them to take their first serious steps toward the airplane.[5] Although news of the sudden loss of the world's best-known aeronautical pioneer sparked a keener interest in flying on the part of the Wrights, it is more accurate to place the beginning of their genuine commitment to the study of human flight in 1899.[6]

Wilbur and Orville had been gleaning bits here and there about aeronautics during the years just prior to Lilienthal's fatal crash. Avid readers of popular and technical literature alike, they had picked up some knowledge of the aeronautical events and personalities that were beginning to creep into the headlines during the 1890s. They became familiar with Lilienthal in particular. There is evidence that the Wrights had read accounts of his exploits as early as 1890. Two brief items about him appeared in one of the Wrights' own short-lived newspapers in the summer of that year.[7] In the September 1894 issue of *McClure's Magazine*, a widely circulated popular journal of the day, there appeared a lengthy, well-illustrated article detailing Lilienthal's inspirational gliding experiments.[8] It cannot be said with certainty that the brothers read this specific story, but it is very likely that this periodical made its way into the Wright household. Through these and other news accounts, Wilbur and Orville had gained a fair degree of familiarity with the field of aeronautics by the summer of 1896.[9]

What happened next has become one of the more melodramatic episodes in the story of the Wrights' path to the airplane. In late August of 1896, Orville was stricken with typhoid and lay delirious for six weeks. Wilbur is supposed to have read of Lilienthal's death, and the tragedy is said to have inspired his first serious thoughts about flight. After Orville's recovery, Wilbur eagerly shared the news with his brother and began to search out literature on flying. It remains unclear whether or not Wilbur read of Lilienthal's death before or after Orville's illness and his resulting incoherence, but this is the way the brothers later recounted the story.[10]

18. Octave Chanute, the elder statesman of aeronautics and the Wrights' faithful correspondent, 1832–1910.

Historical hindsight makes this dramatic Lilienthal crash/Orville sickbed story an appealing opening for the Wrights' legendary achievement. But, in fact, it was something of a false start. The years 1897 and 1898 show little if any aeronautical activity on the part of the Wrights. It was not until the spring of 1899 that their sporadic interest blossomed into earnest study of flight. Aside from a vague reference to reading a book on ornithology,[11] the record is unclear as to what in particular revived the brothers' interest at this point. One thing is certain, however. Once committed to the challenge, the Wrights identified and solved the basic problems of mechanical flight with uncommon insight and startling speed.[12]

The first formal expression of the Wrights' desire to join the growing community of aeronautical experimenters came in a letter Wilbur wrote to the Smithsonian Institution on May 30, 1899. After affirming his belief that human flight was possible—"My observations . . . have . . . convinced me more firmly that human flight is possible and practicable"—he declared his intent to "begin a systematic study of the subject in preparation for practical work."[13] Toward that end, he requested whatever publications on the subject the Smithsonian could make available. Assistant Secretary Richard Rathbun replied with the following suggestions: *Progress in Flying Machines*, by Octave Chanute; *Experiments in Aerodynamics*, by Samuel P. Langley; and *The Aeronautical Annual* for 1895, 1896, and 1897, edited by James Means. Along with this list, he forwarded four pamphlets: *On Soaring Flight*, by E. C. Huffaker; *Story of Experiments in Mechanical Flight*, by Samuel P. Langley; *The Problem of Flying and Practical Experiments in Soaring*, by Otto Lilienthal; and *Empire of the Air*, by Louis-Pierre Mouillard.[14]

Of these references, Chanute's *Progress in Flying Machines* and Means's *Aeronautical Annuals* were especially rich sources of information. Together they provided a compendium of virtually everything that had been done with heavier-than-air flying machines up to the death of Lilienthal.

Octave Chanute, who had built a national reputation as a civil engineer, developed a powerful interest in flight in his later years. During the 1880s and 1890s, he emerged as the aeronautical community's clearinghouse of information. He kept track of most every article and experimenter that had anything to do with flying. Even more important, he disseminated these valuable resources through publication, the organization of meetings and presentations, correspondence with individual experimenters, and the introduction of independent researchers to one another. Along with Augustus Herring and several other younger enthusiasts in his employ, he also supervised the construction and testing of a number of glider designs. One of these aircraft, known as the *two-surface machine*, significantly influenced the basic structural layout of the Wrights' later gliders and powered airplanes with its biplane configuration and its clever manner of bracing.[15]

With the publication of *Progress in Flying Machines* in 1894, Chanute made available in a single volume the wealth of materials and knowledge he had been gathering since the beginning of his interest in aeronautics. For the first time, the scattered and isolated efforts of those attempting to get into the air were assembled in a convenient, comprehensive resource.

James Means, although he never got involved personally with actually building flying machines in any significant way, played a role comparable to Chanute as a chronicler and promoter of aeronautical activity. He corresponded extensively with the foremost experimenters in America and abroad, convincing many of them to contribute articles to his highly influential, though short-lived, journal, *The Aeronautical Annual*. Only three volumes of *The Annual* were published (1895–97), but in them appeared accounts of the work of many of the era's leading figures.[16]

Armed with the annuals and Chanute's *Progress in Flying Machines*, the newcomers to aeronautics hardly had to look elsewhere to apprise themselves of the field. As Wright biographer Fred Howard put it, "Chanute's *Progress in Flying Machines* was a veritable Old Testament of aeronautics, to which the three *Aeronautical Annuals* were a latter-day Gospel bringing the story up to date."[17] Wilbur and Orville quickly read and absorbed this treasure trove of aeronautical experience, along with the other material the Smithsonian had sent them and what they were able to dig up on their own.

The Wrights' literature search is more often characterized in terms of what it failed to turn up rather than how it benefited the brothers. Emphasis is placed on the Wrights' surprise at how little had been accomplished considering the caliber of the people who had addressed the problem of flight and how long it had been a subject of inquiry. Standard accounts stress that pre-Wright flight research provided little concrete information upon which the Wrights could build, leaving them largely on their own at the start of their work. The general view is that their reading served mostly as a catalog of what mistakes to avoid.[18]

All of this was indeed true. There is no doubt that the corpus of aeronautical research produced during the preceding century left many questions inadequately answered and others unaddressed altogether. The Wrights did make numerous essential breakthroughs based entirely on their own ideas and experiments. Nevertheless, the brothers' survey of the still nascent field of aeronautics was not merely a fruitless exercise that simply confirmed that they would have to start virtually from scratch. A careful look at precisely how the Wrights approached the airplane initially reveals the extent to which preexisting ideas and technology were incorporated in their first efforts.

Wilbur and Orville drew advantage from their reading in two important ways. First, they acquired several useful pieces of information that were used directly in the design of their aircraft. Certain concepts about wing shapes and stability, the basic aerodynamic formulas for calculating lift and drag, and fundamental engineering data with regard to sizing and materials needed to design the structure of their flying machines were all in place when the Wrights took up the problem of flight. They would refine this information as they improved their designs and their flying technique, but they used it in its basic form to build and test their initial gliders.

The second benefit Wilbur and Orville derived from their study of previous research was more intuitive. Their observance and analysis of the approaches taken by others greatly aided them in clearly and accurately defining the principle obstacles to human flight and how best to overcome them. They not only had the insight to reject methods and ideas that were obviously unproductive, but they were also able to cull viable techniques and design data from the work of numerous prior experimenters with great clarity of thought.

The advantages the Wrights drew from their preliminary investigation of previous flight research were evident very early in their own work. Less than two months after writing the Smithsonian, they had defined the basic requirements for a heavier-than-air flying machine and successfully built and tested a small, five-foot span aircraft that incorporated, in rudimentary form, the structural design and means of control that would ultimately allow them to take to the air in 1903. Clearly, their insightful and clever approaches to the technical problems of flight were at the center of this rapid start. But their adaptation of the workable and useful ideas present in prior aeronautical research, not to mention the time and frustration saved by the existence of Chanute's and Means's thorough, well-organized documentation of it, is a factor that should not go unnoticed. Unquestionably the Wrights demonstrated a hitherto unknown grasp of the essential problems and an ability for devising practical solutions. As they broke onto the scene, they rapidly made conceptual breakthroughs that raised aeronautics to a completely new level. But in so doing, they did not work from a blank slate, nor was that slate filled entirely with erroneous entries.

As the Wrights conducted their literature search, they began to define the essential barriers to human flight. Initially they reduced the obstacles to three broad categories. First, a successful flying machine would obviously require a structure of sustaining surfaces—a set of wings of some kind. Second, some means of propelling the machine through the air would be necessary. Third, a method of balancing and controlling the aircraft in flight would have to be devised.[19] These starting guidelines may appear rather simplistic from our modern perspective, but they are significant in two important ways.

While it may seem obvious now, conceiving of the airplane as the successful interaction of these three basic elements was apparent to only a few in the nineteenth century. Even though Sir George Cayley had accurately conceptualized the essential components of a heavier-than-air flying machine as lift, propulsion, and control a hundred years earlier, almost none of the many experimenters trying to get airborne prior to the Wrights followed Cayley's pioneering lead. Some experimenters had gone partway. Chanute worked with crude automatic stabilizing devices on his hang glider designs, but he gave little consideration to how his aircraft would be steered during sustained flight. Lilienthal had employed the partially effective weight shifting method of control on his graceful craft, but he failed to see that this was a dead end as far as a large, powered aircraft was concerned. Ader and Maxim attempted to mate brute power to their airframes with no practical thought about control once aloft. Still others chose to build flying machines that perhaps would leave the ground, but which clearly had no future as practical aircraft, simply wanting to be credited with having made the first heavier-than-air flight. Herring, for example, mounted a small, short-duration compressed-air motor on one of his frail hang gliders in 1898. The craft made a brief, uncontrolled hop, but he was obviously at a technological impasse.[20]

The fundamental error made by these experimenters was that none of them thought in terms of the entire problem. They focused on isolated aspects of aircraft design without a clear idea of how their work would relate to the ultimate goal of a practical powered airplane. No one before the Wrights fully recognized that all three of the elements set down by Cayley must be addressed with an eye toward building a powered flying machine in its final form, rather than a stopgap aircraft.

The second reason why the brothers' clear and organized way of initially thinking about the problem of flight is significant is because it reflects the engineering approach that characterized the Wrights' every step. As each new problem presented itself, the Wrights asked themselves the same basic set of questions: What information is needed to solve the problem? Where can it be found or what techniques and tools must be employed to obtain it? How can this information be successfully and practically incorporated into the design? The Wrights' separation of the task of creating a heavier-than-air flying machine into its three essential parts and their assessment of what needed to be accomplished for each in order to make the entire system perform satisfactorily illustrates their engineering instincts operating from the start.

Of the three broad categories of flight research, the Wrights initially concerned themselves the least with propulsion. During the late nineteenth century, several notable examples of lightweight steam-engine technology were produced, as well as some successful pioneering efforts with gasoline engines.[21] Wilbur and Orville believed that they would likely be able to purchase a suitable power plant, or make one on their own, by the time they were ready to begin making powered flights.[22]

Similarly, some useful work had already been done on wing airfoils and aircraft structures. Otto Lilienthal's lift data and his work with curved-wing surfaces provided a sound starting point for Wilbur and Orville's own pioneering aerodynamic work. Octave Chanute and Augustus Herring's classic *two-surface glider* of 1896, in addition to other pioneering multiwing configurations, in part led the Wrights to the trussed biplane structural design they used consistently on all their aircraft.[23]

This is not to say that the Wrights merely adopted the work of these prior experimenters with little revision. Lilienthal, Chanute, Herring, Langley, and everyone else for that matter, were far from a solution to mechanical flight. The Wrights had to rethink and improve upon anything drawn from their efforts, often far more than even they had initially imagined. However, in addition to providing some general starting points for their own investigations, these earlier contributions were important for the brothers in that they demonstrated that some of the crucial problems were on their way toward being resolved. They showed that flying, while still a dream, was no longer an unattainable one.

Unlike aerodynamics and structures, preliminary work on balance and control had barely been addressed. Believing that the other obstacles would be comparatively less difficult to overcome, the Wrights first concentrated on the problem of control. It was not until September of 1901, in an address before the prestigious Western Society of Engineers, that Wilbur first expressed publicly the ideas that he and his brother had formulated on the proper approach to developing an airplane.[24] By this time the Wrights were already experimenting with their second full-size glider. In this speech, Wilbur affirmed, "When this one feature [control] has been worked out the age of flying machines will have arrived, for all other difficulties are of minor importance."[25] In a rare instance of apparent shortsightedness, Wilbur almost dismissed the aerodynamic, structural, and propulsion problems, ones that would at times sorely try his abilities, as well as his patience, over the next two years. Nevertheless, this public statement, his first on aeronautics anywhere, clearly demonstrates the brothers' proper understanding that control was the heart of the flying problem. The Wrights' control system was primarily what made their aircraft unique. It was the main element of their later patent on the airplane, as well as the key aspect of their invention that was drawn upon by virtually all who followed them into the air. The Wrights' recognition of the centrality of control to mechanical flight was among the most significant, if not the premier, conceptual leap that set them apart from their predecessors and their contemporaries.

One of the things that most struck the Wrights as they studied previous aeronautical efforts was the failure by so many experimenters to give the issue of control serious consideration. Most had only the vaguest sense of the relationship between stability and control. A common belief was that air currents were too swift and unpredictable for human reflexes to respond adequately. Many focused on incorporating some form of inherent stability that, independent of the pilot, would return the aircraft to equilibrium if a gust of wind or some other force were to upset it.[26] The technique developed by Alphonse Pénaud in the 1870s, of giving the wings dihedral angle and properly aligning the tail to the wings, was frequently employed. Others tried mechanical means of automatic stability. Octave Chanute, for example, designed a system whereby the wings of his craft were free to rock fore and aft in response to wind gusts. The idea was to vary the center of lifting pressure automatically to compensate for the momentary disturbance from equilibrium. Another technique, one upon which Augustus Herring expended a great deal of effort, was to mount a movable tail fitted with a spring or some other flexible attachment that was intended to act as a damper in response to wind gusts. Herring called it his "regulator."[27]

The problem with these approaches was that they reflected little consideration of the necessity of being able to control an airplane in all three of its axes of motion, or of the airplane's natural operating medium of three-dimensional space. At worst, proponents of inherent stability gave no thought whatsoever to controlling or steering their machines once airborne. Simply getting into the air was enough. At best, as in the case of Chanute and Herring, limited and poorly thought-out means of control supplemented their mechanisms for achieving inherent stability. This generally consisted of weight shifting, as in the manner of Lilienthal. Many reasoned that if simple, stable, straight-line flight was achieved, control could be easily dealt with later.

Few if any before the Wrights saw that this was dead-end thinking. As modern aerodynamics has confirmed, successful flight is possible with either a stable or an unstable aircraft. What is impossible is to fly an airplane that has no adequate means of control. The Wright brothers' aircraft were, in fact, unstable vehicles, but they were fully controllable by the pilot, and as a result capable of practical flight.

As with so many aspects of the invention of the airplane, it was essential to think in terms of the requirements of the final powered aircraft from the beginning, rather than create intermediate designs that had no continuity with the ultimate goal. The control system had to be an integral part of the design from the outset if an experimenter expected his work to conclude with a practical airplane. The Wright brothers were alone in recognizing this and were quite frankly puzzled by the failure of so many of their peers to grasp the concept.

The successful pre-Wright glider pioneers were at least on the right track. The fact that they had some notion of maneuvering their machines beyond maintaining inherent stability demonstrates that they had a sense of the control requirements. In the same 1901 Western Society of Engineers presentation, Wilbur lauded Lilienthal for his approach. "Herr Otto Lilienthal seems to have been the first man who really comprehended that balancing was the *first* instead of the *last* of the great problems in connection with human flight."[28] But, as Wilbur and Orville readily saw, weight shifting held no promise as an effective control system for a large, powered aircraft. Something fundamentally different would have to be developed.

The Wrights were the first to see that control was not merely an adjunct to stability, but the very essence of maintaining equilibrium. Their proper understanding of the relationship between stability and control is not surprising in light of their extensive experience with bicycles. The bicycle is completely unstable, yet it is entirely controllable. Given their familiarity with such a machine, the Wrights did not share the concern of many of their aeronautical peers about sacrificing stability in a flying machine. They recognized that just as a cyclist must make constant control movements to stay on two wheels, the airplane pilot must exercise similar authority over his craft to stay in the air. Equally important, the bicycle showed that controlling instability was possible without superhuman reflexes or extraordinary movements. If this was the case with the bicycle, it was reasonable to think that the same could be true of an airplane. The Wrights' experience with bicycles helped eliminate any potential intellectual barriers to thinking in terms of an airplane devoid of inherent stability.

The glider pioneers of the 1890s, particularly Lilienthal, but also Pilcher, Chanute, and Herring, drew the attention of Wilbur and Orville in an even more important way than with regard to the issues of stability and control. The Wrights were in complete agreement with their approach of gaining actual flying experience in full-size gliders.[29] One of the most significant but rarely commented upon aspects of the Wrights' inventive work was that, in addition to creating the technology, the brothers had to teach themselves to operate it; they had to learn how to fly. Wilbur drew a parallel to an uninitiated rider mounting an untamed horse:

Now, there are two ways of learning how to ride a fractious horse: one is to get on him and learn by actual practice how each motion and trick may be best met; the other is to sit on a fence and watch the beast a while, and then retire to the house and at leisure figure out the best way of overcoming his jumps and kicks. The latter system is the safest; but the former, on the whole, turns out the larger proportion of good riders. It is very much the same in learning to ride a flying machine; if you are looking for perfect safety, you will do well to sit on a fence and watch the birds; but if you really wish to learn, you must mount a machine and become acquainted with its tricks by actual trial.[30]

Here again the influence of the bicycle is revealed. A bicycle requires constant and considerable practice before riding can be mastered. The Wrights correctly reasoned that the same would be true for an airplane. Teaching themselves to fly, they knew, would be just as important as building an airplane that was technically successful.[31]

A few short weeks after they had received the material and references supplied by the Smithsonian Institution, the Wrights had completed the first of their experimental aircraft. They did not begin immediately with a full-size glider. They instead constructed a small kite to test the system of control they intended to incorporate in their first man-carrying machine.

Lateral balance, keeping the wings level, was an obvious requirement. The Wrights decided that an effective way to maneuver their craft in this direction, in *roll* as it is now referred to, would be to alter independently the angle at which each wing-half attacks the air. If one wing-half is presented at a greater angle to the wind than the other, it will generate more lift, cause that side of the airplane to rise, and result in a banking of the entire machine. If the pilot could mechanically and precisely manipulate the wings in this fashion, it would not only be possible to maintain equilibrium, but also to initiate controlled turns when desired. With this idea, the Wrights moved closer to the realization of heavier-than-air flight than anyone had in decades.

To think in terms of banking the aircraft to turn was a familiar and comfortable concept to Wilbur and Orville. The bicycle rider performs precisely the same maneuver when leaning into a turn. If a cyclist attempted to turn without doing so, flatly, as an automobile or ship takes a curve, the result would be a loss of balance and a quick meeting with the ground. Wilbur expressed his analysis of a bicycle turn in a later patent-infringement-suit deposition:

I have asked dozens of bicycle riders how they turn to the left. I have never found a single person who stated all the facts correctly when first asked. They almost invariably said that to turn to the left, they turned the handlebar to the left and as a result made a turn to the left. But on further questioning them, some would agree that they first turned the handlebar a little to the right, and then as the machine inclined to the left, they turned the handlebar to the left and as a result made the circle, inclining inwardly.[32]

Many pre-Wright aeronautical experimenters erroneously believed that maneuvering a flying machine would be a simple matter of steering on a level plane of air, analogous to an automobile on land. The Wrights' knowledge of the dynamics of maintaining the equilibrium of a bicycle afforded them a different and more useful perspective that no doubt aided them in properly understanding the requirements of balancing an airplane in three-dimensional space.

As central as this breakthrough is to the Wright story, it is curious that the actual origin of the idea remains somewhat unclear. It is one of those aspects of the brothers' work that has to a degree fallen between the cracks of their correspondence and recordkeeping at the time and their recounting of the sequence of events in later years.

In May of 1900, in the brothers' first letter to Octave Chanute, Wilbur suggests that they had discovered the principle of angling the wings in opposite directions for lateral control from observing birds:[33]

My observation of the flight of buzzards leads me to believe that they regain their lateral balance, when partly overturned by a gust of wind, by a torsion of the tips of the wings. If the rear edge of the right wing tip is twisted upward and the left downward the bird becomes an animated windmill and instantly begins a turn, a line from its head to its tail being the axis.[34]

Many years later, however, long after Wilbur's death, Orville claimed that their observation of birds had contributed little:

I cannot think of any part bird flight had in the development of human flight excepting as an inspiration. Although we intently watched birds fly in a hope of learning something from them I cannot think of anything that was first learned in that way. After we had thought out certain principles, we then watched the bird to see whether it used the same principles. In a few cases we did detect the same thing in the bird's flight.

Learning the secret of flight from a bird was a good deal like learning the secret of magic from a magician. After you once know the trick and know what to look for you see things that you did not notice when you did not know exactly what to look for.[35]

However the Wrights came upon the idea, whether it was through birdwatching or through conceiving it on their own without any external model, taking advantage of the "dynamic reactions of the air instead

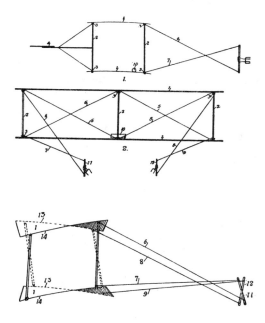

19. Sketch of the Wright brothers' 1899 kite, built to explore the effectiveness of wing warping. Note the removal of the fore-and-aft wire crossbracing, which enabled the wings to be warped.

of shifting weight" for control, as Wilbur put it, was a conceptual leap of immeasurable consequence.[36]

The principle of twisting the wings in opposite directions as a means of lateral control, *wing warping* as it would ultimately be termed, was not entirely new. Two obscure English patents on related systems were granted during the nineteenth century, but neither was ever developed.[37] A version was also invented by a Yale physics instructor named Edson F. Gallaudet a year before the Wrights independently designed their system.

Like the Wrights, Gallaudet built a kite to test his wing-warping control system, although the mechanism for imparting the twist to the wings was entirely different. The Gallaudet kite, mounted on pontoons for trial off water, privately made its one and only flight on November 12, 1898, near Gallaudet's father's Connecticut beach house on Long

Island Sound. After rising into the air, it staggered about momentarily before falling off on one wing into the water. Although the damage was minimal, the kite was stored away and never experimented with again. Gallaudet's colleagues at Yale had gotten wind of his aeronautical work and recommended he dismiss his thoughts of flying if he wished to maintain his reputation as an engineer, as well as his employment. Advanced though his ideas were, Gallaudet's preempted start remained buried for many years.[38]

With no knowledge of Gallaudet's earlier kite, Wilbur and Orville began construction in the summer of 1899 of their own device for testing the concept of wing warping. They would need a system that could easily twist the wings without compromising the structural integrity of the airframe. Orville first sketched out a design in which the outer sections of the wing pivoted on metal shafts. They were geared to move in opposite directions when the pilot operated a lever. Although workable in theory, the weight of the metal shafts, the pivoting mechanism, and the necessary supporting structure would be intolerably high.[39]

Shortly thereafter they arrived at a better solution. One day when Wilbur was minding the bicycle shop alone, a customer stopped in to purchase an inner tube for a tire. After removing the inner tube from the cardboard box in which it was packaged, Wilbur absentmindedly began to twist the box between his fingers as he chatted with his customer. He observed that even when he applied considerable torsion across the box it retained its lateral stiffness. It occurred to him that the same principle likely could be applied to a set of properly rigged biplane wings. Orville related the story years later in a biographical deposition taken in connection with one of the many patent-infringement suits the Wrights filed after making their invention public.

. . . one evening when I returned home . . . , Wilbur showed me a method of getting the same results as we had contemplated in our first idea without the structural defects of the original. He demonstrated the method by means of a small pasteboard box, which had two of the opposite ends removed. By holding the top forward corner and the rear lower corner of one end of the box between his thumb and forefinger and the rear upper corner and the lower forward corner of the other end of the box in like manner, and by pressing the corners together the upper and lower surface of the box were given a helicoidal twist, presenting the top and bottom surfaces of the box at different angles on the right and left sides. From this it was apparent that the wings of a machine of the

Chanute double-deck type, with the fore-and-aft trussing removed, could be warped so as to present their surfaces to the air at different angles of incidence and thus secure unequal lifts on the two sides.[40]

This story, like the one of Wilbur reading about Lilienthal's death at Orville's bedside in 1896, has a touch of the melodramatic. But it is very likely true, as Wilbur later used the same cardboard box analogy to illustrate the wing warping principle to a confused patent office examiner reviewing their application. He in fact sent the examiner a bicycle inner-tube box to try the twisting action for himself.

The twisted box logically suggested a biplane configuration as an obvious form to which the torsion principle could be applied. Through their literature search and their keeping up with the headlines, the Wrights had become familiar with multiwing designs for lifting surfaces. They were aware of the work of Australian Lawrence Hargrave, inventor of the box kite, a structural form that had great influence on future biplane wing design. Descriptions and illustrations of Hargrave's kites and Charles Lamson's modifications of them were published in *Progress in Flying Machines* and *The Aeronautical Annual*. A discussion and drawing of John Stringfellow's triplane design of the 1860s also appeared in these references. Wilbur and Orville knew that Lilienthal had flown a few gliders of biplane configuration, several illustrations of which were reproduced in *The Annual* and elsewhere. Cayley's early man-carrying gliders had employed superimposed wing surfaces, and the Wrights possibly could have been aware of these designs as well. But most significantly, they learned of the successful biplane hang glider developed by Octave Chanute and Augustus Herring.[41]

An article by Chanute appeared in the 1897 issue of *The Aeronautical Annual* describing his recent gliding activities. During the mid-1890s, he and a small band of enthusiasts in his employ conducted tests with a variety of hang-glider designs over the sand dunes at the foot of Lake Michigan, about thirty miles from Chicago. Chanute was in his sixties by this time, so all the actual gliding was done by his younger, more agile colleagues. Included in *The Annual* article was a discussion, with photographs, of the evolution of a craft he and Herring had collaborated on that had achieved flights nearly comparable to those made by Lilienthal. The glider became known as the two-surface machine, and it was one of the most influential aircraft of the pre-Wright era.[42]

20. The influential 1896 Chanute-Herring two-surface machine, with Augustus Herring in the pilot's position.

Usually referred to by the Wrights as the Chanute double-decker, the two-surface machine started out as a triplane. During initial trials, however, the lower wing dragged in the sand and was consequently removed, giving the glider its classic biplane form. With its straight, rectangular wings rigidly secured, one directly above the other with wooden vertical uprights and diagonal brace wires, the two-surface machine foreshadowed the basic aircraft structural design that would dominate the first decades of powered flight. The glider had cruciform tail planes, originally fixed and then later fitted with Herring's so-called regulator for automatic stability. The pilot rode slung through the center section of the lower wing in the fashion of Lilienthal, employing weight shifting to aid in balancing the craft.

Of special interest was the two-surface machine's manner of bracing. It consisted of a crisscross arrangement of steel wires between the open bays of the strut-braced biplane wing cell. This resulted in a simple, but extremely rigid, structure. In developing this design, Chanute drew upon his experience as an accomplished civil engineer and bridge builder. He modified and adapted to his glider a style of bracing commonly used in bridge construction, invented in the 1840s by Thomas Willis Pratt. The *Pratt truss* featured diagonal bracing between the upright members of bridges or similar structures to aid in supporting vertical loads. In his biplane, Chanute replaced the rigid diagonal bracing of the Pratt truss with two crossed steel wires to support the loads imposed on the wing structure due to lift, as well as those generated by the shock of landing.[43]

The Wright brothers saw the trussed biplane as a perfect solution to the dilemma presented by their wing warping concept of maintaining the structural rigidity of a wing that could at the same time be easily flexed for lateral control. By removing the fore-and-aft diagonal wire-bracing of a Chanute-type biplane, but retaining the span-wise trussing, the airframe would take on precisely the same characteristics as the cardboard box with its ends removed. The wings could be twisted across the *chord* (the width of the wing) without loss of strength and stiffness along the length of the wing. The scheme had the added advantage that no complex or heavy mechanism would be required to manipulate the system. Warping was accomplished simply by pulling on thin cables attached to the outer edges of the wings.

Although Orville cites the Chanute glider in his recollection quoted above of the development of the Wright wing-warping control system and the design of the 1899 kite, there is some question as to how directly the Wright craft evolved from the earlier Chanute-Herring glider. At least one historian of the early airplane has argued that the time frame was too short between the Wrights' receipt of the recommended references from the Smithsonian to when they completed their wing-warping kite to reasonably assume that the brothers' design was influenced significantly by the Chanute-Herring two-surface machine.[44]

This contention stems largely from a July 7, 1899, entry in the diary of the brothers' father, Milton Wright, which states: "Milton [the elder Wright's grandson] came up in the eve. to see the flying machine."[45] This suggests that the Wrights located and acquired the literature recommended by the Smithsonian that discussed the two-surface machine and designed and built their kite in only about a month's time. Granted, a rapid sequence of events, but not implausible.

The issue is further muddled by a seemingly contradictory comment by Orville. He stated that Wilbur shared the inner-tube box incident with him during a visit to the Wright home by Harriet Silliman, a friend of their sister Katharine. He went on to say, "We began construction of a model embodying the principle demonstrated with the paper box within a day or two," (i.e., a day or two after Wilbur told him of his experience in the bike shop).[46] The confusion arises from the fact that Harriet Silliman did not begin her stay until July 20, two weeks after Milton Wright's diary refers to the existence of the kite.[47]

Orville's statement about beginning work on the kite during Harriet Silliman's visit was taken twenty years after the fact, and thus could be subject to question. Another possible explanation is that Milton Wright's diary entry refers to a lesser-known, preliminary model of the 1899 kite made of split bamboo, tissue, and thread. The brothers had built this kite to work out the physical details of a craft that, up to that point, had existed only in their mind's eye. But this still does not get around the problem of Orville's claim that Wilbur stumbled onto the twisted-box analogy after July 20. Even the earlier version of the 1899 kite could not have preceded the inner-tube box incident, because it was built specifically to test the wing warping idea on a structural form that was spawned by it.

Beyond the puzzling discrepancy of the dates regarding the time frame of the creation of the 1899 kite, there is also the question of the degree to which the Wright design was influenced by the Chanute-Herring glider and other earlier multiwing craft. It is possible that Wilbur and Orville were able to get their hands on the annuals and the other materials suggested by the Smithsonian, adapt what they found to the wing warping principle, and produce a working prototype based solely on this information by the end of July. It is also possible that they had knowledge of the braced biplane concept prior to reading about the Chanute-Herring machine in the 1897 *Aeronautical Annual,* and that the publications recommended by the Smithsonian merely confirmed ideas they were already formulating. They very likely could have seen pictures of Lilienthal's biplanes in earlier literature, or even newspaper accounts of Chanute's experiments. Similarly, it is not entirely impossible that they could have become familiar with the Pratt truss independently, as it was a fairly standard engineering technique of the day.

The record simply is not clear enough to know exactly and completely how the Wrights arrived at the basic elements that they incorporated in their seminal kite of 1899. There was no doubt a mix of genuinely original thinking with bits of knowledge gleaned during the years after 1896, along with the results from their inquiry to the Smithsonian. What is certain, however, is that this kite, with its biplane configuration, modified Pratt-truss bracing, and rudimentary wing-warping control system for lateral balance, formed the nucleus of the flying machine that would successfully carry a human being into the air over an isolated North Carolina beach in 1903.

After careful study of every movement of the bamboo model, the Wrights proceeded with the flyable version of the 1899 kite. By the end of July, three years after the dramatic death of Lilienthal sparked Wilbur's initial serious thoughts about human flight, the brothers emerged from their workshop with the first Wright machine that would take to the air. The majority of the actual construction was performed by Wilbur. In these early days of their aeronautical work, he was the driving inspiration of the duo. It was primarily due to Wilbur's increasingly passionate interest in the flying problem that the Wrights joined the community of aeronautical experimenters at the close of the century. Before long, however, Orville became equally dedicated to the pursuit of a practical airplane.[48]

The kite was, of course, a biplane.[49] It was five feet in span and had a thirteen-inch chord. The framework was constructed of pine and covered with fabric sealed with shellac to make it airtight. The wing surfaces had a curved, or arched, profile. Although a few experimenters persisted in using flat planes as lifting surfaces as late as the early twentieth century, by the time Wilbur and Orville got involved with aeronautics, it had been clearly demonstrated by a variety of pioneers that curved wings were more efficient in producing lift.[50] The fact that bird wings are curved also suggested the advantage of this form.

The vertical uprights that supported the wing panels one above the other were trussed rigidly across the front and rear of the biplane wing cell in the manner of the Chanute-Herring glider. Across the chord, looking end-on in other words, the kite was left unbraced to allow for warping. Four lines were attached to the top and bottom of the front, outer uprights. The free ends were connected to a pair of sticks held by the operator. When the sticks were tilted in opposite directions, the tension on the lines imparted the twist on the wings, providing control in roll.

Although the kite was built primarily to test the Wrights' system for lateral balance, its climb and descent, known as movement in *pitch*, could also be controlled. The uprights that supported the wings were attached with hinged connections. Fixed to the center uprights was a flat, horizontal stabilizer. When the sticks that actuated the wing warping were operated in unison rather than in opposite directions, the wings shifted fore and aft with respect to one another. This action caused the uprights by which the wings were supported to tilt either forward or backward, angling the attached horizontal stabilizer up or down. Thus, at the operator's command, either the top or bottom face of the stabilizer could be presented to the wind, which in turn caused the kite to rise or fall. Unlike Herring's "regulator," which merely acted in response to wind gusts, the Wrights' method placed pitch control in the hands of the pilot.

The exact date the kite was flown remains unknown. Orville was not present for the tests. On July 24, he, Katharine, Harriet Silliman, and a group of friends left on a camping trip not far from Dayton. Wilbur did not join them until August 6, after he had flown the kite. At some point during this period, he had tested the kite successfully at a nearby field. The only witnesses were a group of schoolboys, who were fascinated by the large, unusual-looking kite this adult in business attire was "toying" with.[51]

The craft responded quickly and precisely to Wilbur's commands, confirming the soundness of the brothers' ideas regarding lateral balance. Its performance made it immediately apparent that wing warping was far superior to weight shifting, automatic stabilizers, or any other means of control that had been employed thus far. The next obvious question was whether or not it could be adapted to a large, heavy glider capable of carrying a human aloft. Not long after flying the kite, Wilbur and Orville decided that the good results warranted taking the next step, and they began designing a full-size glider embodying their wing-warping system of lateral control.

The development of the wing-warping control system was one of the most salient examples of the Wrights' impressive ability to turn abstract conceptual models into practical, concrete technology. They moved deftly from the imaginative theoretical idea of differential lift on opposite sides of the wing to achieve lateral balance to the simple and workable scheme of twisting the wing panels in alternate directions. This ability to merge an abstract intellectual concept for control with a practical understanding of structures and materials to produce an original, effective solution contributed significantly to the Wrights' overcoming several critical barriers to mechanical flight.

It would be an entire year before they actually began to construct their first man-carrying aircraft. Having knocked the door ajar with their relatively simple model kite, Wilbur and Orville now entered a world full of complicated technical problems and seemingly mysterious physical forces. Before the goal of human flight could be realized, they would have to master innumerable challenges with regard to aerodynamics, structures, control, and propulsion, not to mention keeping from breaking their necks in the process. A stumble in any one of these areas, and the invention of the airplane would have taken an entirely different path.

The fact that these two individuals, working almost exclusively on their own, were able to resolve the many problems and take to the air with such dramatic success has to a degree overshadowed the plodding, consuming, and often frustrating experience that was the creation of the first airplane. Despite the insightfulness and skill with which the brothers tackled each aspect of their work, the invention of the airplane should not be mistakenly viewed as a smooth-flowing progression into the skies. Just the difficulties encountered in designing and building their first glider alone were incredibly varied and complex. It is not surprising that these challenges at times caused the brothers to pause and wonder if perhaps they had been too bold in embarking upon such an immense undertaking.

Their highly successful and comparatively rapid initial effort with the 1899 kite launched the Wrights into a new phase that would not only require further fundamental conceptual breakthroughs, but also demand countless practical solutions to the many technical details inherent to so complex a machine as the airplane. Having produced a set of core ideas and design features, they were now faced with the monumental task of transforming these beginning concepts into a fully developed, practical piece of technology.

An indication of how truly involved the Wright achievement was is revealed in the experiences of modern-day builders of reproduction Wright aircraft. Even with the benefit of advanced aeronautical engineering techniques and extensive flight experience, those attempting to reproduce, let alone create originally, what the Wrights did have found it to be an extremely daunting endeavor. To date, the best of the flying reproductions of the Wright brothers' 1903 powered airplane has only been able to cover a small fraction of the distance Wilbur and Orville achieved on their longest flight in 1903; and the Wrights flew their airplane only *four* times.[52]

The tangible results of the 1899 kite, and the broader ideas concerning the general approach to the problem of mechanical flight that the kite represented, were a remarkable achievement and greatly advanced the corpus of aeronautical research that had blossomed during the late nineteenth century. But this was only the beginning. The next major goal, "to mount a machine" and actually fly, would present a myriad of technical and emotional challenges that would increasingly consume Wilbur and Orville's thoughts and energies in the coming years. As the summer of 1899 faded into autumn, the Wrights still had a long and difficult road ahead of them before they would be turning graceful figure eights over the Ohio countryside.

4

Learning the Art of Airplane Design

Having satisfied themselves that they had made a good start on the control problem, the Wrights next began a serious investigation of aerodynamics and structures. It was one thing to design a set of lifting surfaces for a small kite; it was quite another to build a large, heavy glider, climb aboard, and launch oneself into the air. The brothers now began to consider intensely such things as the precise shape of the wing airfoil, the size wings necessary to lift the weight of a man, and the type and sizing of materials needed to construct the glider. They also started to concentrate on developing mechanisms for operating their wing-warping system and for pitch control, and understanding the relationship between the center of gravity of the aircraft and the center of lifting pressure of the wings.

With regard to aerodynamics, the two principal concerns for the Wrights at this point were choosing a proper shape for their airfoil and dealing with the phenomenon known as *movement of the center of pressure*. The first was obvious. The second was less apparent at first, but was also an essential problem that had to be addressed in designing a lifting surface.

What is meant by the movement of the center of pressure? All bodies in air, be they stationary or moving, have pressure exerted upon them by the atmosphere. Let us consider the shape of an airplane wing. The top surface generally has a sharper curve to it than the bottom. If such a form is placed in a stream of air, the rush of wind creates a condition of imbalance. The pressure on the upper surface of the wing is lower than the pressure on the bottom side. The combination of low pressure on top and relatively higher pressure exerted on the bottom will cause

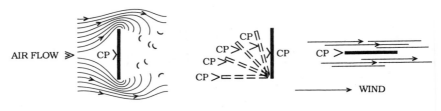

CP = CENTER OF PRESSURE

21. With a flat surface, the center of pressure *CP* is located exactly in the middle when the surface is oriented perpendicular to the airflow. As the angle of attack decreases, the *CP* moves forward toward the leading edge of the surface, ultimately locating itself directly against the front edge.

the wing to rise. This local difference in pressure around the wing is what produces the upward force called *lift*.

In flight, the focal point of this lift-producing pressure, referred to as the *center of pressure*, shifts its position as the angle of the wing to the airflow changes. To simplify matters, first consider a flat plate rather than a curved wing. Picture such a plate with its face oriented perpendicular to a stream of moving air (see Figure 21). In this position, the point described as the center of pressure coincides with the center of the face of the plate. The pressure to one side of this center point will be exactly balanced by the pressure impinging on the area to the other side of the center point. This balance of pressure also exists above and below the center. The point where all these pressures balance is defined as the center of pressure.

If the plate is then inclined in the stream of air, the point around which the pressures balance moves away from the physical center of the plate. This happens because when lift is generated by inclining the plate, the pressure distribution along the plate is altered. As the pressure at particular points changes, the point around which equilibrium pressure exists must also change. For example, if a flat plate is inclined forward into the oncoming flow, the point around which the pressures balance, the center of pressure, moves up the plate, or forward, because of an increase in the relative pressure on the upper portion of the face of the plate exposed to the wind. If the plate continues to be inclined, the center of pressure will continue to move forward, ulti-

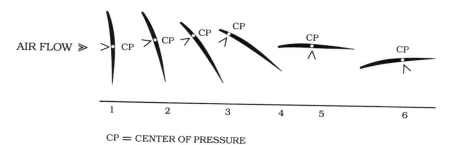

AIR FLOW ⟩

CP = CENTER OF PRESSURE

22. When the angle of attack is decreased with a curved surface, the center of pressure CP moves forward similar to a flat plate, but at a critical angle it rapidly reverses the direction of its travel. This has the effect of pitching the wing downward violently.

mately locating itself on the edge of the plate when it reaches the fully horizontal position.

In the case of a curved surface, such as an airplane wing, the movement of the center of pressure is a bit more complicated. In principle it behaves the same way as with a flat surface, but before reaching the forward edge as the wing approaches the horizontal position, the center of pressure reverses the direction of its travel and begins to move back toward the middle of the surface (see Figure 22).

The majority of early experimenters were ignorant of this fact and designed curved lifting surfaces as if they behaved like flat plates. The Wrights, as they would on so many occasions, clearly thought through the issue before beginning to cut wood and sew fabric. They reasoned that the center of pressure had to reverse with an arched surface when it approached the horizontal because, unlike a flat plate, part of the top surface would now be exposed to the wind, generating an added downward pressure. Since the center of pressure is the point about which the overall pressure on the surface balances, the direction of its travel will be affected when a new component of pressure, oriented in the opposite direction, is introduced.[1]

Although the record shows little specific discussion of these issues by the Wrights before 1901, it is clear from the design of their first glider in 1900 and from several oblique references that they at least had a basic understanding of the reversal of the center of pressure before building their first full-size machine.[2] Just as their initial instincts and ideas regarding control moved them well ahead of their contemporaries, so too did their beginning assumptions concerning aerodynamics.

The reason the movement of the center of pressure is of concern in building a flying machine is because the equilibrium of the craft is dependent upon the relative positions of the center of pressure of the wing and the center of gravity of the aircraft. The airplane is at equilibrium when these two points coincide. When they do not, the machine will pitch in one direction or the other, depending on whether the center of pressure is in front or behind the center of gravity. Since the center of pressure moves about rather freely in response to slight changes in the attitude of the wings, keeping it close to the center of gravity is not so easy. Wilbur summed up the dilemma this way:

The balancing of a gliding or flying machine is very simple in theory. It merely consists in causing the center of pressure to coincide with the center of gravity. But in actual practice there seems to be an almost boundless incompatibility of temper which prevents their remaining peaceably together for a single instant, so that the operator, who in this case acts as peacemaker, often suffers injury to himself while attempting to bring them together.[3]

Wilbur went on to point out that anyone capable of following the course of the constantly changing position of the center of pressure would have to "be very quick of mind" and "very active indeed."[4] This is precisely what Otto Lilienthal tried to do with his weight shifting technique, constantly changing the center of gravity of the glider with his body weight to keep pace with the movement of the center of pressure. This approach required incredible acrobatic movements and ultimately cost Lilienthal his life. Just as with control in roll, the Wrights realized that a better method for dealing with the movement of the center of pressure had to be devised.

The other basic aerodynamic problem initially facing the Wrights was determining the shape of the airfoil. Like the center of pressure, this proved to be a more complex problem than it had first appeared. Before settling on the final form for their 1903 powered machine, Wilbur and Orville spent many hours calculating the aerodynamic efficiency of various airfoil shapes, measuring their properties in a wind tunnel, and experimenting with them in actual practice with their gliders.

By 1900, the greater aerodynamic efficiency of curved over flat surfaces had been established. It was the precise shape of the curve that remained the open question. Many preferred a perfect arc, the high point of the arch being at the center of the wing chord. Lilienthal, Chanute, and others used this form with some success in their gliders.

The Wrights chose to place the high point of the curve closer to the front of the wing. This was done to reduce the amount of surface area of the top side of the wing that was exposed to the wind when the wing was near horizontal. They hoped this would limit the downward pressure that they believed contributed to the reversal of the travel of the center of pressure. The decision broke with tradition but was not without precedent. In the 1870s, Horatio Phillips, using a cleverly designed steam-injection wind tunnel, performed a study of cambered wing surfaces and developed and patented a series of modern-looking airfoils with the high point ahead of the center of the chord.[5]

The other basic characteristic of an airfoil is the depth of the curvature, or the *camber*. Lilienthal used a camber of 1 in 12 on his gliders. This means that the width of the wing, or chord, was twelve times the height of the wing at the peak of the curve. In light of Lilienthal's impressive flights, this ratio became the standard among early glider pioneers. Despite the apparent effectiveness of this curvature, the Wrights again departed from standard practice and chose a much shallower camber of about 1 in 22. The figure for the camber can only be approximate, as it changed continually because of flight loads exerted on the structure when gliding and the natural flattening of the steam-bent wooden ribs over time.

The Wrights reasoned that a flatter camber, with the high point ahead of the center of the chord, would aid in limiting the travel of the center of lifting pressure along the surface of the wing, thereby making the aircraft more stable in pitch and easier to control. They argued that with a highly arched wing with the peak of the curve comparatively far back, a great deal of the upper surface of the wing is exposed to the oncoming flow of air when the wing is at or near horizontal. The significant amount of downward pressure that would be generated by so much upper surface exposed to the wind, they believed, would cause the center of pressure to reverse abruptly and rapidly move toward the rear, resulting in a highly unstable aircraft. If the high point was located close to the leading edge of the wing and the camber was comparatively shallow, far less upper surface area would be exposed to the wind. Under these conditions, the reversal of the movement of the center of pressure would be more gentle and occur at much lower angles of attack because there would be a smaller component of downward pressure acting on the wing.[6] *Angle of attack* refers to the angle of the wings with respect to the oncoming flow of air.

Following this line of reasoning, the Wrights designed their airfoil with the high point extremely close to the leading edge, and with a very shallow, thin overall camber. They believed that while it would be difficult to eliminate the reversal of the center of pressure altogether, with their design the reversal would occur at angles of attack lower than those at which they would normally be flying. Again, the Wrights did not explicitly commit these thoughts to paper until their 1901 glider experiments confirmed their reasoning, but it is readily apparent from examining photographs of the aircraft that this is what they were thinking when they designed the 1900 glider.

Another significant, but at first unforeseen, advantage of the Wright airfoil was the marked improvement in aerodynamic efficiency over the more sharply curved wing used by Lilienthal and others. It also produced much more lift than the wings used by contemporary glider experimenters. Orville later admitted that the enhanced lift-generating qualities of their wing were largely accidental, as the intent of the design focused on controlling the movement of the center of pressure.[7]

As the brothers astutely recognized, trying to keep the center of lifting pressure of the wings and the aircraft's center of gravity balanced by means of shifting body weight was futile. A better method, they reasoned, was to regulate the movement of the center of pressure aerodynamically. Rather than moving the center of gravity in response to a shift in the center of pressure, the Wrights chose to control the movement of the center of pressure with respect to a fixed center of gravity. This would be possible if they could keep the wings at a reasonably constant attitude. The center of pressure would then remain balanced with regard to the center of gravity, and the aircraft would maintain equilibrium in pitch.

The brothers accomplished this with a horizontal surface mounted just ahead of the wings. They called it their *forward rudder*. Since their study of previous aeronautical work was quite thorough, the Wrights undoubtedly knew that Alphonse Pénaud had built a series of model gliders in the 1870s that achieved inherent stability in pitch by setting the wings and the horizontal stabilizing surfaces at slightly different angles to the direction of flight. Pénaud placed the stabilizer behind the wings at a slight positive angle with respect to them. This had the effect of keeping them at a relatively constant angle of attack. Whenever the forward movement of the center of pressure caused the wings to rise, the tail, being at a slight positive angle, would have its underside presented to the wind. The resulting pressure on the tail would force it upward, consequently causing the wings to return to level.

The Wrights chose to place their stabilizing surface ahead of the wing. This is known as a *canard* configuration. To obtain the properties of Pénaud's model glider with the stabilizing surface in front, the Wrights' forward rudder had to be set at a slight *negative* angle relative to the wings, i.e., with its forward edge lower than its rear edge. With the wings near horizontal, the center of pressure would be well ahead of the center of gravity, and the aircraft would be forced to rise. With the forward rudder positioned as described, the pressure on the underside of the wings causing them to rise would be counteracted by a downward pressure on the forward rudder owing to its being angled so that its top surface would be exposed to the oncoming flow. In this way the location of the center of pressure of the wings could be kept fairly constant with respect to the center of gravity, resulting in a state of equilibrium.

Even though by this point the Wrights apparently recognized that the center of pressure reversed with curved surfaces, they initially designed their forward rudder as if they were dealing with a wing having the properties of a flat plate. Since they attempted to design their wing shape such that the center of pressure would only move forward in the range of angles of attack at which they planned to fly, reversing only at minute angles, it made sense that a pitch-stabilizing device similar to Pénaud's would provide the desired effect. The obvious problem with this scheme was that if the wing should dip to very low angles of attack, or the center of pressure reversed at a higher angle than anticipated, a negatively angled forward surface would not only be ineffective but also create a further problem. If the center of pressure reverses and moves to a position behind the center of gravity, the wings will dive rather than rise. In this case, not only will a negatively angled forward surface fail to counteract the pressure that is now causing the wings to dive; it will make things worse by adding further downward pressure to the wing.

Fortunately, the Wrights' forward rudder, or *elevator* as it would later be termed, was able to cope with this situation when it arose. They had added a further degree of sophistication to their device over the simple fixed surface used on Pénaud's models and by previous full-size glider pioneers by linking it to a control lever that enabled it to be flexed in either direction. The pilot was not only able to present the surface at an increased negative angle to level the aircraft if it rose abruptly; he was also able to flex the surface the opposite way to compensate for the diving effect caused by the center of pressure reversing its direction of travel and locating itself behind the center of gravity.[8]

The design of the Wrights' forward elevator provided a simple, responsive control over the movement of the center of pressure. The brothers would continue to experience difficulties with pitch stability for the next several years, not resolving the problem effectively until 1905. But the later solution merely entailed a few refinements to the basic system developed in 1900. Like their concept for control in roll, the Wrights' scheme of a movable elevator to keep pace with a constantly roving center of pressure was fundamentally sound, and it has been the method employed for pitch control on virtually every airplane since.

Wilbur and Orville could have effected precisely the same principle of pitch control by mounting their movable stabilizing surface behind the wings in the manner of Pénaud, Lilienthal, Chanute, Pilcher, and others rather than in front.[9] Indeed, most aircraft designed since the Wrights' have located the horizontal stabilizer at the rear. An obvious question, then, is why did they break from the relatively successful pattern of these earlier glider pioneers?

The Wrights stayed with a canard configuration for years because it offered several benefits that were unique to the design beyond the basic function of pitch control. From an historical perspective, however, documenting their decision to use the forward elevator is as slippery a matter as determining exactly how they arrived at wing warping for lateral control. The brothers, and the many tellers of the Wright story that followed them, invariably point to the advantages derived from the canard arrangement. However, there are only a few, hazy clues as to why they adopted it in the first place. Here again, despite their voluminous records, another of the most significant aspects of their inventive work remains unclear.

One of the most plausible explanations for their choice of the canard configuration relates back to Otto Lilienthal. Lilienthal's fatal crash resulted from a stall of his glider, followed by an uncontrolled nosedive into the ground. Basically, a *stall* is the point at which an aircraft stops flying. As an airplane slows down and the speed of the lift-generating flow of air over the wing decreases, the wing's angle of attack increases to compensate for the loss of lift. This response continues until, at a certain critical point, the flow separates from the top side of the wing. When this happens, turbulence sets in, the local difference in pressure is disrupted, and the wing loses all lift. At this point the airplane is stalled, and an abrupt vertical drop typically follows. If a stall occurs at a relatively high altitude, there is usually enough room for the airplane to regain minimum airspeed and resume flying. When flying close to the ground, however, as in the manner of Lilienthal and the Wrights, a stall invariably results in a crash because there is insufficient altitude to regain flying speed.

When the Wrights built their first glider in 1900, they, and everyone else, were unaware of what a stall was or why it occurred. They did know, based on the experiences of Lilienthal and others, that when an airplane was in an extreme nose-up attitude or lost too much speed, the general result was a violent, uncontrollable crash. Even though they as yet did not understand why this happened, they were acutely aware of the danger and were ever mindful of avoiding such situations.

As it turned out, the Wrights' forward elevator was extremely effective in reducing the violent reaction of a stall. Following a stall at low altitudes, the Wrights' canard design settled to the ground almost parachute style rather than going into a chilling spin common to aircraft with the stabilizer in the rear (see Figure 23). The glider hit with a fairly good jolt upon landing, but it was usually not hard enough to damage the machine or to injure the pilot.

A canard of the type the Wrights used behaves this way because the forward elevator stalls *before* the wing. When a conventional (stabilizer

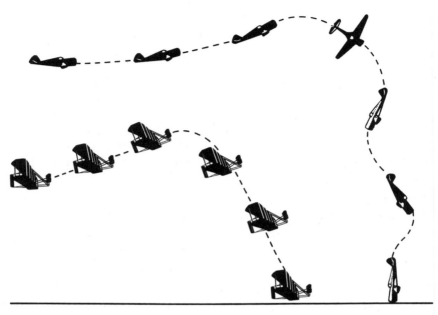

23. The left image illustrates the relatively safe parachute-style response following a stall of the canard configuration used by the Wright brothers. The violent spin and nosedive typical of a rear-tail configuration upon stalling is depicted at the right.

in rear) aircraft stalls, the wings lose all lift and the nose abruptly drops, placing the aircraft in a pronounced dive. When a canard stalls, the much smaller forward elevator loses lift before the main wings and begins to drop naturally, similar to a stalled conventional aircraft. But because the larger wing surfaces are still lifting, the "nose" of the canard does not fall so abruptly. Since the main supporting surfaces have not yet stalled, the violent nature of a typical stall is somewhat dampened. The canard reacts this way on its own, providing an automatic leveling effect of the aircraft. This relieves the pilot from having to respond quickly in such an emergency situation. Conventional aircraft, on the other hand, require an immediate control input from the pilot to regain a normal flying attitude.

At this point the brothers had little knowledge of stalls or of basic flying techniques, so the automatic stall recovery of the forward-elevator design was decidedly beneficial. It saved Wilbur and Orville from serious injury on several occasions before they came to understand stalls and to recognize how to logically avoid them. A stable, well-designed airplane with the stabilizer in the rear will also offer gentle, controllable stall characteristics. But with an unstable aircraft such as the Wrights', a canard configuration offered a far better chance of safe recovery.

Although they were clearly unaware of precisely what a stall was when designing their first glider, it is possible that the Wrights intuitively decided that placing the stabilizer ahead of the wings would help alleviate the deadly nosedive that had claimed Lilienthal's life. They alluded to this in later years. Recalling the experiments of 1900, Orville stated in 1924, "we retained the elevator in front for many years because it absolutely prevented a nose dive such as that in which Lilienthal and many others since have met their deaths."[10] It is difficult to determine, however, whether or not this was hindsight or a genuine accounting of their thinking at the time. But of one thing there is no doubt; once the brothers experienced stalls themselves and saw how effectively their forward elevator dealt with the situation, they steadfastly retained the arrangement for years, long after their improved flying skills permitted them to mount the elevator at the rear in safety. A rear-mounted elevator did not appear on a Wright airplane until 1910, the year the brothers introduced their first production aircraft offered for sale, the Wright Model B.

The forward elevator offered several other advantages that were useful in these earliest days of human flight. One was a purely practical measure necessitated by the conditions under which the Wrights made their first experiments. Because they were flying from sandy terrain, their early aircraft had no landing gear. They merely skidded to a landing on the bottom rails of the aircraft's structure. Locating the elevator out front eliminated the chance of breakage that might occur to a tail-mounted surface if it were to drag in the sand upon landing.

A forward elevator also provided an aerodynamic benefit in that it contributed to the overall lift of the aircraft when climbing. When the elevator was positioned to induce a rise in the aircraft's flight path, the wind hit its bottom side, providing added lift as the machine pitched upward. When a rear-mounted elevator is used to make the aircraft climb, on the other hand, the wind hits the top side of the surface and thus contributes no additional component of lift to the wings.

Another aerodynamic advantage of a forward elevator is that it offers a faster control response than one mounted behind the wing. This was significant in terms of the Wrights' aircraft because they flew at very low airspeeds; in fact, they flew just above stall speed even in full flight. The slower the flow of air over any control surface, the slower the aircraft will react to a control input. Since the performance of the Wrights' aircraft was so marginal, they no doubt benefited from the greater control effectiveness of a forward elevator.

Finally, once airborne, the canard configuration provided the pilot with a visual indicator of the aircraft's attitude in flight. By using the forward elevator as a reference with respect to the horizon, it would be apparent if the machine were diving or climbing. This aid in keeping the aircraft level was especially helpful during the Wrights' first few gliding seasons, when they were teaching themselves how to fly.

By this juncture the Wrights had come a long way from their first small kite built and flown in the summer of 1899. They had carefully considered the forces that would be acting on their lifting surface and came up with a wing airfoil based on a relatively sound analysis. Further, they thoughtfully addressed the issue of pitch stability and control from an aerodynamic standpoint and developed the effective movable forward elevator that coincidentally provided several other benefits, the most significant being favorable stall recovery characteristics. Before they could begin turning their ideas into hardware, however, a number of other design concerns would have to be worked through.

Beyond the fundamental decision to place the horizontal stabilizer ahead of the wing, several other aspects of the general arrangement of the glider had to be decided upon. The brothers continued with the biplane wing structure they had adapted for their wing-warping lateral control system in the 1899 kite. As before, two wing surfaces were arranged one above the other with struts and had wire trussing across the front and rear bays. The fore-and-aft bracing was again eliminated to allow for warping.

There is some evidence that the Wrights originally included a vertical tail on their craft, similar to many contemporary gliders. "The tail of my machine is fixed," Wilbur wrote to his father, "and even if my steering arrangement should fail, it would still leave me with the same control that Lilienthal had at the best."[11] It seems, however, that if a tail was ever on the glider, it was a short-lived addition. Beyond the fact that no tail appears in any of the few existing photographs of the 1900 glider, Wilbur later commented, "After much study we finally concluded that tails were a source of trouble rather than assistance; and therefore we decided to dispense with them altogether."[12] The Wrights would later reconsider this decision and add a vertical rudder to their third glider in 1902, when problems arose with their lateral control system. But for now, they felt it would only complicate matters unnecessarily.

The basic layout of the Wright machine differed in one other significant respect from previous gliders—the position of the pilot. Lilienthal, Herring, Pilcher, and virtually everyone else making tentative glider flights at this time rode their aircraft slung vertically between the wings. Concerned with reducing drag due to wind resistance, the Wrights chose to have the pilot lie prone on the bottom wing. They calculated the total drag of their glider, with the pilot in the horizontal position, to be only one half that of a glider where the pilot was upright, such as the Chanute-Herring two-surface machine. Interestingly, in order to corroborate their estimates of the surface area exposed to the wind of a pilot lying prone compared to one flying upright, they underwent an elaborate analysis of the wind resistance generated by a bicycle rider under known conditions.[13]

Such mathematical reasoning notwithstanding, most of their contemporaries felt that the Wrights' gliding position was a sure ticket to a broken neck. Even Octave Chanute, although impressed with their calculations regarding wind resistance, expressed reservations: "This is a magnificent showing, provided that you do not plow the ground with your noses."[14] Despite such skepticism, the brothers' technique proved to be no more hazardous than any other being employed at the time.[15] They retained this flying position not only on their first three gliders, but also on their 1903, 1904, and 1905 powered airplanes. Because these early aircraft were flying at such low speeds, this seemingly minor difference in design influenced performance significantly. The Wrights' accounting of this factor once again illustrates the thorough consideration they gave to the total sum of elements that make up a flying machine.

The aerodynamics and the general arrangement of components were two major aspects of design the Wright brothers had to address before beginning construction of their first full-size glider. A third obvious question was size. How large a wing area would be required and how light must the craft be in order to lift the weight of a human being into the air? Fortunately, to answer these questions the Wrights were not forced to work from a blank slate. They were able to draw upon a number of well-established mathematical relationships between speed, surface area, lift, and drag in order to calculate the size, weight, and speed requirements for successful flight.

These relationships had evolved over two centuries, largely through experimental analysis and intuitive thinking. The basic physical phenomenon in question was the effect of a flow, liquid or gaseous, on a body. Theorists such as Isaac Newton, who were seeking to explain the laws of motion, as well as practical thinkers concerned with more mundane matters, such as the pressure of water passing through a pipe, had been interested in determining the force of resistance generated by a body moving in a flow.

As long ago as Galileo's time, it was reasoned that an obvious factor related to resistance would be the density of the medium in which the body was moving. Similarly, it seemed logical that the speed of the flow and the surface area of the body would be relevant to calculating resistance. By the midseventeenth century, this intuitively derived relationship between the resistance force and density, speed, and surface area had been demonstrated by Newton.[16]

Over time, these ideas were adapted to a variety of engineering problems. One case that would have particular significance for aeronautics was the work of a well-known, mideighteenth century British engineer named John Smeaton.[17] Among many other subjects, Smeaton was interested in water mills and windmills, and he consequently studied and performed experiments on the flow of water and air against flat plates. Using a whirling-arm device of the type developed by Benjamin Robins and later used by Cayley, Smeaton determined that the pressure on a plate varies in proportion to the square of the velocity of the flow against the plate. (*Pressure* is simply another way of expressing resistance.) This means, for example, that if water were moving through a pipe hitting a flat plate suspended in the flow, the pressure on the plate would increase or decrease in direct proportion to a rise or fall in the square of the speed of the flowing water. For example, if the velocity of the flow were doubled, the pressure on the plate would increase four times.

Smeaton published this work in 1759 in what would become a well-known paper entitled, "An Experimental Enquiry Concerning the Natural Powers of Water and Wind to Turn Mills and Other Machines Depending on Circular Motion."[18] This paper helped to firmly establish the relationship between pressure and velocity among engineers and other technical experimenters. Included in the paper were a set of wind speed and pressure figures compiled by a colleague of Smeaton named Rouse. Others later used the concepts and the data in the paper to derive a constant of proportionality for Smeaton's basic notion of pressure varying as the square of the velocity when it was applied to objects moving in air. A *constant of proportionality* is simply a multiplying factor that allows the general relationship of pressure and velocity to be applied to the specific medium being studied (air, water, oil, etc.). This factor accounts for the density of the medium. The value assigned to this constant for air was 0.005, and it became known as *Smeaton's coefficient*.[19] The constant bears Smeaton's name even though it was arrived at by others from information contained in his paper rather than by the author himself.

The table of wind speeds and pressures that appeared in Smeaton's paper and the so-called Smeaton coefficient became standard values and were used unquestioned for close to 150 years. Using this constant of proportionality, a simple equation for the force of air exerted on a plate can be expressed as

$$F = kV^2S$$

where F is the force on the plate in pounds; V is the velocity, or speed, of the airflow in miles per hour; S is the surface area of the plate in square feet; and k is Smeaton's coefficient, 0.005.

Smeaton had confined his studies to flow oriented perpendicular to the surface. In 1792 another Englishman, Samuel Vince, took Smeaton's work a step further by showing that the force acting on a plate also varies with the *angle* of the plate to the oncoming flow.[20] For example, the pressure on a windmill blade will be different depending on what angle to the wind the blade is set. This would of course be very significant when aeronautical experimenters began to consider the upward force, the lift, generated by a wing at different angles of attack. In order to accommodate various angles of the wing to the flow in the basic pressure/velocity equation, another multiplying factor, or coefficient, had to be introduced. With regard to airplane wings, it is known as the *coefficient of lift* when calculating the lift force, and the *coefficient of drag* when determining the drag force. For every angle of attack of a given wing surface, there is a different coefficient of lift and drag.

During the course of the nineteenth century, the general relationship between pressure, velocity, and density, and the specific equations and information that grew out of the work of Smeaton and Vince, were adapted for aeronautical purposes by experimenters from Cayley to Lilienthal. By the time Wilbur and Orville set about determining the size of their first full-size glider in 1900, the basic equations necessary to calculate lift and drag for a given wing surface were in place. The Wrights did not have to derive them in any way. They were published by Lilienthal in his book *Der Vogelflug als Grundlage der Fliegekunst*, and they subsequently appeared in *The Aeronautical Annual* and other sources available to the Wrights. Lilienthal had even compiled and published a set of actual lift and drag coefficients for the specific wing shape he used for his gliders.[21] With these equations and the Lilienthal coefficients in hand, the Wrights were able to calculate with relative ease the appropriate dimensions of their own glider.

Expressed in terms of lift and drag respectively, the formulas available to the Wrights were

$$L = kV^2SC_L$$
and
$$D = kV^2SC_D$$

where L is the lift in pounds; k is Smeaton's coefficient, 0.005; V is the velocity of the airflow over the wing in miles per hour; S is the surface area, i.e., the wing area, in square feet; and C_L is the coefficient of lift. (C_L will of course be different for different angles of attack.) In the second equation everything is the same, except that now the Wrights were calculating the drag D in pounds and had to assign a coefficient of drag C_D for the specific angle of attack with which they were concerned.

Using these equations and the Lilienthal table of lift and drag coefficients, determining the size wing necessary to fly was a matter of basic algebra. Beginning with the simplest case, the minimum amount of lift

L required to carry an aircraft aloft would have to at least equal the total weight of the glider and the pilot. Knowing their own body weight and that of the materials they planned to use, the Wrights could estimate the final weight of the aircraft fairly closely. From here they could substitute values into the equation for the other terms they knew. The value for *k* was a known constant, 0.005. The velocity of the air *V* could be easily measured with an anemometer. The coefficient of lift was taken directly from Lilienthal's table. Now all the brothers had to do was solve for *S* to obtain the wing area necessary to lift the total weight of the aircraft and the pilot.

Using this result for the wing area, the Wrights could then perform a similar operation using the drag equation and Lilienthal's drag coefficients. In this way they were able to determine what the drag would be on a wing of the size calculated with the lift equation. The drag equation, however, only accounts for aerodynamic drag produced by the wing. The brothers also had to calculate and add in *parasitic drag*, the drag resulting from the wind resistance of the aircraft's structure and the exposed pilot.

Although the Wrights did estimate the drag on their gliders and measured the actual drag during trials, this information did not play a significant role in designing the gliders. Knowing the drag only becomes essential when designing a powered aircraft. Because the drag force is oriented horizontally, thus operating against thrust, the value for the drag is necessary to calculate the required thrust of the propellers. This, of course, is not a concern with an unpowered machine.

In light of this, it remains somewhat unclear as to why the Wrights calculated the drag at all when designing their gliders. One possibility is that they may have wanted to get a sense of how steep the glider's angle of descent would be with reference to the ground. For long glides, as shallow an angle of descent as possible is desired, necessitating a wing with a minimum amount of drag for the lift produced. Unfortunately, the Wrights never explain whether they calculated and measured drag on their gliders for this purpose.

Although Wilbur and Orville were able to take advantage of the equations and the data that had been developed by a variety of people over the previous two centuries, there was one critical problem that would confound their efforts well into 1901. Smeaton's coefficient, the constant of proportionality for air that virtually everyone had taken for granted as correct for so long, was in fact nearly forty percent off. The proper value is closer to 0.003. The problem caused by this error was an overestimation of the predicted lift of a given wing by forty percent when using the standard equations.

It was not until the middle of 1901, when the Wrights were having continued lift problems with their second full-size glider, that they began to seriously question the heretofore unchallenged coefficient. Shortly thereafter, they calculated a much more accurate value of 0.0033. Modern aerodynamicists have subsequently confirmed this figure to be correct within a few percent. But it would be two gliders and nearly two years before the Wrights made this important breakthrough. In designing their first aircraft in 1900, they used the equations with the same flawed constant that had evolved through practical experimentation and which had been used by everyone else.

Using these existing formulas and the available data, the Wrights began to transform their design ideas into an actual aircraft of specific dimensions and tangible materials. They began construction in mid-August of 1900, more than a year after the successful tests of their comparatively simple wing warping kite.[22] In only a few short weeks, the Wrights had prefabricated the majority of the parts for their first glider. Nearly every piece—the ribs, the struts, the metal fittings, even the fine French sateen fabric that would cover the spruce-and-ash framework—was carefully prepared to allow for simple assembly upon reaching the site of their gliding experiments, Kitty Hawk, North Carolina. Only the eighteen-foot lengths of spruce they planned to use for the wing spars were to be obtained and cut to size near Kitty Hawk. Such long pieces were too unwieldy to transport easily from Dayton.

Finally, after much hard work sorting out numerous complex problems, the brothers were ready. They had worked through the basic aerodynamic questions, developed a mechanical control system for both roll and pitch, designed the general layout of components of their glider, calculated how large the aircraft needed to be, and engineered and fabricated the individual parts. The time had come to test their ideas in actual practice. By early September 1900, almost a year and a half after the elder brother's eloquent letter to the Smithsonian Institution requesting information on the subject of human flight, Wilbur and Orville were ready to make their first tentative leaps into the air.

Even though the Wright brothers were still a long way from successful powered flight in the late summer of 1900, their glider was by far the most advanced and sophisticated heavier-than-air flying machine yet created. It represented the most thorough understanding of aerodynamics and control up to that time. The Wrights' initial design phase amply illustrates that many key aspects of their inventive method were operating from the start. Their engineering approach was readily apparent, as was the degree to which knowledge of previous experimenters' work guided their beginning research and design decisions. Their conceptual skills and rapidly growing understanding of the basic problems were also evident.

Perhaps the most striking element of the Wrights' method revealed in these early stages of their aeronautical work was their use of visual thinking. Certainly nonverbal thought was at work when they conceived the wing warping method for lateral control and adapted the twisted inner-tube box idea to the Pratt trussed-biplane wing structure. Their introduction of a longitudinal twist along the wing to produce different angles of attack on either side, followed by their realization that removal of the fore-and-aft bracing of a Chanute-Herring type biplane glider would allow for warping without compromising structural strength, clearly emanated from within their mind's eye. They had to have visualized these structures and movements in order to work them through conceptually and then turn them into a working mechanism. The Wrights' development of their basic ideas regarding stability and control also had a visual component. When the brothers looked to the bicycle to analyze how the rider stays upright and in control, they had to have depicted in their minds what was happening.

Even the Wrights' understanding of lift and the travel of the center of pressure was in part derived from such images. Considering the movement of the lifting pressure along a wing surface necessitates drawing a mental picture of what is going on. Similarly, the Wrights' belief in the advantage of locating the high point of the camber far forward clearly was derived from their envisioning the wing in the airstream. Their conclusion that this would help limit the travel of the center of pressure because less of the top surface of the wing would be presented to the flow, resulting in the reduction of downward pressure, would have been difficult to comprehend without such a concrete mental picture. Visual analysis was also prominent in the brothers' understanding of the function and placement of the forward elevator. Again, they clearly had to have "seen" the surfaces and forces in their minds' eyes to reason through matters as they did.

Obviously, the Wright brothers did distinguish themselves from many of their contemporaries by their effective use of reasoning and verbal information. Their understanding and use of the basic lift and drag equations and the realization of the error in Smeaton's coefficient are conspicuous examples. But repeatedly, the use of nonverbal, in combination with verbal, thinking and information is evident in the development of the Wrights' aircraft and in their understanding of aeronautics. The brothers' strong capacity to think and analyze problems using mental images was among the most fruitful elements of their inventive method.

5

Riding the Winds

In the spring of 1900, when Wilbur and Orville were in the midst of working through the many aerodynamic and design problems presented by their first full-size glider, they took a step that would have a long-term impact on their work and personal lives. They decided to write to the grand old man of aeronautics, Octave Chanute. Their success with the 1899 kite and the wing-warping system, as well as the work they had done so far in planning the 1900 glider, convinced the brothers that their ideas were basically sound and that they were ready to consult with someone of Chanute's stature in the aeronautical community. This opening letter had a twofold historical significance. It not only introduced a new, prominent player in the Wright story, but also launched a string of correspondence that would in great measure document the invention of the airplane.[1]

When Wilbur sat down to write Chanute on May 13, 1900, he could hardly have known that this would be the first of some four hundred letters they were to exchange until Chanute's death ten years later. Although Wilbur displayed deference and struck a self-effacing tone in this introductory contact, he was very forthright in the presentation of his ideas on the flying problem and how he planned to approach it. Despite the fact that it was common for Chanute to correspond with well-known engineers and scientists from around the globe, he was particularly impressed with the thoughts expressed on these first examples of pale blue Wright Cycle Company stationery that would now begin to appear regularly at his Chicago address. He was always eager to lend whatever support he could to promising and enthusiastic young experimenters and lost no time in responding to this obviously intelligent, capable bicycle shop proprietor from Ohio.[2]

Mutual admiration grew quickly out of the growing exchange of letters that in turn evolved into a warm friendship between the Wrights and Octave Chanute. During the Wrights' experimental years, and for a long period after their success, it was widely believed that Chanute played the role of mentor to Wilbur and Orville because of his prominent position in the aeronautical field and his seniority. But while they were in nearly constant communication, the Wrights were in no way pupils of Chanute. Throughout the years of their association, Chanute provided the Wrights with little genuine technical assistance and few if any useful theoretical ideas. In fact, he often misunderstood and incorrectly expressed to others the ideas and principles the Wrights shared with him. In making a case for Chanute's technical contribution, one could point to the influence of the Chanute-Herring two-surface glider of 1896 on the Wrights' early designs. But the brothers greatly modified and improved upon the ideas embodied in this craft preceding their personal contact with Chanute.

Chanute's significant contribution to the Wrights' invention of the airplane was as a source of moral support and a confidence builder to Wilbur and Orville during times of difficulty and frustration. He was an ever-enthusiastic correspondent to whom the brothers articulated proposed solutions and nascent ideas. It was only on rare occasions that Chanute was able to point out errors or correctly suggest that they were exercising bad judgment. But just the fact that he was always ready and willing to respond promptly to their latest letter was a major source of encouragement to Wilbur and Orville and played no small part in their seeing the project through to completion. Even though Chanute may have at times had problems comprehending entirely what the Wrights were doing, he understood one thing fully. He astutely recognized that Wilbur and Orville Wright had done more in the short time that they had been at work on human flight than the numerous other young experimenters he helped and sometimes supported financially. Consequently, he eagerly assisted them however he could.

Wilbur's first letter to Chanute went on for several pages, but it was not until the last few sentences that he actually got around to asking advice of this established leader of pioneer flight research. After a thoughtful and well-written outline of their work up to that point and their plans to build and test a full-size man-carrying glider, Wilbur inquired about suitable locations to fly such a craft. Chanute's prompt and cordial response of May 17 suggested San Diego, California, and St. James City, Florida, as sites of open spaces and steady winds. He further recommended investigating the Atlantic coasts of South Carolina and Georgia.[3] The Wrights also contacted the National Weather Bureau in Washington, D.C., and received publications containing tables of average wind speeds for a variety of places around the country.[4] Strong and regular breezes were essential for their glider tests. Without an engine, the wind was the only means of achieving the necessary lift-generating flow of air over the wing. Also desirable were open, sandy terrains, which would allow for relatively safe gliding and landing.

Among the sites that seemed promising, the Wrights selected a spot known as Kitty Hawk, located on an isolated strip of beach off the coast of North Carolina. "I chose Kitty Hawk," Wilbur explained to his father,

> because it seemed the place which most closely met the required conditions. In order to obtain support from the air it is necessary, . . . to move through it at a rate of fifteen or twenty miles per hour. . . . It is safer to practice in a wind, provided this is not too much broken up into eddies and sudden gusts by hills, trees, &c. At Kitty Hawk, which is on the narrow bar separating the Sound from the Ocean, there are neither hills nor trees, so that it offers a safe place for practice.[5]

Of the sites that met their basic criteria of open spaces, steady winds, and soft sands, Kitty Hawk also provided the brothers with the privacy they desired while still being reasonably accessible from their home, Dayton, Ohio.

There are a number of legends regarding the origin of the name *Kitty Hawk*. Among them are that during the period of early English settlement, it became an anglicized version of "Killy Honk," a local Indian expression for killing the geese that migrated to the area every fall. Another version suggests the name is derived from *skeeter hawk*, an insect eater that frequents the area and feeds on the prodigious mosquito population.[6]

Beyond these pragmatic reasons, the Wrights' choice of the site was also influenced strongly by two letters they received in response to an inquiry Wilbur made to the weather station at Kitty Hawk on August 3, 1900. The observer at the station, Joseph J. Dosher, after penning his own positive response, passed on Wilbur's original letter to William

J. Tate, a local resident considered the best-educated person in the modest little fishing village. Tate also answered the letter, enthusiastically endorsing Kitty Hawk as a "fine place" to conduct the "scientific kite flying" experiments the Wrights described and graciously offering to help in any way he could. "If you decide to try your machine here & come I will take pleasure in doing all I can for your convenience & success & pleasure, & I assure you you will find a hospitable people when you come among us," Tate wrote.[7] This expression of welcome settled the issue for the brothers. They looked no further and immediately set about making travel preparations for themselves and the carefully fabricated parts of the glider they had painstakingly designed during the previous year.

At 6:30 P.M. on Thursday, September 6, 1900, Wilbur Wright set off for Kitty Hawk, North Carolina, for the first time. Other than a trip to the World's Columbian Exposition in Chicago in 1893, he had not traveled farther than a bicycle ride from Dayton in more than a decade. In addition to a suitcase and trunk borrowed from his sister Katharine, he carried in crates the premade parts of the glider and all the necessary tools and equipment for conducting the experiments. He also brought along a large tent in which to camp and assemble the glider. The only essential he did not bring from Dayton were the cumbersome lengths of spruce for the wing spars, which he intended to acquire nearer to Kitty Hawk. The brothers agreed that Wilbur would go down ahead, get situated, and ready the glider. Orville would stay behind to make arrangements for running the bike shop in their absence and join his brother as soon as he was able.[8]

Wilbur's initial journey to Kitty Hawk turned out to be far more trying than he had anticipated. The first part of the trip was no great problem. Wilbur's 6:30 Thursday train from Dayton delivered him to Old Point Comfort, Virginia, the next day. From there he took a steamer ship to Norfolk, where he lodged Friday evening.[9]

He spent Saturday canvasing local lumberyards for the eighteen-foot lengths of spruce he needed for the glider's wing spars. The decision to acquire this material en route proved to be a mistake, for the best Wilbur could find were sixteen-foot strips of white pine. This not only meant that the strength of the glider would be slightly compromised, as pine is a somewhat less resilient wood than spruce, but, even more importantly, substituting shorter spars would reduce the overall wing area. This, of course, meant a smaller lift-generating surface than what the Wrights had planned. Frustrated but left with few alternatives, Wilbur purchased the sixteen-foot pieces and continued on. With the temperature near one hundred degrees, he loaded the lumber and his other cargo on board the 4:30 PM train from Norfolk to his next stop, Elizabeth City, North Carolina.[10]

Getting to North Carolina had been simple enough. The real difficulty lay in traversing the remaining thirty-five miles from Elizabeth City to Wilbur's more remote final destination. Kitty Hawk is located on the Outer Banks, a two-hundred-mile strip of sand that faces the Atlantic on its eastern shore and is separated from the North Carolina mainland by a series of shallow bodies of water. Today a popular getaway for urban dwellers, the Outer Banks are now accessible by road. But in 1900 there was no such convenience. Wilbur would have to secure passage by boat.

William Tate had indicated in his letter that Wilbur could cross Albemarle Sound to Kitty Hawk by hitching a ride on the mail boat that left three times a week from Manteo, North Carolina. But Manteo was fifty miles from Elizabeth City. Eager to get started with his experiments, Wilbur decided to go down to the waterfront and see if he could hire a boat to take him directly to Kitty Hawk from there.[11]

Curiously, no one Wilbur talked to in Elizabeth City seemed to know much about Kitty Hawk or how to get there. Finally, on his third day in town, Wilbur made the acquaintance of Israel Perry, a local fisherman who lived on a boat anchored nearby and who claimed to have been born in Kitty Hawk. A deal was made, and Perry helped Wilbur load his suitcase, trunk, and the pine spars on board a leaky, dilapidated skiff that would take Wilbur and his belongings to Perry's fishing boat three miles down river. The crates containing the remaining glider parts and tools would be transported to Kitty Hawk later on one of the freight boats that left Elizabeth City on a weekly basis.[12]

Upon arriving at Perry's schooner, Wilbur was shocked to see that the boat was in even worse condition than the skiff. He later recounted, "The sails were rotten, the ropes badly worn and the rudderpost half rotted off, and the cabin so dirty and vermin-infested that I kept out of it from first to last."[13] Anxious to conclude what had already been a long, tiring journey, Wilbur continued on with Perry.

What followed was a rather perilous voyage across the Sound during

24. Bill Tate, the Wrights' host and enthusiastic assistant at Kitty Hawk, with his family.

which the craft became caught up in gale-force winds, springing numerous leaks and sustaining some damage. The weather-torn schooner and its beleaguered occupants finally made it to Kitty Hawk Bay on Wednesday evening, September 12. Wilbur spent the night on board Perry's boat and made his way to the home of William Tate the next morning with the help of a local boy named Elijah Baum. It had been two arduous, fright-filled days since leaving Elizabeth City, and a full week after his departure from Dayton, but Wilbur Wright finally had arrived at the place he and his brother would make famous.[14]

Wilbur found Bill Tate and his family to be as hospitable as Bill's letter had suggested. When Mrs. Tate realized Wilbur had eaten nothing for forty-eight hours but a small jar of jelly that Katharine had slipped into his suitcase, she made him a hearty ham-and-eggs breakfast. This was more than a modest gesture, as eggs were not terribly plentiful in

25. The Kitty Hawk lifesaving station, 1900.

this area. Wilbur asked if he could stay with the Tates for several days until his brother Orville arrived with their cots, other camping equipment, and provisions. They graciously agreed.[15]

The residents of Kitty Hawk for the most part split their time between fishing and manning the local lifesaving station, one of seven that had been built along the Outer Banks in response to the many shipwrecks caused by treacherous shoals just off the North Carolina coast. A church, a store, and a U.S. Weather Bureau facility were the only other notable structures beside the small collection of rude frame houses that made up the village. Bill Tate was an unofficial leader of this tiny hamlet. In addition to his activities as a fisherman and his serving with the lifesaving crew, he was postmaster, notary public, and a local county commissioner. Although extremely austere even by the standards of 1900, he lived in one the nicest houses in Kitty Hawk.[16]

After a few days of rest, Tate introduced Wilbur around and showed him the terrain he had described in his letter. By then the crates containing the rest of the glider parts had reached Kitty Hawk, and Wilbur eagerly got to work. Outsiders were a rarity, so it did not take long for the villagers to learn what this well-dressed man from the north was up to. When they realized the sticks of wood and the French sateen fabric Wilbur brought with him were being assembled into a flying machine, their friendliness was balanced with a degree of suspicion. As Bill Tate would write in a future recollection of his association with the Wrights, Kitty Hawkers believed "in a good God, a bad Devil, a hot Hell, and more than anything else . . . that the same good God did not intend that man should ever fly."[17]

The first thing Wilbur did on the glider was to trim two feet from the center of the presewn fabric covering, which had been prepared to accept eighteen-foot spars, to compensate for the sixteen-foot pieces acquired in Norfolk. He then carried Mrs. Tate's sewing machine into the yard and spliced the halves of the covering back together. Twenty-eight years later, the citizens of Kitty Hawk would erect a five-foot marble shaft on this spot to mark the place where Wilbur began work on the Wrights' first glider.[18]

While his brother was finding his way to the Outer Banks, Orville had secured the services of a young man named Harry Dillon to look after the bike shop and a boyhood friend, Cord Ruse (builder of Dayton's first automobile), to do the repairing while he and Wilbur were away. Orville left for Kitty Hawk on September 24 and arrived four days later. Like Wilbur's, his trip across Albemarle Sound was problem ridden and also took two full days. The delay was for lack of winds rather than because of storms, however. The Tates played host to the two of them for a few more days before the brothers set up their own camp a half mile from the Tate house.[19]

They pitched their large twelve-by-twenty-four-foot tent adjacent to a lone, haggard oak tree that somehow managed to survive in the harsh, sandy environment. The arduous aspects of the trip to Kitty Hawk were not confined to crossing the sound. Sudden squalls would frequently blow up off the ocean, making for more than a few sleepless nights of holding down the tent and trying to stay warm. Orville related something of the experience in a letter to Katharine:

This is "just before the battle," sister, just before the squall begins. About two or three nights a week we have to crawl up at ten or eleven o'clock to hold the tent

26. The Wrights' camp on the desolate Kitty Hawk beach in 1900.

down. When one of these 45-mile nor'easters strikes us, you can depend on it, there is little sleep in our camp for the night.[20]

Orville went on humorously,

A cold nor'easter is blowing tonight, and I have seen warmer places than it is in this tent. We each of us have two blankets, but almost freeze every night. The wind blows in on my head, and I pull the blankets up over my head, when my feet freeze, I reverse the process. I keep this up all night and in the morning am hardly able to tell "where I'm at" in the bedclothes.[21]

The wind conditions were a source of other annoyances as well. The ubiquitous sand was constantly being blown and sifted about, finding its way into every corner and crevice of their tent, cots, and clothes; there was no escaping it. "But the sand!" Orville exclaimed, "The sand is the greatest thing in Kitty Hawk, and soon will be the only thing."[22] During wind storms, he reported, "When we crawl out of the tent to fix things outside the sand fairly blinds us. It blows across the ground in clouds. . . . We came down here for wind and sand, and we have got them."[23] Years later Orville remarked that the place was "like the Sahara, or what I imagine the Sahara to be."[24]

An unexpected problem regarding the wind was its variability. The Wrights did not realize that the figures of fifteen and twenty miles per hour reported by the weather bureau were monthly averages. On a daily basis, the wind speed would reach as high as sixty miles per hour on some occasions and be dead calm on others. This meant that conditions suitable for testing the glider were far more irregular than the brothers had assumed they would be.

Insects, especially mosquitoes, were constant companions, as Orville reported to Katharine during the brothers' second trip to Kitty Hawk in 1901. "They chewed us clear through our underwear and socks. Lumps began swelling up all over my body like hen's eggs. . . . Misery! Misery!"[25]

To add to these hardships, there was always the problem of food. Even though Kitty Hawk was a fishing village, the need for cash forced the locals to ship the majority of what they caught north to Baltimore and other East Coast cities for sale. The few cows that existed were so pitiful it was a wonder that they were able to deliver any milk at all. The same was true for chickens and the eggs they produced. There was a fair amount of wild game to be had for those willing to hunt for it, but much of that was also sold rather than consumed. Invariably, the provisions the Wrights brought with them on their several trips to the Outer Banks were more diverse and plentiful than what the local stores had to offer.[26]

But Kitty Hawk was not all problems and unpleasant conditions. Orville wrote to his sister in October 1900,

The sunsets here are the prettiest I have ever seen. The clouds light up in all colors in the background, with deep blue clouds of various shapes fringed with gold before. The moon rises in much the same style, and lights up this pile of sand almost like day. I read my watch at all hours of the night on moonless nights without the aid of any other light than that of the stars shining on the canvas of the tent.[27]

Most importantly, Kitty Hawk, with its clear, expansive stretches of soft sand, rolling dunes, and hearty breezes, was an ideal place to do what the Wright brothers principally came there for—to fly. Despite the

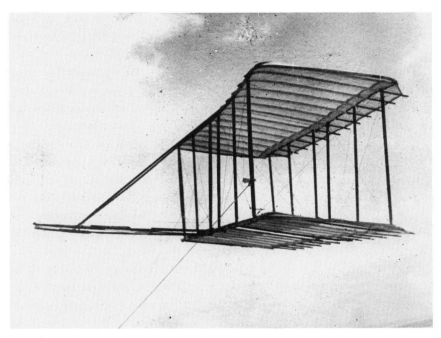

27. The 1900 Wright glider, the brothers' first man-carrying aircraft.

hardships, Wilbur and Orville always viewed their trips to Kitty Hawk as vacations. They enjoyed periodically escaping from the tedium of city life, grew fond of the Tates and the other local folk they came to know, and found the opportunity to experiment and test their ideas in the field exhilarating. They always returned to Dayton feeling more fit than when they left, and in later years the brothers looked back on their times on the Outer Banks as some of the happiest in their lives.

Wilbur had hoped to have the glider ready for trial by the time his brother joined him. But the unexpected modification of the covering, along with a few other problems, left a fair amount to be done after Orville reached Kitty Hawk. With a second pair of hands, however, the work went quickly, and by the first week in October they were ready to put their efforts of the past year to the test.

Originally intended to be of 200 square feet, the wing area of the biplane glider had to be reduced to 165 square feet because of the shorter sixteen-foot spars the Wrights were forced to use.[28] With wooden bows added to the ends to complete the wing panels, the total span of the craft came to 17½ feet. The chord was five feet, and the final weight without pilot was fifty-two pounds. The wing ribs were cut from ash strips and steam bent to a camber of approximately 1 in 22.[29]

There was only a single layer of the French sateen-fabric covering on the glider. The ribs were slipped into pockets sewn into the underside of the covering. The white-pine spars that formed the leading edge of the wings were triangular in cross section. The rear spars were square and located on top of the ribs and the fabric covering about a foot from the trailing edge. An extra piece of cloth was applied over the rear spar to lessen wind resistance. The construction was interesting in that the wooden structure was not rigidly fastened together; it merely "floated" inside the pockets sewn into the fabric covering. An added ingenious feature regarding the fabric was that it was applied to the wing structure with the direction of the weave on the bias. This imparted stiffness across the frame without hindering its ability to be warped for lateral control. Making the fabric an integral part of the structure in this way also eliminated the need for internal bracing, which saved weight. An eighteen-inch-wide space in the center of the lower wing where the pilot would lie was left completely uncovered. Unlike the 1899 kite, the fabric on the 1900 glider was not varnished or sealed in any way.[30]

In the manner of the earlier kite, the biplane wings were wire-trussed lengthwise across the front and rear bays but left unbraced fore and aft to allow for wing warping. Each half of the wing cell had a single fifteen-gauge spring-steel wire fed through the entire structure so that all the rigging on the glider could be tightened by adjusting just two wires. Originally, the wings had been rigged with a few degrees of dihedral angle, but they were put straight after just a few flights because side gusts of wind hitting the underside of the wing contributed to difficulties in controlling the glider.[31]

The forward elevator was flexed up and down by means of horizontal levers mounted to the rear of the surface that extended back to the pilot lying prone. For the wing-warping system, a wooden crossbar to which the warping cables were connected was mounted at the rear of the lower wing such that the pilot's feet rested on it. Control to the right or left was achieved by pushing on the crossbar with the appropriate foot.

When the Wright brothers surveyed the efforts of previous glider pioneers, they recognized that in addition to their flawed approach to balance and control, most were also hampered by their limited and sporadic time in actual flight. Lilienthal had been the first to understand that extensive flight testing was essential to achieving success in the air:

One can get a proper insight into the practice of flying only by actual flying experiments. . . . The manner in which we have to meet the irregularities of the wind, when soaring in the air, can only be learnt by being in the air itself. . . . The only way which leads us to a quick development in human flight is a systematic and energetic practice in actual flying experiments.[32]

The Wrights agreed that consistent and appreciable amounts of time in the air must be achieved if flying was to advance at any sort of reasonable pace.

The skills required to pilot an aircraft demand sustained and intensive practice. Unlike driving an automobile, for example, which requires maneuvering in only one plane of motion, an airplane must be controlled in three planes of motion. The pilot must control the aircraft's movement from side to side. This motion, known as *yaw*, related to pointing the nose of the airplane toward the right or left and is comparable to the plane of motion in which an automobile turns. In addition, the pilot must also balance the wings of the machine, control in *roll*, and attend to vertical motion, control in *pitch*. To stay airborne, simultaneous coordination of the airplane's movements about all three of these axes is required. Learning to fly an airplane has the added complication that, once in the air, you are committed to flying the machine back to the ground. One cannot simply hit the brakes and start over when trouble arises, as can be done in an automobile.

Because of the complexity involved in controlling an airplane, making only brief glides such as those achieved by earlier pioneers made it difficult to gain the experience necessary to become proficient at flying. The Wrights noted that, even as impressive as Lilienthal's flights had been, he had accumulated a total of only five hours in actual flight over a period of five years. This was hardly adequate to master so difficult an activity as flying, thought Wilbur. He wrote Chanute, "Even the simplest intellectual or acrobatic feats could never be learned with so short practice, and even Methuselah could never have become an expert stenographer with one hour per year for practice."[33] In his 1901 speech to the Western Society of Engineers, Wilbur again returned to the bicycle analogy. "It would not be considered at all safe for a bicycle rider to attempt to ride through a crowded city street after only five hours' practice."[34]

Attentive to this drawback evident in their predecessors' efforts, Wilbur and Orville decided that they must gain a significant amount of practice flying their aircraft if they were going to make any serious headway with their glider program and ultimately be prepared to pilot a powered machine. Toward this end, they devised a method they believed would allow them to stay airborne for extended periods with their first full-size glider. The device consisted of a tower with a pulley at the top over which ran a rope that was attached to the glider. On the other end of the rope was a counterweight intended to balance the glider as the force of the wind caused it to pull on the line running over the tower. In this manner, the Wrights felt they could practice handling their glider by the hour rather than for only a few seconds at a time. Wilbur explained to Chanute, "if the plan will . . . enable me to remain in the air for practice by the hour instead of by the second, I hope to acquire skill sufficient to overcome . . . [the] difficulties . . . inherent to flight.[35]

As it turned out, the suspension device proved to be of little value and was abandoned after only a few trials. Like their fellow experimenters, the brothers were going to have to brave the winds in free flight in order to learn how the forces of flight acted upon their craft.[36]

Despite the limitations of the tower scheme, the Wrights' emphasis on gaining extended practice in the air illustrates an important aspect of their methodology. They always thought in terms of the final goal of a practical powered airplane, correctly conceiving it as a complex technological system comprised of several distinct units, all of which needed to operate in concert in order to achieve successful flight. This system included not only the physical structure and mechanisms for controlling and propelling the airplane, but also the pilot as an integral component of the craft. Having a pilot with the appropriate skills was just as crucial to success as a sound control system or a suitable engine. Recognizing this, Wilbur and Orville gave an equal degree of attention to learning to fly as they did to designing and constructing their aircraft.

The precise dates are not known, but the Wrights made the initial flights of their 1900 machine during the first week in October, probably on the 5th and 6th. After a few brief attempts at flying the glider as a tethered aircraft with a man on board, it was flown from two to four hours each day as an unmanned kite with lines running to the ground to operate the controls. They tried it unloaded as well as with a ballast of fifty pounds of chain. Because of excessive winds on their third day out with the glider, October 10, they did not make any piloted attempts at all, confining their efforts entirely to kiting the machine with no one aboard.[37]

That afternoon the brothers tested the suspension apparatus. On a dune a short distance from their camp, they erected a tower from which they would suspend their glider and hopefully gain extended experience controlling it by manipulating lines from the ground. After an hour of only modest success, they brought the glider down to make some adjustments to the control lines. As they attended to the tower, the glider was tipped up and carried away by a gust of wind. It smashed into the sand twenty feet away and was damaged severely. Fittingly, the Wrights thereafter referred to this dune as the Hill of the Wreck. Greatly discouraged, they nearly gave up and went home. But leaving with so little accomplished would have bothered them even more, so they decided to piece their flying machine back together and continue their experiments.[38]

Three days later the glider was back in flying shape and ready for another trial. The suspension device was abandoned in favor of flying the glider as a kite. The Wrights flew their aircraft in this manner for the majority of the remainder of their stay, mixing in a few manned tethered flights when the conditions permitted. Occasionally Tom Tate, the young son of Bill Tate's half-brother, Dan, took the pilot's position when the winds were not strong enough to carry one of the Wrights. The younger Tate would come to be a familiar and welcome face in the Wrights' camp. His talent for telling tall stories made him an entertaining as well as useful helper. All of the Tates became interested in the Wrights' flying experiments and frequently assisted the brothers during this and future visits to Kitty Hawk. They often provided the necessary additional hands required to handle the aircraft.[39]

During the week and a half since they had begun flight testing their machine, the Wright glider had amassed quite a few hours in the air as a kite, but neither Wilbur nor Orville had as yet experienced even a second of free flight. Even the few instances when a pilot rode the aircraft while tethered had accounted for only a total of ten minutes.

The techniques by which they planned to improve upon their predecessors' time in the air had not panned out. The Wrights realized that there was no substitute for climbing on board the glider and actually making true flights in the manner of Lilienthal, Herring, and Pilcher.

On October 18, the brothers carried their by now somewhat tattered flying machine down to a group of small but steep hills about a mile south of their camp, from which they planned to make their first attempts at true gliding. Unfortunately, the wind died down as they arrived on the site. In order to keep the long trek through the sand from being a total waste, they made several launches of the glider unmanned down the hillside to observe its behavior in free flight. Despite some minor cracks and breaks upon hard landings, they were pleased with the way the glider reacted.[40]

The following day they made an even longer journey to the largest of three dunes collectively known as Kill Devil Hills, some four miles away. As with the name Kitty Hawk, Kill Devil Hills is also the subject of many stories. Some say the dunes got that name "because sailors say it is enough to kill the devil to navigate this part of the sound." Other legends cite devilish apparitions seen among these hills.[41]

The dominant sand hill of the group jutted approximately one hundred feet above the beach and had about a ten-degree slope. This time just the opposite occurred. The winds were so strong that the Wrights felt a piloted glide would be unsafe, and they returned to their camp having made no attempts at all. Finally, on October 20, conditions at Kill Devil Hills permitted a trial, and, for the first time, one of the brothers felt the unique sensation of unfettered flight. Wilbur did all of the free gliding in 1900 and 1901. It was not until they flew their third glider in 1902 that Orville tried his hand at the controls.

During the brief periods when they rode the glider as a tethered kite, the Wrights found that their arrangement of the wing-warping and forward-elevator controls made it very difficult to operate them simultaneously. So difficult, in fact, that it nearly discouraged them from attempting any free glides at all. They did not have the necessary materials or tools to change the control set-up on the spot, so as a stopgap solution they decided to try some glides with the wing-warping control wires secured, leaving only the forward elevator operable.[42]

With Wilbur positioned along the lower wing, Orville and Bill Tate each grasped a wing tip and ran down the slope with the glider until it began to lift on its own. As the machine floated over the sand, they continued alongside it, pressing down whichever wing tip wanted to rise to maintain lateral equilibrium. This allowed Wilbur to focus on balancing the glider fore and aft with the front rudder. When the glider reached a speed where Orville and Bill Tate could no longer keep up, Wilbur settled the aircraft gently into the sand with a slight downward turn of the elevator.[43]

Ever cautious, the brothers started slowly. At an altitude of no more than a foot, the first few attempts were between five and ten seconds in duration. The best glides of the day lasted between fifteen and twenty seconds and covered three hundred to four hundred feet. Wilbur was amazed by the ease and precision with which he was able to control the glider in pitch. He did not have to resort to the violent, acrobatic movements employed by Lilienthal and others. He was able to lie still on his craft and deftly command its flight path with hand and mind working in precise unison.[44]

Having gained a little experience with the forward elevator, the Wrights loosened the wing warping cables for the last three or four glides; however, operating the two control systems together still proved too much of a challenge. With this the gliding for 1900 came to a conclusion. Altogether, Wilbur had made a dozen trips down the hillside for a total of two minutes in actual flight. Three days later, on October 23, the brothers left for home.[45]

The Wrights discarded their glider upon completion of the trials. Everything was scarce in Kitty Hawk, so it was not surprising that Bill Tate asked if he could salvage the glider for materials. Mrs. Tate put the French sateen wing covering to particularly good use, making it into dresses for her two young daughters, Irene and Pauline.[46]

On the surface, the Wrights' first season at Kitty Hawk appeared to be something of a disappointment. Their original plans to spend long periods learning to pilot their glider had proven to be overly optimistic. Nonetheless, there were numerous other successes. The failure to gain extensive flight experience was more than made up for by the data they had collected regarding the lift and drag of their aircraft and their confirmation of various ideas that heretofore had only existed on paper. As Wilbur later summed it up, we were very much pleased with the general results of the trip, for setting out as we did, with almost revolutionary theories on many points, and an entirely untried form of machine, we considered it quite a point to be able to return without having our pet theories completely knocked in the head by the hard logic of experience, and our own brains dashed out in the bargain.[47]

To begin with, the Wrights demonstrated that many of their working assumptions and beginning design concepts were sound. Their belief that practice in actual trial was a key to learning the art of flying was borne out. They gained more knowledge about flying in those two minutes of sailing down the slope at Kill Devil Hills than in all the hours of kiting the glider. The basic effectiveness of their wing-warping system that was exhibited in the trial of the 1899 kite was confirmed by the full-size aircraft. In addition, their hope that the movable forward elevator would help limit the travel of the center of pressure and enable the pilot to control the aircraft in pitch with great precision was more than fulfilled. They and others had always considered fore-and-aft balance to be more difficult to achieve than lateral balance. As such, the brothers were particularly pleased with how well the forward elevator dealt with the problem. Further, the flight testing at Kitty Hawk substantiated the structural integrity of their design and showed it to be easily repaired when damage did occur. Another significant result of the experiments was the validation of the Wrights' belief that flying and landing with the pilot lying horizontal was practical and safe.

Despite these positive results, the experience at Kitty Hawk also revealed some disturbing things concerning the aerodynamic performance of the glider. In the long run, however, the questions raised by these problems ultimately led the brothers to several important breakthroughs that were crucial to their later triumph in 1903. Extensive kiting of the glider gave the brothers an opportunity to make a series of direct readings of the lift and drag generated by the machine. They measured these values in pounds using a grocers-type pull scale. Surprisingly, the drag, or *drift*[48] as the Wrights referred to it, proved to be far less than anticipated. The fifty-two-pound glider registered a total horizontal pull of only 8½ pounds, a figure much lower than had been estimated.[49]

The lift produced by the glider, on the other hand, was terribly disappointing. Based on the data recorded by Lilienthal and using the standard lift equation, the Wrights calculated that a machine the size of theirs, using a wing curvature of the type they had selected, should be able to lift its own weight plus a pilot in a wind of about twenty-one miles per hour at an angle of attack of three degrees, flight parameters they considered favorable. Actual performance was nowhere near this good. Winds over twenty-five miles per hour and an angle of attack of nearly *twenty degrees* were required to lift the glider with a man aboard.

That high an angle of attack was unacceptable for several reasons. Under such conditions a tremendous amount of drag is generated compared to lift, and an almost total loss of effectiveness of the forward elevator results. Beyond these immediate problems, the poor performance of the 1900 glider presented a greater, more basic dilemma for Wilbur and Orville. It placed in question the data and the equations they had been relying upon to design their aircraft. They had carefully calculated the size of the glider and designed the wing shape to meet a set of general flight parameters they considered desirable. Even though drag readings were better than expected, the lift produced was only about half of what their calculations had predicted it should have been. For all their precise planning, something was obviously very wrong.

Several possible causes for this immediately sprang to mind. Perhaps they had made a mistake in departing from Lilienthal's flight-tested curvature of 1 in 12, opting for a flatter camber of 1 in 22. The fact that they did not make the fabric covering airtight by sealing it as they had on the 1899 kite may have diminished the lift as well. The Wrights also entertained the possibility that data obtained from Lilienthal's work, or the lift and drag equations themselves, might have been in error. The poor performance of the 1900 glider placed genuine doubt in their minds concerning the established values and formulas they had used. This last possibility was most unsettling for Wilbur and Orville. If the published data were in error, the brothers faced major rethinking of a number of fundamentals that had been widely accepted as correct.

Despite the puzzling results concerning certain aspects of their tests and their failure to gain much time in the air, the Wrights were generally pleased with their first visit to Kitty Hawk. They were able to validate quite a few of their ideas regarding control and structural design, and they found their stay on the Outer Banks, on balance, very enjoyable. The 1900 glider cost them a mere fifteen dollars to build, and the experiments had proven to be relatively safe. All things considered, they saw no reason not to continue their aeronautical work and made plans to return to the little fishing village with a new glider the following year.[50]

On November 16, 1900, Wilbur wrote Octave Chanute a long letter detailing the glider and the results of its trials. Beyond the account of the experiments, the letter is interesting in that for the first time Wilbur gives an indication that he was not working alone. Up to this point, all of his correspondence with Chanute, the Smithsonian, even his father, continually referred to "my experiments," "my glider," "my ideas." Even though in future letters Wilbur would often continue to use "I" when referring to the work of both of them, it was now clear that Orville was as involved in the project as himself. By this point, Wilbur's initial interest in aeronautics had evolved into a true team effort.

The Wrights' growing uncertainty regarding Lilienthal's lift tables prompted them to conduct a number of experiments in order to validate their concerns. They mounted small wing surfaces to either end of a V-shaped structure made of wood and exposed the device to the wind. By this method they hoped to determine the relative lifting forces of various curved surfaces and discover if these measurements compared favorably to Lilienthal's published values. The crude nature of the tests did not allow for accurate readings, but, as Orville wrote, "the results of these experiments confirmed us in the belief already formed that the accepted tables of air pressures were not to be altogether relied upon."[51]

Despite their suspicions, the Wrights were still not prepared to throw out the published data and equations upon which they had based their first glider. Who were they, the brothers modestly believed, to reject the work of internationally recognized scientists and engineers? Nevertheless, their brief series of experiments did convince them that some change was necessary to gain greater lift.

To deal with the lift problem of the 1900 glider, the Wrights simply increased the size of the aircraft. The new glider, as they described it to Chanute in May of 1901, would "be built on exactly the same general plan as our last year's machine but will be larger and of improved construction in its details."[52]

This statement reveals an important aspect of the Wrights' approach to aircraft design. One of the things that most distinguished their aeronautical research from other early experimenters was the great degree of continuity in their work. Unlike their contemporaries, who jumped from one completely different design to another, the Wrights built upon the same basic structures and concepts from beginning to end. The similarity between their initial full-size craft of 1900, their subsequent gliders, and their later powered airplanes is clear and very significant. Every step they took and each new component they developed was thoughtfully incorporated into an ever-evolving single, basic design. Their series of gliders were never intended to be anything more than preliminary aircraft to test out various aeronautic, structural, and control concepts essential to the complete, unified system of elements that would become the airplane.

The new 1901 glider was again a biplane. It had a span of twenty-two feet and a seven-foot chord, giving it a net wing area of 290 square feet after making the opening for the pilot in the lower wing. It weighed ninety-eight pounds unloaded. As a further measure toward curing the lift deficiency of the 1900 machine, the brothers also increased the camber of the wing from 1 in 22 to 1 in 12. This seemed a reasonable move given that the Lilienthal data they had used in their earlier calculations were derived from a 1 in 12 airfoil, a curvature the German pioneer had seemingly proven successful. Not to be locked-in to this change, however, the Wrights cleverly constructed their new glider so that the camber could be altered during their experiments in the field.[53]

The Wrights' 1901 glider was the largest anyone had yet tried to fly. Compared to their own 165-square foot craft of 1900, Lilienthal's 151-square foot monoplane glider, and the Chanute-Herring two-surface machine of 134 square feet, the Wrights' latest was mammoth in dimension. Not only were the numbers impressive, but the Wright 1901 glider marked a significant point of divergence in the invention of the airplane in another, more important, sense as well.

It would have been impossible to fly so large an aircraft without some mechanical means of control such as Wilbur and Orville had developed. Weight shifting would have been totally ineffective on a machine of this size. Similarly, a powered airplane of sufficient size to carry the weight of an engine and a pilot would also require a mechanical control system. The door to the development of a powered airplane that other experimenters had closed to themselves by pursuing weight shifting for control was opened by the Wrights with their wing-warping system and their movable forward elevator. The much larger Wright 1901 glider was a tangible step beyond the limiting designs of previous glider pioneers because its size unquestionably illustrated the advantage of mechanical control, and the relationship of mechanical control to coping with the minimum size requirement of a powered flying machine. There was no appreciable difference in the aerodynamic, structural, or control principles embodied in the first two Wright gliders. But the unprecedented size of the 1901 machine contributed to establishing the fundamental breakthroughs that were present in both gliders in a very visible way and in this sense showed the aeronautical work of Wilbur and Orville Wright to be on an entirely new level.

On their second trip to the Outer Banks, the Wright brothers were able to leave together, arriving at Kitty Hawk during the second week in July 1901. The previous month, they had hired a machinist named Charlie Taylor on a full-time basis. This turned out to be an important event for the invention of the airplane. Not only did Charlie Taylor's presence free up more time for the brothers to concentrate on their aeronautical work and make their trips to Kitty Hawk; it would be Taylor who would later do most of the designing and machining of the gasoline engine that powered the Wrights into the air in December of 1903.[54]

Aside from the Tates and other locals who lent a hand, this year the brothers would be joined in their camp by a few other aeronautical experimenters. Shortly before leaving for Kitty Hawk, Wilbur and Orville had their first meeting with Octave Chanute in late June. He stopped off to visit them in Dayton while en route to Tennessee to confer with Edward C. Huffaker, a somewhat experienced member of the late nineteenth-century aeronautical community who was building a new glider for Chanute to his specifications. The name Huffaker was not unfamiliar to the Wrights. He had worked for Samuel Langley and was the author of one of the pamphlets the Smithsonian had sent them in 1899. During this visit to Dayton, Chanute delivered a French-made Richard anemometer he had earlier promised to lend them for taking accurate wind speed measurements on their upcoming trip to Kitty Hawk.

The Chanute-Huffaker machine was a hopelessly designed five-winged contraption featuring in-flight variable wing curvature and constructed of paper tubes, of all things. Chanute was dissatisfied with some of the changes Huffaker had made in his design, in particular the paper tubes, but decided to test the glider anyway. He wrote the Wrights two days after visiting with them and asked if they would not mind Huffaker joining them at Kitty Hawk to try the glider. Chanute indicated that he also wished to send George A. Spratt, a new enthusiast he had recently hired. The Wrights no doubt thought little of Chanute's new machine, but they politely agreed to share their camp and lend whatever assistance they could provide. Chanute himself would also come to Kitty Hawk for a time to see to his own interests as well as to observe the Wrights.[55]

The trip south was a bit easier this time given that the brothers were now familiar with the territory, but the weather was again a problem. The day before reaching Kitty Hawk, the winds topped ninety miles an hour, and for a solid week after that it rained. To avoid the four-mile hike from Kitty Hawk to Kill Devil Hills, the Wrights set up camp about 1,500 feet from the largest of the three dunes, known as "Big Hill." Although closer to the slopes, drinking water was a problem this far from Kitty Hawk, and the mosquitoes were more plentiful. The insect problem was made still worse, as the heavy rains left standing water all around, providing ideal breeding grounds for the swarming pests.[56]

The size of the new glider necessitated the building of a shed, so in addition to their tent, the Wrights erected a rough hangar sixteen by twenty-five feet. The hanger featured large doors at either end hinged along the top to simplify moving the glider in and out. The doors also made convenient awnings when propped up, offering shelter from the sun. With delays because of the rain, the week required to build the hangar, and the time spent assembling the glider, it was not until July 27 that the Wrights were ready to resume the exciting gliding experiments begun the previous fall.

The first day out with the 1901 glider started slowly. Following up on the technique used in 1900, Wilbur took the pilot's position on the lower wing, and Orville and another assistant picked up the glider at the wing tips. They then ran down the side of the dune until the glider began to lift on its own, whereupon they released it to the full control of the pilot. The first several launches ended abruptly with the glider quickly settling into the sand after being released. On each successive

28. The Wrights' more substantial camp building, erected in 1901. The ends of the structure opened upward to afford easy removal of the glider, as well as to provide welcome shade from the scorching Kitty Hawk sun. Seated left to right are Octave Chanute, Orville, and Edward Huffaker, with Wilbur facing them.

attempt, Wilbur inched back a little further on the wing to move the center of gravity closer to the rear. Finally, positioned about a foot behind where he had started, Wilbur got off several successful glides, a few covering as much as 300 feet, and one distancing 370 feet. The best flight in terms of duration was a nineteen-second effort that measured 315 feet. The first day's flying totaled approximately seventeen glides.[57]

There were two flights that day that were significant not for their duration but for the way they ended. During one of the longer glides, Wilbur lost speed at an altitude of about eighteen feet. The glider stalled, and in response Wilbur lurched himself forward and turned the elevator downward. Still the glider continued to stall, but rather than crashing uncontrollably, it made a flat descent without damaging the machine or injuring the pilot. For the first time, the Wrights had exper-

29. Wilbur on board the 1901 glider, with Bill and Dan Tate lending a hand with launching the machine.

ienced the deadly stall and benefited from the favorable recovery characteristics of the canard configuration. A similar reaction occurred when the glider lost too much forward speed on a second occasion. The Wrights did not fully understand what had happened or why the canard contributed to a safe landing, but they knew it had prevented a fatal nosedive. From that moment onward their confidence in the forward elevator was established, and they faithfully retained the arrangement for many years.[58]

Although those present were quite impressed with the day's flying, Wilbur and Orville were somewhat discouraged. Pitch control on the new glider was not as solid and responsive as it had been on the 1900 machine and, even with its large wing area, the lift and speed of the aircraft were disappointing. Also, unlike the 1900 glider, the total resistance of the machine was higher than estimated. In nearly all significant respects, the glider simply failed to perform in the manner the Wrights' calculations predicted it should. On the positive side, the

30. Wilbur making a free glide with the 1901 machine. Although successful by the standards of the day, the brothers were dissatisfied with both its lift and its control performance.

wing-warping control for lateral balance did continue to perform well.

Initially, the Wrights thought that the size of the elevator was causing the problem with pitch control, so they reduced the area from eighteen to ten square feet. This step made no improvement. Frustrated, they decided to fly the glider as a kite to try and determine what was wrong. These tests provided no clues concerning the front rudder, and the lift problem became even more apparent. At an angle of attack of three or four degrees, the glider required a wind of nearly twenty-five miles an hour to fly. To the brothers' dismay, this meant that the new machine was generating only one-third of the lift their calculations predicted it should. This was even worse than the performance of the 1900 glider.[59]

Their next move was to check the porosity of the fabric covering to see if that had any bearing on the deficiency of lift. A tightly woven

31. The Wrights' second glider being flown as a kite in 1901. The Wrights' methodical program of flight testing always began with kiting the gliders before attempting free glides.

muslin called Pride of the West that Wilbur had purchased in Dayton replaced the French sateen used on the 1900 glider. The Wrights had again left the covering unsealed to save weight and speculated that the cloth might not be sufficiently airtight. They applied the fabric to two small test surfaces, varnishing one and leaving the other untreated. They found that there was no difference in lift between the airproofed and untreated samples.[60]

By this point it had been more than three weeks since the Wrights had left Dayton. They had endured harsh weather, fought off ravenous hoards of mosquitoes, invested a week in building a hangar, and spent several frustrating days testing the glider. Spirits in their camp were ebbing. Discouraged and at somewhat of a loss to explain the poor performance of the new glider, the brothers considered a suggestion for the cause of the trouble offered by their guests, Huffaker and Spratt.

They pointed to the reversal of the center of pressure as a possible cause for the erratic behavior of the machine. Both Huffaker and Spratt had gained familiarity with the phenomenon from their own work. The Wrights were initially reluctant to accept this possibility. They had, of course, addressed this issue in the design of their 1900 glider. Their use of a wing with a comparatively flat curve with the high point far forward was intended to limit the travel of the center of pressure at low angles of attack. The poor performance of their first glider, however, placed doubt in their minds about their choice of wing profile and contributed to their reverting to the seemingly well-proven 1 in 12 camber of Lilienthal's machines. After all, they had no indication that Lilienthal had experienced the kind of discrepancies with predicted performance they were now facing. Moreover, in response to Huffaker's and Spratt's thoughts regarding the center of pressure, the Wright believed that the change in camber did not sacrifice the benefits of the 1900 wing profile in this regard because they still retained the forward position of the high point of the curve. But lacking any better ideas, the decided to follow up on their guests' suggestion.[61]

The brothers devised a simple but clever means of experimentally determining how the center of pressure was behaving with their wing surfaces. They removed the top wing of the glider, attached two short lines to the leading edge, and flew it in varying winds by itself. They observed that in light winds the wing exerted an upward pull on the lines, indicating that the center of pressure was ahead of the center of gravity, which caused the leading edge to rise. In stronger winds, the wing flew at a lower angle of attack and pulled down on the lines. This demonstrated that the center of pressure had moved behind the center of gravity, forcing the trailing edge up.[62]

The Wrights realized immediately that the center of pressure was reversing at low angles of attack, so that the 1901 glider required frequent and pronounced movements of the forward elevator to maintain stability in pitch. The reversal did not occur on the 1900 wing until it reached even lower angles of attack than the three or four degrees at which the Wrights were flying. As a result, the earlier aircraft exhibited very smooth control in this axis. Aside from helping them resolve their immediate pitch problem, this simple test was the Wrights' first experimental confirmation of their earlier assumption regarding the reversal of the center of pressure with curved surfaces.

The brothers' forethought in constructing the 1901 machine with a means for adjustment of the wing curvature paid off. It was a fairly sim-

32. The rain-soaked wreckage of Huffaker's hopeless paper-tube glider at Kitty Hawk in 1901.

ple matter to retruss the new glider's wings to a flatter airfoil. The adjusted camber was about 1 in 19. While the Wrights were reworking the wings, they also made a change to the contour of the leading edge. Originally, the lifting surfaces of the new machine had a very blunt leading edge that contributed to a greater than estimated wind resistance. The 1900 glider had favorable drag characteristics, so the brothers returned to the sharper leading-edge form of the previous machine.[63]

Octave Chanute had arrived at the Wright camp on August 4, just as the revisions to the 1901 glider had been completed. The following day the machine was flown as a kite with good results. The true test, of course, would come when it was flown as a free glider.

As Chanute anxiously anticipated his first opportunity to see a Wright glider in the air, he had to suffer the embarrassment of seeing the crumpled mass that was his own glider. The heavy rains had weakened the paper-tube structure and caused the machine to fall apart even before a single attempt to fly it could be made. To make matters worse,

Huffaker's abrasive personality and incompetence, not to mention lax personal hygiene, had sorely tested the Wrights' patience. He would often borrow tools and personal items belonging to the brothers without the slightest concern about asking for them or taking care of them. Upon their return to Dayton, Katharine noted in a letter to their father, "They haven't had much to say about flying. They can only talk about how disagreeable Huffaker was."[64] Chanute felt more than a little regret for imposing this trying companion on Wilbur and Orville. The brothers did enjoy the company of the affable and humorous George Spratt, however, and would maintain a cordial and helpful association with him in the future.[65]

On Thursday, August 8, the Wrights' resumed free gliding with the reconfigured 1901 machine, and the smooth, responsive action of the forward elevator that had impressed the Wrights in 1900 returned. Wilbur was able to follow the undulating contour of the dunes closely with amazing ease and precision. He turned in several good glides that day, the two best covering 366 feet and 389 feet. The next day witnessed continued success with consistent flights of thirteen seconds or more.[66]

With the pitch problem apparently solved, Wilbur took the next step and attempted to make an intentional turn with wing warping. Because of the great difficulty the Wrights experienced in operating the elevator and wing-warping controls simultaneously on the 1900 glider, they now used a different setup. They connected the warping cables to a laterally sliding hip cradle mounted at the center of the lower wing. The pilot actuated the mechanism by swinging his body in the direction he wanted to turn. This was far easier to coordinate with the arm-operated forward elevator than was pressing with the feet as before.[67]

Up to this point, the Wrights' system for lateral balance had presented no problems, but now, as Wilbur warped the wings to make a turn to the left, a startling thing happened. The turn began normally. The right wing was twisted leading edge up and the left leading edge down. The right wing then rose because of increased lift on that side, and, as it should, the glider began to bank to the left, pivoting about the low, left wing. But partway into the turn, the glider reversed direction and began to turn about the high wing, to the right. Wilbur was taken aback by this confusing action of the glider, and he quickly straightened it out and landed. A repeat attempt ended with the same

33. The 1901 glider upon landing. Chanute cautioned the Wrights about the dangers of flying the gliders prone, favoring an upright pilot's position. The brothers never experienced any problems with the arrangement, however, and it offered the advantage of less wind resistance.

result. Not only did this baffle the Wrights, but it added to their frustration in that having apparently solved the problem with pitch, their heretofore reliable system of lateral control was now going awry. Wilbur later lamented to Chanute, "we proved that our machine does not turn (i.e., circle) toward the lowest wing under all circumstances, a very unlooked for result and one which completely upsets our theories as to the causes which produce the turning to right or left."[68]

Their luck continued to worsen when on the last and best glide of the day, 335 feet, Wilbur became preoccupied with a dropping left wing and momentarily neglected the forward elevator. The result was a sudden dive into the ground, throwing him forward into the front rudder. The elevator was damaged slightly, and he suffered a bruised nose and a black eye. Despite the mishap, Octave Chanute was much impressed with the Wrights' technical skill and their aircraft. With his favorable instincts about the polite gentlemen from Dayton more than confirmed, he departed on August 11.[69]

Before leaving the following week themselves, the brothers got in a few more gliding sessions after repairing the elevator but were able to record only a handful of short flights of two hundred feet or less. With another spate of rain to further dampen their already dispirited camp, the Wrights left for home on August 20.[70]

All in all, it had been a very discouraging several weeks for Wilbur and Orville. Even though they had achieved far more gliding time than during the previous year, their experiments seemed to raise more doubts and puzzling questions than concrete steps toward a powered airplane. The pitch problem seemed to be in hand at the moment, but the dismal performance of their glider in terms of lift remained a mystery. Further, the mysterious behavior of their heretofore reliable wing-warping system raised a raft of new, unexplored aerodynamic questions. True, they had successfully flown a glider far larger than any before, but the Wrights recognized that such an achievement held little meaning if it did not lead to a final resolution of the basic problems of mechanical flight. They were not interested in isolated records. Their eyes were on the ultimate goal of a practical true airplane.

In retrospect, this was clearly the nadir of the Wrights' aeronautical work. Recounting this most disconsolate moment in their path to the airplane in 1908, Wilbur admitted that on the trip back to Dayton he had told Orville dejectedly "that men would not fly for fifty years."[71] In the 1940s, when Orville shared the story with Wright biographer Fred Kelly, the statement was emboldened to "not within a thousand years would man ever fly!"[72] Whether or not Wilbur ever truly uttered these words is open to question, but the sentiment they reflect certainly gripped the brothers as they made the long trip north in August of 1901. For the moment, at least, Wilbur and Orville were more than happy to get back to their bicycles.

6

Seeking Answers:
The Wrights Build a Wind Tunnel

The disheartening mood that overtook Wilbur and Orville as they departed from Kitty Hawk fortunately did not last long. Not two weeks after their return to Dayton, Katharine lamented to their father, "We don't hear anything but flying machine and engine from morning till night. I'll be glad when school begins so I can escape."[1] After receiving her degree from Oberlin College, Katharine taught classics at Steele High School in Dayton.

The brothers' renewed enthusiasm was in part spawned by the arrival of some new equipment for their workshop. A drill press and a band saw were added, along with overhead line-shafting and belts to operate them. The engine Katharine referred to was a small, one-cylinder example, fueled by illuminating gas, that Wilbur and Orville built to drive the new machinery. It was a rather crude device, as this was their first experience with internal combustion engines, but it worked. Fortunately, their new assistant, Charlie Taylor, was an able machinist and brought with him a modest familiarity with the still nascent propulsion technology. His skills in these areas would prove indispensable when building the motor for later powered airplanes. With these enhancements to their shop, the brothers were able to produce airplane components and structures of increasing sophistication, not to mention improved bicycle manufacture.[2]

The Wrights' flagging interest in flying was also rekindled in their home darkroom.[3] As they developed the glass plates recently exposed at Kitty Hawk, the brothers were able to relive the exhilaration of skimming over the dunes on board their manmade wings.

the excitement of gliding experiments does not entirely cease with the breaking up of camp. In the photographic darkroom at home we pass moments of as thrilling interest as any in the field, when the image begins to appear on the plate and it is yet an open question whether we have a picture of a flying machine, or merely a patch of open sky.[4]

Any lingering doubts the Wrights may have had about continuing their aeronautical work vanished with an invitation to Wilbur from Octave Chanute to speak before the Western Society of Engineers on the recent gliding experiments he and Orville had conducted at Kitty Hawk. Wilbur was both flattered and a bit apprehensive about speaking before so august a body of engineers and technical people; he had never before made a public presentation on aeronautics. But with a little good-natured nagging from Katharine, he put his concerns aside and, in a self-effacing reply to Chanute's invitation, agreed to deliver "a brief paper of a rather informal nature" at the society's next meeting in September. As the date of Wilbur's talk approached, his brother and sister queried him on whether the speech was to be witty or scientific. He quipped that he thought it would be "pathetic."[5]

Wilbur took an early morning train to Chicago on the day of his speech, September 18. Orville did not join him, but the elder brother did go off "arrayed in Orv's shirt, cuffs, cuff links and overcoat."[6] Orville was by far the more sartorially conscious of the two. So much so that family members often commented upon his dapper, tidy appearance, even after just having emerged from the workshop. The Wrights' favorite niece, Ivonette, later recalled, "I don't believe there ever was a man who could do the work he did in all kinds of dirt, oil and grime and come out of it looking immaculate. . . . when the job was finished he'd come out looking like he was right out of a band box."[7] Wilbur, on the other hand, although always in proper attire for a man of his station, was far less concerned with matters of style and fit. Katharine often had to kindly remind him that his suit needed pressing or that something did not match. His dress on the morning of the Chicago speech, however, was cause for her to remark in a letter to their father a few days later, "We discovered that to some extent 'clothes do make the man' for you never saw Will look so 'swell.'"[8]

Wilbur's presentation before the Western Society of Engineers was hardly "pathetic." It focused on the 1900 and 1901 gliders and the brothers' flying experience at Kitty Hawk. Wilbur touched on many of the fundamental concepts that he and Orville had developed during the preceding two years and the lessons they had learned through actual trial of their aircraft. In particularly clear and precise terms, he discussed the importance of control, wing warping, the movement and reversal of the center of pressure, the stall characteristics of the forward elevator, the necessity of actual practice on board the glider, and so on. Illustrated with lantern slides of the Wrights' gliders, as well as other experimenters' machines, the speech was a remarkably concise and insightful statement of the problem of flight as it stood in the fall of 1901.

The presentation was well received by those in attendance, and after a transcript of it later appeared in the society's proceedings, it quickly became one of the most sought-after pieces of aeronautical thinking yet published. It was reprinted or abstracted in numerous scientific and engineering journals in the United States and Europe. The lucid, thoughtful paper, modestly entitled "Some Aeronautical Experiments,"[9] became a benchmark in pioneer aeronautical literature, supplanting *Progress in Flying Machines* and *The Aeronautical Annuals* as the state-of-the-art references for experimenters entering the field.

The opportunity to present their work to the highly regarded Western Society of Engineers marked an important step in the Wrights' path to the airplane. The invitation extended from so well known a figure as Octave Chanute to share their ideas before other experienced engineering professionals did much to dissuade them from giving up after the recent disappointments at Kitty Hawk. The positive reception of their work legitimized the brothers' position in the aeronautical community. It no doubt instilled in them an extra degree of confidence that gave them the incentive to forge ahead with their own ideas—even if those ideas ran counter to accepted tenets of established experimenters.

This event illustrates perhaps better than any other the role Chanute played in the Wrights' work. His recognition, if not complete understanding, of their progress led him to offer consistent encouragement through active correspondence and dissemination of their ideas to other knowledgeable experimenters. By embracing Wilbur and Orville as he did, Chanute afforded them the ear and the connections of one of the most respected engineers in America. His reputation and position provided the brothers with valuable personal reinforcement at critical times, as well as giving them an entrée into the aeronautical establish-ment that further strengthened their self-confidence.

As Wilbur and Orville edged closer to successful flight, they moved farther and farther ahead of their peers. By the time they were about to fly their first powered airplane in late 1903, their ideas and designs were so advanced that they stood virtually alone at the door to human flight. The type of moral support and professional legitimacy provided by their relationship with Chanute was a great help as the Wrights began to face more and more uncharted territory on their own. Although Chanute's technical contributions were quite limited, his personal assistance went beyond simply lending an occasional ear and was an important factor in the Wrights' seeing through to conclusion so complex and demanding a project as the invention of the airplane.

The confidence-building impact of Wilbur's speech to the Western Society of Engineers and the brothers' growing friendship with Chanute began to manifest itself shortly after Wilbur returned from Chicago. Ever since the poor performance of the 1900 glider, the Wrights had been suspicious of the lift and drag data drawn from Lilienthal's published work. Their immense respect for the great German pioneer, however, made them cautious about rejecting his values. But now, in light of the continued lift problems with the 1901 glider and their growing knowledge and experience in aeronautics, they de-cided the time had come to check Lilienthal's table carefully, as well as the other aerodynamic data they had drawn from fellow experiment-ers to design their gliders.

In a letter dated September 26, 1901, Wilbur informed Chanute that he was "arranging to make a positive test of the correctness of Lilien-thal's coefficients."[10] Unlike the crude qualitative tests performed on small curved surfaces in 1900, this new series of experiments was de-signed to accurately evaluate the specific values listed in Lilienthal's table.

The entries that the Wrights were about to check were coefficients of lift and drag. Recalling the basic lift equation discussed in Chapter 4, the coefficient of lift C_L is the term in the equation that related the specific angle of attack of the wing to the force of lift generated by the wing. The Wrights had taken this coefficient directly from Lilienthal's table to calculate the lift of their first two gliders, but after the poor performance of these machines, they now believed Lilienthal's values might be flawed.

Another critical term in the lift equation that the Wrights were by now regarding with increasing uncertainty was the time-honored Smeaton's coefficient, 0.005. This was the constant of proportionality developed in the eighteenth century for use with the relationship between pressure and velocity from which the lift and drag equations were derived. The Wrights had used the established value in designing their first two gliders. An error in this constant would have provided another explanation for the less than expected lift of these machines, independent of any problems with Lilienthal's lift coefficients.

Even though the Wrights were confident that at least one, or possibly both, of these values was in error, determining which one(s) presented a confusing dilemma for them. A quick review of the standard lift equation and the way in which Lilienthal compiled his table will reveal the problem facing the brothers.

The established relationship between lift, wing area, and velocity in use at the time was generally written

$$L = kV^2 S C_L$$

where L is the lift in pounds; k is Smeaton's coefficient, 0.005; V is the velocity in miles per hour; S is the surface area of the wings in square feet; and C_L is the coefficient of lift. Using this relationship, Lilienthal calculated a set of values for the coefficient of lift at various angles of attack. (Lilienthal actually worked in metric units of kilograms, meters per second, and square meters, but the relationship was the same.)

He began by first experimentally collecting direct readings of the lift of a test wing-surface using a whirling-arm device similar to the type pioneered by Benjamin Robins, John Smeaton, and George Cayley in the eighteenth century. The test surface measured one half square meter in area, with a span to chord ratio of 4.5 to 1. The total resultant aerodynamic force (combined lift and drag) exerted by the wing in the flow was balanced by a counterweight and measured in kilograms. A simple calculation was then employed to give just the lift component of the total aerodynamic force. This was Lilienthal's L in the above equation.

Next he inserted into the equation the other terms he knew. The surface area S was acquired by simply measuring the dimensions of the wing. Similarly, the velocity of the whirling arm V was an independently measured quantity. And of course, Smeaton's coefficient k was also known, and presumed to be correct. From here it was a simple matter of elementary algebra to solve for the coefficient of lift C_L. Lilienthal went through and calculated C_L for his standard 1 in 12 camber airfoil for angles of attack ranging from −9 degrees to 90 degrees, thus creating the famous table to which everyone was referring.[11]

As Wilbur and Orville pondered the possibility that Lilienthal's table was inaccurate, one obvious source of error that occurred to them was his direct measurements of lift from the whirling arm. Decades of experience had shown that these devices introduced misleading factors such as centrifugal forces and friction, which placed their reliability in question. An even greater problem was that the rotation of the arm imparted a swirling effect to the air around the test surface that significantly effected the measurement of the velocity of the flow. Each of the other terms in the equation was either a known constant or an easily and independently measured quantity, so it was a logical possibility that errors in determining the actual lift of the test surface had led Lilienthal to calculate inaccurate coefficients of lift.

But the Wrights' growing doubt about Smeaton's coefficient supplied them with reason to suspect another cause for the inaccuracy of Lilienthal's lift coefficients. Even though the Smeaton value of 0.005 had remained unquestioned for many years, it had been experimentally derived in the preceding century and was not easily measured like surface area and velocity. By the time Wilbur and Orville had become immersed in aeronautics, more than a few individuals interested in the subject were considering the accuracy of the accepted figure. Chanute had collected forty or fifty values for k ranging from 0.0027 to 0.0054. The extreme variation was due to imperfect techniques of measurement, changes in air temperature and density, and nonuniform air speeds of his testing device. He had also assembled a list of coefficients derived by other experimenters varying from 0.0033 to 0.0049. Langley had come up with comparatively low values of below 0.0035. Charles F. Marvin of the U.S. Weather Bureau suggested 0.004 as a suitable air pressure coefficient. By 1901, the time-honored Smeaton figure of 0.005 was no longer unquestioned and had in fact become a growing point of debate.[12]

The Wrights recognized that because Lilienthal had used Smeaton's coefficient to compute the coefficient of lift, an error in this constant would have thrown off the calculated value for the crucial C_L. This, of course, was complicated by the fact that an inaccurate Smeaton value would have also undercut the Wrights' own lift calculations for their gliders, apart from the effect it had on Lilienthal's table. Because Lilienthal's coefficients of lift and Smeaton's coefficient were related in this way, it was difficult for the Wrights to isolate the two factors and verify their accuracy independently. At this point, they had no way of determining if in fact the lift coefficients were really off, or merely that a potentially erroneous value for k was making them appear wrong. But whether the coefficients of lift in the table were genuinely in error or Lilienthal had simply used a flawed value for k to calculate them, the Wrights were all but certain that they had found the reason for the disappointing results of their first two gliders. Having carefully reasoned through the problem, they now set about checking Smeaton's coefficient and the data in the Lilienthal table.

To investigate the accuracy of the factors in question without isolating the terms and measuring their absolute values, the Wrights cleverly devised a test mechanism that produced an actual, physical result that would reflect what the lift equation expressed mathematically. The device held a small model wing that when exposed to the wind moved in relation to an opposing force. If the lift equation genuinely mirrored the true forces that were acting on the wing, the test device would move to a position in accordance with what the equation predicted mathematically. If, however, any of the values that were substituted into the equation were off, the device would not respond in accordance with the calculated results because it would of course still be reflecting the actual aerodynamic forces that were acting upon it. In this way, the Wrights could determine indirectly the accuracy or inaccuracy of the coefficients of lift and Smeaton's coefficient without actually having to measure their specific values.

The Wright brothers' testing device incorporated the same basic principle of evaluating the relative lifting force of a wing with regard to an opposing counterforce that Lilienthal and others had developed, but it utilized a different method to achieve this. Rather than using a whirling arm where gravity served as the counterforce, they choose to balance the lifting force of the curved surface against the pressure exerted by the airflow upon a flat plate oriented perpendicular to the

34. The Wrights began their tests of model wing surfaces to check the accuracy of the aerodynamic data
they had been using to calculate the size of their machines using this makeshift bicycle apparatus.

wind. They would first record the actual angle of attack at which the
lift of the curved surface balanced the opposing pressure generated by
the wind hitting the flat plate. They would then calculate what that
angle *should* be based on the values in Lilienthal's table. From a comparison of the two results the Wrights would be able to evaluate the
accuracy of Lilienthal's coefficients.

In building their device to test these coefficients, the brothers again
tapped their familiarity with bicycles. They mounted two small surfaces
vertically on a bicycle wheel laid on its side. The wheel was free to turn
in response to the wind striking the surfaces. One surface was a flat
plate mounted perpendicular to the flow. The other was a model wing

35. The Wrights built a wind tunnel in late 1901 to generate
a more reliable set of aerodynamic data than that provided
by the bicycle apparatus.

patterned after the curve used by Lilienthal. According to the German
pioneer's table, the model wing set at a five-degree angle of attack
would generate enough lift to balance the flat plate exactly.[13]

Simply exposing the device to the natural wind failed to yield good
results, so the Wrights mounted the horizontal wheel to the front of
a bicycle in order to create a steady flow. Riding both with and against
the wind at a constant speed to average out any differences, the tests
seemed to bear out their doubts regarding Lilienthal's values. The
model-wing surface required an angle of attack of *18 degrees* to balance
the plate, more than three times what the table indicated it should be.
The Wrights were able to conclude definitively from this that either
Lilienthal's lift coefficients or the Smeaton value was in error.[14]

Although the tests thus far supported their suspicions, the Wrights
recognized that the apparatus they were using was not very reliable.
To verify the results, Orville built a makeshift wind tunnel out of an
old starch box. It was eighteen inches long and fitted with a plate glass
window on top to observe the interior during tests. A small fan running

off their new workshop engine supplied the flow of air. Inside the tunnel the Wrights placed what they called their balancing vane. It consisted of a vertical rod upon which were mounted two 1 inch by 3¼ inch surfaces, one curved and one flat. Again, the lift generated by the curved surface was balanced against the pressure on the flat plate. The arrangement was in theory similar to the bicycle tests, but the apparatus was far more precise.

"When exposed to the wind," Wilbur reported, "the vane took up a position to one side of the line of the wind direction thus showing that the curve required a less angle of incidence than the plane."[15] The deflections were recorded on some leftover scraps of wallpaper laid in the bottom of the tunnel. This tunnel was in use only for one day, but the results again showed clear discrepancies with Lilienthal's data. "I am absolutely certain," Wilbur wrote to Chanute on October 6, "that Lilienthal's table is very seriously in error."[16] It was still unclear whether the coefficients in the table were genuinely wrong or the problem lay in Lilienthal's use of an inaccurate value for k, but the Wrights now knew that the poor performance of their gliders was definitely linked to an error in the data or in a term in the equations they were using, and not in their own design or construction. The next step would be to develop a means of analyzing these two factors independently to determine which was incorrect.

Not only did the second set of tests with the wind tunnel confirm what the Wrights had believed for quite some time about Lilienthal's data; the new apparatus worked so well that the brothers recognized its utility for accurately and efficiently collecting extensive lift and drag data on a large number of different surfaces. Lilienthal's highly touted table was actually only one set of determinations for one specific curvature. The Wrights' use of the wind tunnel would allow them to test a whole range of wing shapes and curvatures, thus creating a genuine array of data from which an aircraft could be designed to meet desired flight parameters in terms of lift and drag. With these goals in mind, and a heightened resolve toward their work, they immediately set about building a larger, more sophisticated wind tunnel.[17]

Among all of the distinct aspects of their invention of the airplane, the Wrights' wind tunnel work best demonstrates their brilliance as engineers. They first defined the problem: Which term or terms in the lift equation were in error? Then, after developing a conceptual model for answering the question, they devised a practical, mechanical means of realizing the solution. But while the discovery of the flawed terms in the lift and drag equations was among their more crucial breakthroughs, the manner in which the Wrights arrived at this conclusion exemplifies their reasoned, systematic handling of every problem they faced. Of all the experimenters who preceded them, none exhibited a more refined engineering style than Wilbur and Orville Wright. In order to fully comprehend their achievement, the importance of understanding the brothers' strict and skillful engineering approach cannot be overemphasized. They never got bogged down in theoretical matters that were not directly related to the problem at hand. Even though the sophisticated wind tunnel experiments they were about to commence did a great deal to advance the understanding of aerodynamics, the Wrights consciously focused only on those practical questions that would provide them with specific information necessary to building a successful flying machine. They left it to their successors to develop a body of theory that would explain the underlying scientific principles of aerodynamics.

As Wilbur and Orville planned their wind tunnel investigation of the coefficient of lift and drag, they took a separate look at the validity of Smeaton's coefficient. Lilienthal had used the standard figure of 0.005 derived in the eighteenth century. (Actually, he used the metric equivalent of 0.005, which is 0.13. Although in calculation the Smeaton value was used as a dimensionless constant, it does in fact have units and must be adjusted accordingly depending upon the system of units in which the lift, the wing area, and the velocity are measured.)

By 1901, there were literally dozens of different values for Smeaton's coefficient being gathered and discussed. Based on an assessment of the techniques and conditions under which the various suggestions for k were obtained, the Wrights judged the range for the coefficient published by Charles Marvin of the U.S. Weather Bureau to be the closest to the correct figure thus far recorded. "I am inclined to think that the value . . . obtained by the Weather Bureau . . . is the best yet obtained," Wilbur informed Chanute. "Their estimate varies from 0.0035 to 0.0025 at speeds from 20 miles to 40 miles indicated velocity; and 0.004 for corrected velocities at all speeds."[18]

The Wrights compared these values with estimates for Smeaton's coefficient they had made based on their recent gliding experiments at

Kitty Hawk. Using the actual lift measurements of their 1901 glider, they computed the lift equation again, this time solving for k. Their calculations produced a value for Smeaton's coefficient that would make predicted and actual performance concur. Repeating this computation using the lift data from a number of glides yielded an average value for k of 0.0033, very close to what Marvin and several others had estimated. "Using . . . 0.0033 . . . we get results corresponding very well with our Kitty Hawk observations," Wilbur reported to Chanute. "It is evident that in our observations at least the value 0.0033 should be used for indicated speeds from 18 to 22 miles per hour."[19] Similar calculations convinced the Wrights that Lilienthal's use of the time-honored 0.005 (0.13 metric) was a mistake: "We think he is in error in using 0.13, so that altogether his estimate of the lift of his machine . . . is about double what seems reasonable to us."[20]

As early as the first week in October, with the wind tunnel experiments barely begun, the Wrights were confident that their adjusted value for Smeaton's coefficient was close to the proper figure. "If in our [original] Kitty Hawk calculations we had used a coefficient of 0.0033 instead of 0.005 the apparent advantage of our surfaces over the plane . . . would have been much greater. I see no good reason for using a greater coefficient than 0.0033," Wilbur proclaimed.[21] Although Wilbur and Orville hint that they intended to confirm this more precisely later, it appears that they never did.[22] They make no mention of any further corroboration of their value after 1901 and used 0.0033 in designing every subsequent aircraft they built. Their initial finding proved to be sound. Modern aerodynamicists have since confirmed 0.0033 to be accurate within a few percent. Having satisfied themselves that they had a usable Smeaton value and that they had solved half of the riddle presented by Lilienthal's data, the majority of the Wrights' further aerodynamic research focused on the wind tunnel and the coefficients of lift and drag.

The Wright brothers did not invent the wind tunnel. Nearly a dozen such devices had been built during the last quarter of the nineteenth century, beginning with the instrument produced by Francis Wenham and John Browning in 1871.[23] Despite the fair amount of experimentation in this area, these early tunnels yielded little useful aerodynamic information. They provided some general confirmation of the behavior of flat and curved surfaces in a flow from a qualitative perspective but were often operated with only a vague sense of how the data obtained could be practically employed in aircraft design. The Wright wind tunnel of 1901, however, marked a significant departure from prior instruments. Besides being well-designed and producing accurate results, it was the first used to systematically collect specific data on a wide range of prospective wing shapes to be used in conjunction with the established lift and drag equations. Moreover, this was the first time anyone had used such an instrument to obtain aerodynamic data in a form that could be incorporated directly into the design of an actual aircraft. Aside from the technical superiority of the tunnel, it was the manner in which the brothers used their device that made it so much more effective than anything that had preceded it.[24]

The Wrights' new, larger wind tunnel was complete and in use by mid-October 1901. The outward appearance was comparatively crude. The tunnel itself was a simple wooden box six feet long and sixteen inches square with a glass window on top for viewing the interior during testing. As with their earlier starch box tunnel, a fan belted off the overhead line shafting run by the one-horsepower shop engine provided the airflow, generating a wind of approximately thirty miles per hour.[25]

Using accurate reproductions of the tunnel and the testing instruments, the Wright brothers' wind tunnel experiments have been recreated at the National Air and Space Museum on several occasions, most recently in April 1985 and January 1988. Paired with a careful study of the Wrights' own documentation of their experiments, the recreations have contributed immeasurably to the following analysis of the brothers' wind tunnel research. It was possible thereby to get a sense of the procedures and problems associated with running the tests not always apparent from the literary evidence. Even more importantly, the opportunity to examine and operate the test instruments provided a unique insight into how the devices worked and how they had been designed.

The first thing the Wrights had to do was ascertain that their tunnel was set up properly. "Our greatest trouble was obtaining a perfectly straight current of wind," Wilbur reported to Chanute.[26] To correct this problem, a metal shroud at the fan end directed the air through a honeycomb grid in an effort to ensure a straight, smooth current down the tunnel.[27] "We spent nearly a month getting a *straight* wind," Wilbur later admitted.[28] This difficulty was confirmed by the recently recreated experiments with the National Air and Space Museum reproduction Wright wind tunnel. It took an extraordinary amount of adjustment and leveling of the tunnel to achieve a consistent, unwavering flow.

What made the Wrights' apparatus truly unique were the instruments used for making the actual lift and drag measurements. The brothers called them *balances* because they operated on the principle used before of balancing the lift of a model wing surface against an opposing force in order to evaluate the surface's lift and drag properties over a range of angles of attack. As before, the balances were basically a mechanical representation of what the lift and drag equations expressed mathematically. In other words, they were designed to measure values related to the actual aerodynamic forces acting on the model surface in terms that could be substituted directly into the equations. This was a particularly astute concept upon which to design the balances and lay at the heart of their effectiveness in providing useful data that could be practically applied to the creation of an aircraft. After the fact, designing the balances in this manner would appear to be a fairly self-evident thing to do. But looking at it from the perspective of the Wrights' time, it was an especially imaginative way to have made use of a wind tunnel.

Using readings from the balances in the wind tunnel, along with the actual measurements of lift, drag, and velocity yielded by the trials of the full-size gliders at Kitty Hawk, the Wrights ultimately were able to derive values experimentally for each of the variables and constants in the equations. This not only allowed them to verify Lilienthal's data and Smeaton's coefficient independently, but also to generate their own table of lift coefficients, which in turn enabled them to build an aircraft that would perform in accordance with prior calculations. This artful interweaving of a clear, straightforward conceptualization of the problem and a clever, effective means of experimentally obtaining results illustrates the Wrights' engineering talents at their finest.

Fashioned from bicycle spokes and old hacksaw blades, the balances were deceptively crude in appearance. In reality they were marvels of simplicity and sophistication. Originally, the Wrights tried to measure both lift and drag with a single instrument. But the data using this balance was, as Wilbur reported to Chanute, "subject to errors of perhaps ten percent."[29] They then decided to build separate balances for measuring lift and drag.

The lift balance was in theory very similar to the earlier bicycle apparatus and the balancing vane used in the first tunnel. "The essential principle of it is the use of a *normal* [ninety degrees to the flow] plane in measuring the pressure on an *inclined* surface," Wilbur explained.[30] The lift of the model wing surface was measured in terms of an opposing force exerted on a flat plate oriented perpendicular to the airstream. In other words, the lift force generated by the curved surface would be measured as a fraction of the oppositely directed force resulting from the wind hitting the flat plate. Put even more simply, they were expressing lift as the ratio of these two forces. This meant that the pressure on the flat plate would serve as the common standard against which the lifts of the various wing shapes tested would be measured.

The significant improvement of the new lift balance over the previous methods was that accurate readings of the forces involved could be taken in such a way as to directly arrive at the coefficient of lift for a given surface and at a specific angle of attack. The great advantage of this technique was that it enabled the Wrights to determine C_L *without* having to use Smeaton's coefficient. This was one of the most ingenious features of the design because it isolated one of the two variables the Wrights were in doubt about, eliminating the problem presented by Lilienthal's method of calculating C_L using Smeaton's coefficient.

With the new balance, the model wing surface, which could be set at various angles of attack, and the flat plate were mounted to an arrangement of arms and crossmembers that were free to pivot. During initial trials the plate created a disturbance of the flow in the tunnel, so the brothers replaced it with four narrow strips of an equivalent area. The fingerlike attachments added to the ungainly look of the device. With the wind turned on, the ratio of the force of lift generated by the wing to *both* the force exerted on the plate plus the drag force produced by the wing was indicated by an angle traced out by a pointer connected to the arms carrying the surface and the four strips that replaced the plate. But at this stage the Wrights wanted to record only the lift of the model wing. To eliminate the effect of the drag component of the total aerodynamic force acting on the wing, a mechanical readjustment of the arms of the balance was required. After resetting the balance, a second reading was taken. The angle now traced out by the pointer only indicated the component of aerodynamic force generated by the wing owing purely to lift.

36. The cleverly designed lift balance used to collect accurate coefficients of lift. The model-wing surface was mounted to the top crossmember. With the fan turned on, the total aerodynamic force generated by the wing (lift and drag) was balanced against the drag of the four resistance fingers attached to the lower crossmember. Readjusting the top tier carrying the airfoil after the initial reading was taken factored out the drag due to the model wing, thereby giving the Wrights a measurement of the lift force alone.

Constructing the balance in such a way as to factor out the effect of drag mechanically was one of the most remarkable features of the instrument's design. Even from a modern perspective, this aspect of the balance was an incredibly impressive piece of engineering.

The next step involved the most ingenious aspect of the balance. To analyze what was happening in terms of the aerodynamic forces acting on the balance and the surface, as represented by the movement of the pointer, the Wrights drew diagrams illustrating the various individual components of lift and drag generated by the model wing and by the four resistance strips. Using basic geometry, the Wrights were then able to conclude from their schematic drawings of the force components

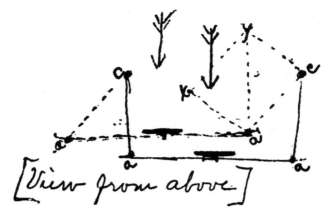

37. To analyze the aerodynamic forces acting on the
wind tunnel balances, the Wrights drew schematic
force diagrams. This one illustrates the forces acting
on the lift balance.

that the coefficient of lift of the test surface could be obtained by merely
taking the sine of the angle indicated by the pointer.[31]

This method proved to be an amazingly rapid and direct way of obtaining C_L. "We can make a complete chart of lifts of a surface from 0° to
45° in about an hour," Wilbur reported.[32] Systematically performing
this operation with a variety of airfoil shapes through a wide range of
angles of attack, the Wrights generated an extensive table of accurate
lift coefficients. Once properly set up, the National Air and Space Museum reproduction apparatus confirmed the ease with which data could
be collected using the Wright balance.

Even though collecting the data was rather easy, it is not immediately obvious from looking at the balance why the angle traced out by
the pointer should lead directly to the coefficient of lift. After all, the
pointer is moving in response to the force of lift generated by the model
wing surface. As noted earlier, the lift L in the equation is expressed
in pounds. C_L has no units; it is a dimensionless coefficient. How could
it be then that in reading the value for the force of lift shown by the
balance the Wrights were able to reduce this to a dimensionless C_L simply by taking the sine of the indicated angle?

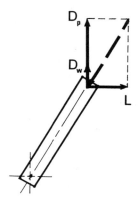
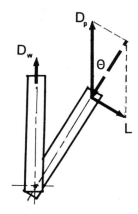

38. Force diagrams of the lift balance. The left image shows the balance in the first equilibrium position. D_p is the force due to drag on the resistance fingers. D_w is the aerodynamic drag force on the model-wing surface. L is the lift force generated by the wing. The right image shows the balance after being reset to eliminate the effect of the drag force generated by the model wing. Now the resistance fingers are acting against the lift force alone, not the total aerodynamic force of lift *and* drag. C_L can now be obtained by simply taking the sine of the indicated angle Θ.

The reason in large measure has to do with the basic principle they employed to evaluate the lift of a given surface. The lift balance *balanced* the force due to lift against the force exerted on a flat plate (the four strips in actual tests). Because the Wrights expressed lift in terms of the pressure on a plate—in other words, as a ratio of the two pressures—the dimension of pounds per unit area for each pressure canceled out one another. The balance was constructed in such a way that the units of the lift and the pressure on the four strips did not come into play, thus producing the desired dimensionless value for C_L with only a one-step reduction of the data, namely, taking the sine of the indicated angle.

Upon explanation, the mathematics involved in the Wrights' lift balance is comparatively simple. But a careful examination of what was done reveals a sophistication to the arrangement that reflects a keen understanding of geometry and trigonometry. Although both brothers excelled in these subjects, Orville in particular had distinguished himself as a mathematician during his school years.[33] The success of the wind-tunnel balances owed a great deal to the younger Wright's exceptional facility in this area. Unfortunately, Orville's identification with this important contribution has often been overlooked, since Wilbur was the principal communicator of their work to Chanute and others. "Will seems to enjoy writing, so I leave all the literary part of our work to him," Orville later explained.[34]

The lift balance also illustrates another instance of the use of graphic imagery in the Wrights' inventive work. Creating the physical arrangement of the device and working through the geometry clearly involved visualizing the direction and the interplay of the forces acting on the balance and the model wing surface. To have conceptualized the function of the balance literally necessitated picturing what was happening in the tunnel. Performing an analysis of this type by any engineer usually includes some form of visual representation to make the ideas clear. This is precisely what the Wrights did. Wilbur's explanations of the brothers' lift measuring instrument to Chanute often featured diagrams of the balance and schematic drawings depicting the forces.[35]

Beyond their skill as mathematicians and their talent for visual thinking, the Wrights' lift balance also demonstrates their practical and fruitful approach to invention of creating a piece of technology that replicated a conceptual model of a problem, which could then be used to gain the information needed to forge ahead with their main goal of building a successful flying machine. The lift balance is among the most brilliant examples of how the Wrights merged their many talents to produce a useful resolution to a problem. Their ability to think through a problem clearly, their technical skill, their engineering sense, and their consistent focus on what specifically was required to proceed with the overall project came together in a particularly impressive and effective way. Over and over again, the combination of these attributes enabled the Wrights to find solutions to daunting challenges.

The second balance, the drag balance, was equally masterful in its design and function. Just as before, the Wrights sought a means of obtaining values that could be substituted directly into the equations they were using to calculate the performance of their aircraft, in this case the drag equation. Recalling from Chapter 4, the drag equation was basically the same as the lift equation except that to determine the drag on a wing surface rather than the lift produced, the wing area, the velocity, and the constant of proportionality k are multiplied by a coefficient of drag C_D, instead of C_L. Thus the equation for calculating the aerodynamic drag of an airfoil can be written

$$D = kV^2SC_D$$

where D is the drag in pounds, k is the constant of proportionality for air (Smeaton's coefficient up to this point), V is the velocity in miles per hour, S is the wing area in square feet, and C_D is the coefficient of drag.

Just as with C_L, for every specific angle of attack there is a different coefficient of drag. In order to compare the performance in terms of drag of various airfoil shapes in preparation for designing a new full-size aircraft, the Wrights needed to generate a table of drag coefficients for different wing curves over a range of angles of attack similar to the one they created for C_L.

At this point, the Wrights took advantage of one of the few genuinely useful technical ideas they received from someone else. During the 1901 gliding season at Kitty Hawk, Wilbur and Orville discussed with George Spratt, the young experimenter hired by Chanute, the possible methods for determining the aerodynamic forces acting on a model wing surface. Spratt had been performing experiments of his own in this area, and he suggested that measuring the ratio of drag to lift might be easier than trying to measure either force independently. When the Wrights turned their attention to finding the drag acting on a wing, they recognized that Spratt's suggestion offered a practical way of obtaining the coefficient of drag C_D. If they measured the volume of the ratio of drag to lift, it would be a matter of simple arithmetic to obtain C_D, because they already had an accurate way of finding C_L independently. When looking at the lift and drag equations together this becomes clear. The Wrights knew that

$$\text{Drag} = kV^2SC_D$$

and

$$\text{Lift} = kV^2SC_L$$

If they compared drag to lift as a ratio, they could write

$$\frac{\text{Drag}}{\text{Lift}} = \frac{kV^2SC_D}{kV^2SC_L}$$

Since k, V^2, and S are the same in both expressions, it followed that

$$\frac{\text{Drag}}{\text{Lift}} = \frac{C_D}{C_L}$$

To isolate C_D, they could write

$$C_D = \frac{\text{Drag}}{\text{Lift}} C_L$$

They could find C_L using the lift balance, so if the value of the drag-to-lift ratio was known, computing C_D would be a case of simple multiplication.

Seeing this relationship between C_D and C_L, the Wrights adopted Spratt's idea of measuring the ratio of drag to lift as an expeditious means of generating a table of drag coefficients. However, they did so using a balance of an entirely different design from Spratt's.

In 1909, after the Wrights had become famous, Spratt complained to the brothers that he felt he had not received adequate credit for his contribution to their wind tunnel experiments. He argued that the information the Wrights had given him in return for his suggestion "cannot be considered in any degree a fair compensation."[36] A bit taken aback by this charge, Wilbur pointed out to him that he and Orville had shared far more of their own ideas regarding aerodynamics with him, including their specific values for lift and drag. Even so, Wilbur graciously offered "to place at your disposal any scientific information or practical knowledge which we have gathered in ten years of investigation and practical experience." Wilbur went on to assure Spratt, "We have not wished to deprive you of the credit for the idea, and when we give to the world that part of our work, we shall certainly give you proper credit."[37]

The Wrights first attempted to measure the drag-to-lift ratio by modifying their lift balance slightly, but they found "that it was not well adapted to that purpose, as it was necessary to place it in a position where it slightly affected the direction of the wind."[38] They then built an entirely new device specifically designed to measure the drag-to-lift

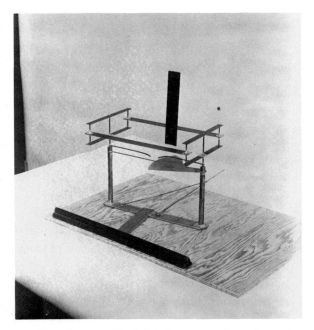

39. The drag, or "drift," balance, used to determine
the drag-to-lift ratio of the model airfoils.

ratio. They called it their drift balance, *drift* being the Wrights' term
that was analogous to the modern *drag*.[39]

Like the lift balance, the drift balance gave a reading of the ratio
of two forces. However, rather than comparing lift against a common
standard—the four metal strips on the lift balance—the drift balance
expressed the ratio of the forces due to lift and the pressure from drag
of the various model airfoils being tested. The drag force was not measured in terms of the force on a separate plate, as was the case with
the other balance.

Running the tests and reducing the data with the drag balance was
even easier than with the lift balance. The same model wings used to
obtain C_L were mounted on the drift balance. The angle of attack was
set by orienting the entire device in the flow at the desired angle. The
wind was turned on, the balance assumed an equilibrium position, and,
as before, a pointer traced out an angle that represented the ratio of

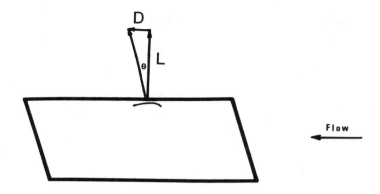

40. Force diagram of the drag balance. In this case, no direct measurement of lift or drag is obtained, only the ratio of drag to lift. *D* indicates the drag force acting on the model wing. *L* is the lift force. The tangent of the indicated angle Θ equals the ratio of these two forces.

the two opposing forces. This was the drag-to-lift ratio. Since the Wrights were not trying to measure drag independently, there was no need to readjust the balance to factor out the effect of any other forces.

Obtaining the actual values for drag-to-lift ratio C_D/C_L was again a matter of analyzing the basic geometry of the forces involved. First, the angle indicated by the pointer was added to the angle of attack set when initially placing the balance in the flow. The Wrights called this total angle of displacement the *gliding angle*. To obtain the drag-to-lift ratio, all that was then required was to take the tangent of the gliding angle. From here, as shown above, the drag coefficient C_D resulted from multiplying the C_D/C_L obtained from the drift balance by the previously derived values for C_L. As with the lift balance, because the drift balance expressed the ratio of two pressures, the dimensional units of lift and drag did not figure into the reduction of the data. Using this procedure, the Wrights were able to compile a list of drag coefficients for wing shapes and angles of attack that corresponded to their table of lift coefficients.

Like their instrument for measuring lift, the Wrights' drift balance was cleverly designed to measure the aerodynamic forces acting on a wing in terms that could be substituted directly into the lift and drag equations they were using to predict the performance of their aircraft. The drift balance again showed the uncommon ability of the Wrights to develop practical mechanical devices that mirrored their conceptual analysis of a problem. The fluid manner in which their intellect and their mechanical aptitude meshed to solve a complex task was central to their inventive creativity and their final accomplishment.

During late October and early November of 1901, Wilbur and Orville conducted preliminary tests on as many as two hundred different model wing shapes. This phase of the wind tunnel experiments served primarily to perfect the operation of the tunnel and the balances, to determine how best to fabricate the model surfaces, and to get a general feel for how varying the planform and the depth of curvature of the surfaces would affect the pressures they were investigating.[40] "After almost numberless small changes," Wilbur enthusiastically reported to Chanute, "we think our machine will now give results within two or three percent of the real truth. . . . The comparative lifts of different surfaces will be obtained with almost absolute correctness."[41] Chanute was most impressed with what he had learned about the tests so far. "It is perfectly marvelous to me how quickly you get results with your testing machine. . . . You are evidently better equipped to test the endless variety of curved surfaces than anybody has ever been."[42] By November 22, the Wrights were ready to begin a series of systematic, carefully recorded aerodynamic experiments that would be the single most important aspect of their aeronautical work.[43]

For the formal tests, a total of thirty-eight different model airfoils were made, mostly of twenty-gauge steel. "With a pair of tin shears, a hammer, a file, and a soldering iron you can get almost any shape you want," Wilbur explained to Spratt.[44] To make wings with thickened leading edges, the brothers simply added an extra piece of tin, some solder, or wax to the front of the surface. They tested cambers ranging from approximately 1 in 6 to 1 in 20 on curvatures with the high point forward as well as perfect arcs. The outlines of the model wings included perfect squares, elongated rectangles, ellipses, surfaces with

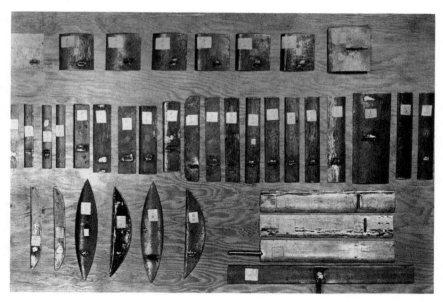

41. A sample of the many different model wing surfaces the Wrights tested in their wind tunnel.

raked tips, and half circles. Several of the surfaces were tested in tandem or superposed above one another to investigate the aerodynamic effect of the gap between multiplane wing arrangements.[45]

The Wrights formally recorded the results of forty-three surfaces and multiwing forms tested on their lift balance, and another forty-eight on their drift balance. They evaluated the surfaces from zero to forty-five degrees angle of attack. When running the determinations, they took great care to maintain consistency in their procedure and to ensure that no outside influences would adversely affect the readings.

After we began to make our record measurements we allowed no large object in the room to be moved and no one except the observer was allowed to come near the apparatus, and he occupied exactly the same position beside the trough [tunnel] at each observation. We had found by previous experience that these precautions were necessary, as very little is required to deflect a current a tenth of a degree, which is enough to very seriously affect the results.[46]

It took about three weeks to complete the entire series of experiments and collect the raw data that would be used to prepare the tables of lift and drag coefficients. Some of the measurements surprised the brothers, so they built a "recheck vane" to verify several of the more disturbing findings.[47] The recheck device corroborated the few puzzling readings and confirmed the Wrights' confidence in their technique. Even so, when plotting the data in graphic form, Wilbur occasionally struggled to keep his gut instincts from interfering with objectivity.

I have myself sometimes found it difficult to let the lines run where they will, instead of running them where I think they ought to go. My conclusion is that it is safest to follow the observations exactly.[48]

In addition to collecting data that would be used to produce an accurate set of lift and drag coefficients, the Wrights also investigated a number of other aerodynamic properties of curved surfaces. Among the most important was *aspect ratio*. This refers to the ratio of the span of the wing to the chord. Wilbur and Orville learned from their wind tunnel experiments that long, narrow wings typically generate more lift than short, wide ones of the same area. Their next full-size glider featured wings of this more favorable layout and produced far greater lift than their 1901 machine, with only a slight increase in wing area.

Other significant tests included thick versus sharp leading edges and the effect of varying the gap between biplane and triplane wing arrangements. A year later, in January 1903, the Wrights used their wind tunnel to test the drag properties of various shapes of vertical struts that supported the planes of their aircraft.[49]

By the second week in December 1901, Wilbur and Orville regrettably discontinued their experiments. During the weeks the brothers had been closeted away in the back of the bike shop so absorbed in their aeronautical work, they had relied on Charlie Taylor to keep things running out front. They thoroughly enjoyed the opportunity to lose themselves in their investigations, but the bicycle business was their livelihood, and they knew they could no longer neglect their responsibilities. "The boys have finished . . . their experiments. As soon as the results are put into tables, they will begin work for next season's bicycles," Katharine reported to their father.[50]

Considering the Wrights' methodical inventive style, their decision to discontinue the wind tunnel experiments is not all that surprising or inconsistent with their general approach to the problem of flight. Through each aspect of the project, they always concentrated on precisely what they needed to know to move on to the next step—no more, no less. Even though they were fascinated by this phase of their work, once their wind tunnel provided them with the answers they sought, they had the discipline to return their focus to the overall project of a practical flying machine. "We got all that we originally set out for, so we thought it a favorable time to take a recess," Wilbur explained. The brothers also wanted to be sure that they had enough time to build a new glider for 1902 based on what they learned over the fall and winter: "We saw that any further time consumed now would seriously impair our chance of a trip to Kitty Hawk next fall."[51] In an earlier letter, Wilbur had lamented to Chanute,

I regret that we did not have time to carry some of these experiments further, but having set a time for the experiments to cease, we stopped when the time was up. At least two thirds of my time in the past six months has been devoted to aeronautical matters. Unless I decide to devote myself to something other than a business career I must give closer attention to my regular work for a while.[52]

Disappointed by the Wrights' decision to stop, Chanute offered to use his connections to secure funding for them to continue their experiments. "I happen to know Carnegie," Chanute informed the brothers. "Would you like for me to write him?"[53] Not wanting to be beholden to anyone, the Wrights preferred to conduct their investigations from the profits of their own business. Wilbur diffused the matter with a tongue-in-cheek response to Chanute's inquiry: "A salary of ten or twenty thousand a year would be no insuperable objection, but I think it possible that Andrew is too hardheaded a Scotchman to become interested in such a visionary pursuit as flying."[54]

Despite having cut their work short, the Wrights had completed a body of wind tunnel research that would become the basis of the first successful airplane. Their work was impressive not only from a technical perspective, but also for the expediency with which it was accomplished. The wind tunnel experiments conducted in late 1901 were arguably the most significant single step in the brothers' path to mechanical flight. But as with their earlier development of wing warping, their design work regarding the aerodynamics and the layout of the 1900 and 1901 gliders, and their gaining actual flight experience at Kitty Hawk, the wind tunnel should be understood as an integral part of the Wrights' *overall* approach to flight. The tunnel was built expressly to find usable information concerning specific questions related to the design of a successful flying machine. What they derived from it was straightforward enough—accurate lift and drag coefficients and a better understanding of the aerodynamic properties of prospective wing shapes.

The Wright brothers' invention of the airplane was characterized by numerous distinct intellectual and technical achievements that ultimately were linked together to produce a complete technological system capable of flight. The wind tunnel certainly was one of the single most impressive segments of the Wrights' program of flight research. But the manner in which the brothers integrated its use with the many other problems they had to solve offers great insight into how, from a general point of view, innate creativity and skill are applied to produce complex pieces of technology. Independent discoveries, no matter how revolutionary, rarely result in a new invention. It is only when such discrete achievements are synthesized with other discoveries and technical knowledge that practical innovations typically come about. What made the Wright brothers special was that they understood and defined their inventive method in these terms and had the talent to follow through with the entire set of problems presented by the creation of a complex mechanical device. The Wrights' wind tunnel experiments can stand alone as a crowning achievement, but they are even more meaningful when examined in the context of the Wrights' entire body of inventive work.

7

Turning the Corner

By December of 1901, in only a few short weeks, the Wright brothers had accumulated all the aerodynamic data they needed to build a successful flying machine. They had developed a thorough understanding of the lift and drag equations. They had arrived at an accurate value for Smeaton's coefficient and, uncertain of Lilienthal's coefficients, they had compiled a reliable set of their own lift and drag coefficients for a wide variety of wing cambers. They had also investigated the aerodynamic effects attributable to factors such as airfoil shape, aspect ratio, and wing configuration. This impressive body of work not only answered the questions that initially prompted the Wrights to conduct their wind tunnel experiments, but also produced an array of data that enabled them to predict with great precision the performance of potential designs over a range of flight parameters.

Were the Wrights' initial doubts regarding the accuracy of Lilienthal's published data correct? Did they find the Lilienthal coefficients to be in error after all? There is some evidence to suggest that the brothers' wind tunnel experiments demonstrated Lilienthal's data to be fairly accurate given the crude test instrumentation he used. The inference from this is that it was only the Smeaton value that was drastically inaccurate, so that this error was the sole source of the trouble with the 1900 and 1901 calculations. This common interpretation suggests that the Wrights' earlier high regard for Lilienthal's work was ultimately reaffirmed.

But a closer examination of what took place in the Wright shop during the last few months of 1901 reveals this to be a misleading assessment of the brothers' comparison of their own results with Lilienthal's work, as well as an inaccurate representation of the place of Lilienthal in the overall Wright achievement. In fact, *both* Lilienthal's published figures and Smeaton's coefficient turned out to be wrong. Moreover, once Wilbur and Orville began gathering lift and drag data of their own, Lilienthal's coefficients ceased to play any role at all in their work.

Much of the misunderstanding surrounding the Wrights' seemingly positive reassessment of Lilienthal's lift and drag coefficients stems from two letters written to Chanute while the brothers were performing their wind tunnel experiments. On October 16, a scant ten days after Wilbur had declared to Chanute, "I am now absolutely certain that Lilienthal's table is very seriously in error," he recanted. "It would appear that Lilienthal is very much nearer the truth than we have heretofore been disposed to think," Wilbur admitted. A month and a half later, when he and Orville were in the midst of the systematic tests from which they would derive their own table of coefficients, Wilbur wrote, "The Lilienthal table has risen very much in my estimation since we began our present series of experiments for determining lift."[1] On the surface, these statements would seem to support the interpretation that Lilienthal's data was indeed usable, and that it was not the principal cause of the poor performance of the Wrights' first two gliders. A more careful reading of these letters and the rest of the correspondence during this period, however, indicates that the Wrights' wind tunnel work confirmed their initial belief that Lilienthal's data collection methods were flawed and the resulting coefficients suspect. Even more important, it quickly becomes apparent that the Wrights dismissed any possibility of using Lilienthal's coefficients, no matter how accurate, shortly after they began testing surfaces in their tunnel. Another look at Lilienthal's procedures and a comparison of his data to the values the Wrights obtained testing a similar wing surface makes this clear.

Recall from the previous chapter that Lilienthal accumulated his data using a whirling arm. A one-half square meter wing of 1 in 12 camber was spun on the arm, generating an aerodynamic force measured in kilograms. This experimentally obtained value was then substituted into the standard lift equation along with the other measured quantities of wing area and velocity and Smeaton's coefficient. The expression was then solved for the coefficient of lift C_L:

$$C_L = \frac{L}{kV^2S}$$

The immediate problem Lilienthal's method presented for the Wrights was that Smeaton's coefficient k was used to calculate C_L. They believed that one or both of these factors was in error. Lilienthal's technique frustrated them because it precluded isolating the terms and determining which of the two was inaccurate. As we have seen, this was the principal reason the Wrights designed their wind tunnel balances to measure the coefficient of lift and drag without using Smeaton's coefficient. Their independently derived coefficients could then be compared to Lilienthal's calculated ones.

Beyond the problem of using Smeaton's coefficient to calculate C_L, there were other aspects of Lilienthal's method that had a bearing on the Wrights' comparison of his data with their own results. Among these were his measurements of lift L and velocity V. Because the circular motion of a whirling arm imparts a swirling effect to air surrounding the test surface mounted on the end, it is virtually impossible to obtain a consistent and accurate reading of the velocity of the flow over the wing. Centrifugal forces and friction in the arm also contribute to the problem. These inaccuracies in the measurement of the velocity in turn lead to mistaken values for the lift. If the recorded velocity is higher or lower than the actual speed of the air moving over the surface, there obviously will be a misreading of the aerodynamic force generated by the wing. Returning to the rearranged lift equation,

$$C_L = \frac{L}{kV^2S}$$

it becomes readily apparent that, in addition to a flawed k, errors in the physical measurement of lift and velocity because of inherent defects in Lilienthal's test apparatus could also have contributed to erroneous values for the coefficient of lift.

When Wilbur reported to Chanute in December of 1901 that "the Lilienthal table has risen very much in my estimation," he was referring only to coefficients over a very small range of angle of attack. "Below ten degrees," Wilbur went on, "our measurements run below his (at small angles much below), but at larger angles we are above him."[2] In other words, it was only around an angle of attack of ten degrees that

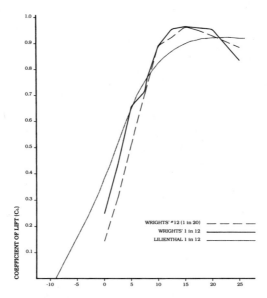

42. A combined graph of Lilienthal's data and that of the surfaces tested by the Wright brothers in their wind tunnel. Plotted are coefficients of lift versus angle of attack for Lilienthal's 1 in 12 cambered wing, the Wrights' data for a 1 in 12 surface, and the brothers' surface #12, their most efficient airfoil, which had a camber of 1 in 20. Close correlation between Lilienthal's and the Wrights' data occurs only between five and eight degrees angle of attack, illustrating the coincidental nature of the apparent accuracy of Lilienthal's coefficients of lift.

the Wrights found any correlation at all between their own data and Lilienthal's.

If the coefficients of lift for Lilienthal's 1 in 12 wing surface are graphed versus their corresponding angles of attack, and the same is done for the 1 in 12 model wing similar to Lilienthal's that the Wright brothers tested in their wind tunnel, the results reflect Wilbur's statement (see Figure 42). The coefficients of lift of each experimenter are similar only from about five to eight degrees angle of attack. Moreover, this correlation is due only to a gradual intersection of the graphs in this area. It is not an indication of corroboration of either set of data; the curves are quite different in character.

What does all this mean? It shows that the seeming accuracy of Lilienthal's coefficients was minuscule and coincidental. This is apparent for a number of reasons. The difference in the graphs shows clearly that Lilienthal's problem went beyond merely an inaccurate Smeaton value. If this multiplying factor were the only error, Lilienthal's coefficients would have differed from that of the Wrights by a consistent amount. That there is a varied amount of error in his C_Ls indicates that Lilienthal substituted other flawed values into the lift equation, namely, his measured lift and velocity. It then follows that the only explanation for Lilienthal's coefficients being reasonably accurate between five and eight degrees angle of attack is that, in calculation, a coincidental combination of errors in the values for k, the lift, and the velocity fortuitously yields usable C_Ls in this small range. Given the fundamentally different shapes of the graphs and their intersection, this has to be the case. Part of what made the results tantalizing is that five to eight degrees angle of attack was precisely the range at which Wilbur and Orville planned to fly. Interesting as this agreement was, it was completely unpredictable and entirely coincidental.

One obvious question that arises from all this is that if Lilienthal's data were wrong, why was he able to make successful glides while the Wrights, designing their first gliders using his coefficients, had difficulties? The answer is that there is no way of knowing if Lilienthal's actual glides agreed with predicted performance. Because the coefficient of lift changes with the angle of attack, in order to evaluate the lift of a wing for a particular C_L, the angle of attack must be kept constant. The Wright brothers tested the actual efficiency of their wings by flying their gliders as kites, a procedure that allows for a constant angle of attack. Lilienthal, on the other hand, simply flew his gliders down a hillside. Because gliding requires a constant change of angle of attack during flight to maintain pitch stability, i.e., to keep the craft level, there is no way to determine accurately the efficiency of a wing for a given coefficient of lift while in flight. Lilienthal made successful glides, but it is impossible to know if his performance correlated with his highly touted published table of aerodynamic data. The Wrights of course made glides, but because they also flew their machines as kites, they were able to learn precisely how well their aircraft were performing. Despite a certain reticence on Lilienthal's part, Wilbur suspected that the German pioneer had doubts about his glider performance: "I am led to think that Lilienthal himself had noticed that there was a discrepancy between his glides and his tables."[3]

Beyond these numerous problems with Lilienthal's data, the table had an even greater drawback. The Wrights had to test only a few different surfaces in their wind tunnel before they realized that the published coefficients for Lilienthal's 1 in 12 surface, regardless of their accuracy, would not be suitable for the shallower cambers of 1 in 22 and 1 in 19 that they had used on their 1900 and 1901 gliders. "It will not do at all to attempt to apply his table indiscriminately to surfaces of different aspect or curvature," Wilbur explained to Chanute.[4] The brothers' early wind tunnel tests proved that they had made a mistake in applying Lilienthal's coefficients to their flatter wing curvatures. Wilbur also told Chanute, "It is very evident from these measurements that a table based on one aspect and profile is worthless for a surface of different aspect and curvature."[5] Graphing the results for one of the Wrights' shallow airfoils makes this apparent. Laying such a graph over the one prepared for Lilienthal's 1 in 12 surface, the curves intersect sharply with no correlation of any kind.

The experiments also confirmed the Wrights' long-held belief that surfaces with the high point forward were much more efficient than the perfect arcs that Lilienthal and others had used. "The arc and the parabola . . . lift exactly the same at about 8° [angle of attack], but at 12.5° there is a difference of nearly one third!" Wilbur excitedly reported to Chanute.[6] From all this the Wrights surmised that the poor performance of their gliders in part reflected the error of using Lilienthal's data universally. "This no doubt explains why we have had so much trouble figuring all our machines from Lilienthal's table."[7]

These initial tests convinced the Wrights that it was pointless to use the Lilienthal table at all. Even before building the wind tunnel, Wilbur and Orville had discarded the idea of using a camber of 1 in 12. They believed so sharp a curvature would not be terribly efficient and would very likely generate a great deal of drag. Once the preliminary wind tunnel experiments demonstrated what a dramatic effect a difference in camber had on the lift coefficient, the Wrights never again considered using Lilienthal's data in designing one of their gliders. From then on they concentrated on collecting and working with their own values based on the flatter curvatures they believed to be more efficient.

In light of the limitations of Lilienthal's testing apparatus, the problems with his method of calculating lift and drag coefficients, the lack of any serious effort to confirm his experimental data in actual practice, and the pitfalls of applying his coefficients to a variety of airfoils, it becomes clear that Wilbur and Orville were absolutely correct in their initial uncertainties and suspicions regarding Lilienthal's published values. Their statements suggesting that they may have been hasty in their judgment of the German experimenter's work merely reflect the coincidental correlation they had noticed between Lilienthal's values and their own over a small range, and of course this was only for the 1 in 12 surface. The letters in which the Wrights make these statements are full of qualification, and it is obvious that early on they recognized the stumbling blocks presented by Lilienthal's table.

Even though their doubts were confirmed, these realizations did not dampen the Wrights' respect for Lilienthal. They always maintained that, however flawed, his work laid an important foundation for others to build upon. Referring to Lilienthal's book, *Der Vogelflug als Grundlage der Fliegekunst*, Wilbur wrote, "It is certainly a wonderful book. Although, as I see it, errors are not entirely absent, yet considering that it was a pioneering work, developing an entirely new field, it is remarkably sound."[8]

Lilienthal's mistakes are not so important; they pale next to his many contributions to the advancement of aeronautics. The significance of this analysis of the comparison between Lilienthal's aerodynamic work and that of the Wrights is that it sheds greater light on the way in which the brothers' wind tunnel experiments led them to a clear understanding of how to generate and evaluate aerodynamic data, and how to incorporate it into a full-size aircraft. This aspect of their wind tunnel studies, along with the physical design and data collection techniques discussed in the previous chapter, illuminate in great detail the analytical skill and judgment that was at the center of the Wright brothers' inventive approach and creativity.

Despite the success of the wind tunnel experiments and the Wrights' confidence in their results, Wilbur and Orville did not immediately attempt to realize their ultimate goal of a powered airplane. They had no assurance that the data obtained from a six-square-inch model wing would hold true for a full-size aircraft. The only precedent for extrapolating such experimental results was Lilienthal's work, and that had proven to be not without its uncertainty. Further, they still had to contend with the mysterious lateral control problem that surfaced during the final trials of the 1901 glider at Kitty Hawk. By this point the Wrights had moved so far ahead of any of their contemporaries that every step moved them into totally uncharted territory. Understandably, they felt some reluctance in moving directly to a powered airplane. It was one thing to fly a model wing in a wind tunnel; it was quite another to risk life and limb on board a several-hundred-pound, untried powered flying machine. In view of these factors, Wilbur and Orville decided to build one more glider.

The next machine continued to reflect the evolutionary nature and continuity of design that characterized the entire Wright aeronautical program. The new glider retained the generally successful layout, control system, and construction of its predecessors, as well as effectively incorporating the valuable information the Wrights had accumulated over the fall and winter. All the key breakthroughs made with the wind tunnel were deftly merged with the brothers' basic design to produce a final, much superior, experimental glider.

The major problem the Wrights had experienced with their previous gliders was inadequate lift. Wilbur and Orville resolved this failing in their new aircraft in several ways that stemmed directly from their wind tunnel research. This went beyond determining coefficients of lift and drag. First, their experiments enabled them to select a new wing shape with a favorable *lift-to-drag ratio*. This refers to the trade-off of drag for lift for a given surface. Every wing, even a flat plate, produces lift and drag when placed in a flow at an angle of attack. The most efficient wings are those that generate the least drag for the most lift, and this of course is what aircraft designers typically seek. Unlike Lilienthal, who never wavered from the inefficient 1 in 12 surface, the Wrights grew to understand that a good lift-to-drag ratio, as well as accurate coefficients of lift and drag, were essential to designing a successful aircraft. This is largely why the brothers tested so many different model wings in their wind tunnel. Using the tunnel, they methodically and rapidly narrowed down the broad range of prospective wing shapes they considered to be the most efficient.

For the new machine, the Wrights chose a camber that varied from 1 in 24 to 1 in 30, depending upon how the wings were rigged. In actual gliding, they found that curvatures close to the 1 in 30 end of the range produced the best results. This was much shallower than the final 1 in 19 of the 1901 glider and the 1 in 22 of the 1900. The high point of the 1902 curve was one-third of the way back from the leading edge, also a departure from the earlier wings, which had the high point well forward.[9]

Interestingly, despite the extensive and wide-ranging evaluation of model wings conducted by the Wrights, the precise wing shape used on the 1902 glider was never actually tested in their wind tunnel. "We never tested a surface exactly corresponding to those used in our 1902 machine, and consequently are compelled to make various allowances in our estimates," Wilbur explained to Chanute.[10] The wing was based for the most part on characteristics of three of the more promising model surfaces, one of which Wilbur recorded as having the "highest dynamic efficiency" of all the surfaces tested.[11] The term *dynamic efficiency* is a bit vague. What Wilbur meant by this was the best lift-to-drag ratio.

Particularly puzzling was their selection of a maximum camber of 1 in 24. Even though the Wrights evaluated as many as two hundred model wings and recorded precise data for nearly fifty, they tested none with a camber flatter than 1 in 20. In light of how quickly and easily the Wrights said it was for them to make the test surfaces, it is rather mysterious that they would not have made and evaluated one in the range that they ultimately used for the full-size glider.

One possible explanation may be related to the fact that the Wrights finished running their determinations and dismantled the wind tunnel before graphing all the data. Once the tunnel was shut down, it would have been difficult to recreate conditions exactly, which would have made a comparison of data collected subsequently somewhat suspect. Plots of surfaces that were tested ranging from 1 in 12 to 1 in 20 show fairly similar lift performance up to a camber of 1 in 16, but a striking rise in efficiency with the 1 in 20. It may be that Wilbur and Orville saw a clear trend toward better efficiency with the shallower curvature and extrapolated the results for cambers of 1 in 24 or less. This, combined with an intuitive judgment based on their experience in varying the camber on the first two gliders, may have prompted them to go with an even flatter airfoil than they had tested. Even if this suggestion is plausible, it still does not explain the apparent inconsistency of this move with regard to the Wrights' typically methodical and systematic experimental approach. Unfortunately, they never addressed this issue beyond stating that the 1902 glider wing did not correspond to any shape evaluated in the wind tunnel. What actually led to their decision to use an untested camber remains one of the more inexplicable gaps in the Wright story.

Regardless of the reason, the brothers' choice of a very shallow curvature proved to be sound. The effectiveness of the new wing shape was keenly reflected in the size and performance of the Wrights' gliders. The 1902 machine had a wing area of 305 square feet, which was only slightly greater than the 290 square feet of the 1901 craft, yet it generated far greater lift. The Wrights were able to make numerous sustained flights with the new glider, finally fulfilling their initial hopes for their first trip to Kitty Hawk in 1900 of spending a good deal of time in the air learning to fly. Equally significant, the glider flew in accordance with calculated performance. This notable improvement was due in part to the good lift-to-drag ratio of the wings. They produced significantly less induced drag than the wing shapes of the two previous gliders. *Induced drag* refers to the drag generated in the process of producing lift. As lift increases with greater angle of attack, more and more drag is induced.

This dramatic effect of airfoil efficiency on flight performance of the Wrights' gliders was displayed quite visibly when the aircraft were flown as kites. Both the 1900 and 1901 machines maintained equilibrium at very high angles of attack, with the lines running to the ground at about a forty-five degree angle. The 1902 machine, on the other hand, could be kited at a low angle of attack, with the lines nearly vertical. A comparison of photographs of the 1900 and 1902 gliders being flown as kites shows this difference quite vividly. The earlier aircraft had to fly at high angles to generate enough lift to compensate for the relatively high drag of their specific wing shapes, which became even greater at large angles of attack. Because the 1902 surface produced more lift at a smaller angle of attack with significantly less induced drag, i.e., a favorable lift-to-drag ratio, it could support itself in near level flight. "In a test for 'soaring' as a kite," Wilbur reported, "the cords stood vertical or a little to the front on a hill having a slope of only $7\frac{1}{2}°$.

43. The 1900 glider being flown as a kite. The poor lift-to-drag ratio of the machine is exhibited by the high angle of attack and the comparatively horizontal position of the lines running to the glider.

This is an immense improvement over our last year's machine."[12]

Another aspect of the Wrights' wind tunnel experiments that contributed to the vastly improved lift of the 1902 glider was their investigation of aspect ratio, the ratio of wingspan to chord. The brothers compared various planforms of the same wing area and recorded significant differences in efficiency depending upon the outline of the surface. They examined the comparative lift of various multiwing arrangements of the same area as well.

The results showed that, in general, longer, narrower wings produced more lift for the same area than short, wide ones. The previous, 1901 glider had had a span of twenty-two feet and a chord of seven feet, giving it a comparatively low, inefficient aspect ratio of three. On the 1902 machine, the wings were extended another ten feet, and the chord was reduced to five feet, doubling the aspect ratio to six. As the wind tunnel tests had predicted, this change greatly enhanced performance. It also added to the gracefulness of the aircraft from an aesthetic point

44. The 1902 glider being flown as a kite. The low angle of attack and the near vertical lines indicate the much superior lift-to-drag ratio of this machine over the earlier gliders.

of view and was one of the more visible and directly apparent manifestations of the Wrights' wind tunnel work.

Recording accurate coefficients of lift and drag, developing an airfoil with a favorable lift-to-drag ratio, and determining an efficient aspect ratio for the wing planform were three critical aspects of wing design that resulted from the Wrights' wind tunnel experiments. They also used the device to examine the effect on lift of different leading edge forms and of variable gaps between biplane wing arrangements.

The Wrights' recognition of these important areas of aerodynamic investigation stemmed from a careful analysis of the lift problems they had experienced with their 1900 and 1901 gliders. They designed and built the wind tunnel expressly to generate data and to answer questions concerning these facets of airfoil design. The information acquired was then incorporated directly into the new glider, completing a brilliant phase of the Wrights' characteristic process of problem assessment, research, and practical solution. Others had previously employed wind tunnels for aeronautical research. But the Wrights were the first to develop and use the instrument to answer specific questions directly related to the design and construction of an actual aircraft. The procedures they devised for data collection and analysis established a model for aerodynamic investigation upon which most all subsequent wind tunnel research has been based. This methodological precedent was as significant a contribution to aeronautical engineering as the Wrights' many technical achievements.

The wind tunnel experiments performed by the Wrights in late 1901, and their practical application in the form of the 1902 glider, carried the progress toward mechanical flight to another new plateau. In many respects, this phase of the Wrights' work stands as the technological and psychological turning point in their path to the airplane. From their investigation of model wings, they overcame what had been the central stumbling block up to that point, the inefficiency of their lifting surface. And, as will be seen later, the solutions to several remaining technical challenges critical to the design of the powered airplane were also anchored in the wind tunnel experiments. The airplane that first carried a human being aloft on December 17, 1903, was the product of a thoughtful and precise program of engineering, the heart of which was the wind tunnel. So inextricable are the Wrights' aerodynamic research and their design of the first successful flying machine that, when defining their invention of the airplane from a technical point of view, both the wind tunnel and the aircraft itself should be understood as two essential components of a single creative achievement.

Equally important, the wind tunnel experiments served to change profoundly the Wrights' attitude toward the soundness of their research and their confidence in their ability to achieve the ultimate goal of a powered flying machine. Prior to deciding to check the accuracy of Lilienthal's coefficients, the brothers, although possessed of a strong self-confidence in their basic skills, clearly saw themselves as newcomers to aeronautics. They held in high regard the great names of the field such as Lilienthal, Chanute, and Langley and were slow to reject their "wisdom," even when their own ideas seemed closer to the truth.

After completing the wind tunnel experiments, Wilbur and Orville recognized how far ahead of everyone else they were. Years later Orville stated,

earlier experimenters had so little accurate knowledge concerning the properties of cambered surfaces that they used cambered surfaces of great inefficiency, and the tables of air pressures which they possessed concerning cambered surfaces were so erroneous as to entirely mislead them. . . . I believe we possessed in 1902 more data on cambered surfaces, a hundred times over, than all of our predecessors put together.[13]

In February 1902, while still putting all the data into tables, Wilbur wrote the following sarcastic passage in a letter to Chanute that reflected clearly the new assessment the Wrights held of their position in the field.

The newspapers are full of accounts of flying machines which have been building in cellars, garrets, stables and other secret places. . . . They all have the problem "completely solved," but usually there is some insignificant detail yet to be decided, such as whether to use steam, electricity, or a water motor to drive it. Mule power might give greater ascensional force if properly applied, but I fear would be too dangerous unless the mule wore pneumatic shoes. Some of these reports would disgust one, if they were not so irresistibly ludicrous.[14]

In the now-famous letter that Wilbur wrote to the Smithsonian Institution on May 30, 1899, he humbly stated, "I wish to avail myself of all that is already known and then if possible add my mite to help on the future worker who will attain final success."[15] By 1902 it was apparent that the Wrights believed *they*, not a "future worker," would attain final success. Almost three years to the day after the Smithsonian inquiry, on May 29, 1902, Wilbur responded to Chanute regarding a request to publish drawings of the new glider. "I do not think that drawings will reveal very much of the principles of operation of our machines, unless accompanied with somewhat extended explanations, so our secrets are safe enough."[16] It was clear that by now the brothers realized their findings must be guarded to prevent someone else from gaining fame and fortune based on their own research and hard work. This comment was among the earliest references to a sentiment that after 1905 became a near obsession on the part of the Wrights. After achieving success, they spent much of their time, particularly Wilbur, trying to ensure public recognition of the magnitude of their contribution and establish that they were indeed the inventors of the airplane.

As Wilbur and Orville prepared to make their third journey to Kitty Hawk in the spring of 1902, they knew they had turned the corner. They still had many uncertainties and problems yet to solve, not to mention numerous unforeseen snags. Their decision to build one more glider reflected well-grounded caution against rushing ahead too quickly. But they were no longer groping tentatively in the dark either. The Wrights had assembled a body of aeronautical knowledge and experience that enhanced their ability to make informed decisions. They now proceeded with a confidence that was not based on faith in the work of others, but supported by their own original research. In retrospect, the wind tunnel experiments clearly emerge as the center of this major leap forward, both technologically and psychologically.

Through the wind tunnel, the Wrights dealt with the questions of lift and drag and the determination of the size, airfoil, planform, and configuration of the wings, all factors related to the inadequate lift of the earlier gliders. Wilbur and Orville next tackled the other major problem that had surfaced during the 1901 gliding season—the mysterious failure of their apparently proven lateral control system to respond properly under certain conditions.

During the final trials of the 1901 glider, Wilbur had experienced control reversal[17] when attempting to make an intentional turn. After placing the glider into a left bank by warping the wings, the aircraft suddenly reversed direction partway into the turn and started back to the right. Wilbur leveled the wings immediately and landed. A repeat attempt produced the same result. This further exasperating dilemma, on top of the numerous delays, bad weather, and time-consuming adjustments and repairs made to cure lift and pitch problems, sent a frustrated Wilbur and Orville home to Dayton on the verge of giving up completely.

During the fall and winter, the brothers were preoccupied largely with issues of lift and drag. Early in 1902, with the wind tunnel experiments completed and the basic design estimates for the new glider in place, the Wrights began to give serious attention to the puzzling control problem that continued to trouble them. By February, they felt they had an answer. "The matter of lateral stability and steering is one

45. Wilbur gliding in 1902. The Wrights added a vertical tail to their third glider to deal with the lateral-control problems experienced in 1901. The more graceful appearance of the 1902 machine over the previous gliders is shown here to good advantage.

of exceeding complexity," Wilbur wrote Chanute, "but I now have hopes that we have a solution."[18] This solution was the addition of a fixed vertical tail, or rudder, to the rear of the glider.

The turning problem was related to the drag produced when warping the wings. The basic principal of the Wright system of lateral balance was to generate unequal amounts of lift on either side of the aircraft by twisting the wings in opposite directions. More lift from one wing caused that wing to rise and to initiate a turn. The increased lift of the rising wing half, however, also produced greater drag on that side. This resulted in a difference in the forward speed of the wing tips. If the drag induced by the increased lift of the high wing slowed the forward speed of that side of the glider so much that the opposite wing tip—the low one—began to overtake it, the pilot would experience control reversal. The low wing would begin to "slide" forward, lurching the machine in the opposite direction in an unsafe, stall-provoking, attitude. The Wrights did not encounter this phenomenon every time banking was attempted, but it happened enough for them to realize that their wing warping method of control still had a fundamental flaw.

The addition of a fixed vertical tail as a remedy for this problem was the product of yet another instance of the brothers' thoughtful analysis of their experience. The Wrights reasoned that if control reversal was due to the low wing advancing ahead of the high one in a turn, it could be prevented by regulating the forward speed of the individual wing tips. A fixed rudder was a simple, but clever, means of achieving this. If the low wing began to overtake the high one, a fixed surface mounted at the rear would present itself to the wind on the side of the low wing, causing the forward movement of that tip to be retarded. This uncomplicated device would regulate the tip speeds automatically, the Wrights believed, thereby maintaining the intended direction of the turn.

By this point, the Wright brothers had assessed the basic problems that arose during the 1901 gliding season and conceived practical solutions based on intensive original research and careful analysis. They were ready to once again test their ideas in actual practice. As winter drifted into spring, however, the busy season for bicycles fell upon them, and the pace of their aeronautical work had to be tempered by the realities of earning a living.

Throughout the period of the wind tunnel tests and into early 1902, the volume of correspondence between the Wrights and Octave Chanute greatly intensified. In addition to serving as a sounding board for Wilbur and Orville's theories and ideas, the elder statesman of aeronautics offered his services for the laborious task of reducing the data the brothers had collected in their wind tunnel. In the days before handheld electronic calculators, doing the arithmetic and taking the sine or tangent of the hundreds of angles the Wrights measured was a long and tedious process. The Wrights and Chanute spent weeks compiling the tables and reporting to one another discrepancies and interesting findings. Interestingly, in 1895, Orville had designed and built a crude mechanical calculator capable of addition and multiplication. It was not used in conjunction with any of the Wrights' aeronautical work, however.

The many letters exchanged over these months not only reflect the Wrights' growing self-assurance regarding final success, but also illustrate a subtle shift in their view of their dear and respected old friend from Chicago. Wilbur and Orville never looked upon Chanute as a mentor. From Wilbur's first contact with Chanute in May of 1900, the brothers always expressed their thoughts and proposals clearly and with forthright confidence. Their communications with their friend usually just informed him of their plans or what they were thinking on a particular issue, and only rarely requested direct advice. Nevertheless, in their first years as aeronautical experimenters, the Wrights recognized that they were newcomers and that Chanute was among the most highly regarded people in the field. Even though they generally pursued their own ideas, they always valued his opinions.

By 1902, however, it had become clear to the Wrights that their advances had gone well beyond Chanute's understanding of aeronautics. The accomplished engineer had little to offer Wilbur and Orville at this point, and more often than not he ruminated over antiquated or wrongheaded theories and designs that the brothers had long since discarded. By now, the Wrights' sharing of information with him was far more an act of courtesy toward a respected, well-liked friend than a forum for substantive intellectual exchange. On more than a few occasions after 1902, Wilbur wrote lengthy, detailed responses to Chanute, setting him straight on issues that had by now become rudimentary to the brothers. This dilemma of wishing to afford Chanute the respect and courtesy he deserved, yet wanting to avoid being hindered by his well-intentioned, but fruitless, suggestions and offers of assistance became frustratingly acute as the Wrights planned their next journey to Kitty Hawk.

Chanute wanted Wilbur and Orville to supervise the reconstruction and testing of two of his previous gliders. "I propose to rebuild my 'multiple-wing' and my 'two-surfaced,' so as to have comparative tests when you go out again [to Kitty Hawk]. Could you build these at my expense in your shop?"[19] Chanute also contracted Charles Lamson, a California kite experimenter, to build a new glider based on Lamson's oscillating wing principle. With this questionable design, the wings were free to rock fore and aft, which was intended to achieve balance automatically; automatic, or inherent, stability was a concept that had long preoccupied Chanute. He hoped the Wrights would direct the flight testing of this machine as well.

It seems that Chanute was now less interested in pursuing his own aeronautical work than he was in linking his somewhat half-hearted efforts to the Wrights' clearly ground-breaking experiments.

Lamson is building a folding machine for me of which I shall ask your acceptance as well as two former types which I expect to have rebuilt. I think I will not experiment any more myself, but I desire you to test the comparative merits of what I have done in the hope that you will get some good out of it.[20]

The only result the Wrights could see deriving from experimentation with these antiquated designs was a delay of their own work. They did their best to disengage themselves from these propositions without affronting their well-intentioned friend.

We consented to undertake the building of machines for you for the good of the cause. If you make other arrangements, it will be all right with us. To tell the truth, the building of machines for other men to risk their necks on is not a task that I particularly relish, and if Mr. Herring is at leisure to take charge of the matter for you, it will relieve us.[21]

These exchanges concerning the brothers' involvement with Chanute's machines went on for months. In the end, Wilbur and Orville did live up to their commitment and assisted Chanute and his people as best they could, however reluctantly. A letter of masterful diplomacy to Chanute dated June 2, 1902, sums up the Wrights' reservations about spending valuable time on what they knew were fruitless efforts, while at the same time not wishing to hurt the feelings of a man whom they had clearly surpassed as pioneers in the field of aeronautics.

If I understand you properly, you propose to build the multiple-wing and double-deck machines and give them to us as presents. You hinted something of this kind in a former letter, but it surpassed our capacity for belief that you were intending to exercise the virtue of benevolence on so magnificent a scale as your words seemed to imply. The kindness and enthusiasm in the case which prompted such a generous offer strike a very deep chord in our hearts. We thank you most earnestly. Yet the question rises whether it would be wise to spend so much for such a purpose. It is not certain that we would be able to find opportunity for such extended use of the machines as would justify so great an expenditure on your part. Our use of the machines ought to be an incident rather than the primary purpose of their construction. We are yet in hopes that you may decide to resume experiment on your own account. A friendly spirit of emulation is a spur to progress in every line of human endeavor, and I really think that we would derive more good from seeing the machines in operation in the hands of one of your experts than if they were our own property.[22]

The Wrights' suggestion that Chanute use his own "experts" to conduct the trials of his gliders, however, created another potential burden for the brothers. On the one hand, to relieve themselves from too much responsibility, Wilbur contended that it would not be advisable for he and his brother to fly the aircraft personally. He went so far as to suggest that if "the results obtained should fail to equal those obtained by Messrs. Herring and Avery it might raise a suspicion that we had not acted fairly."[23] But the Wrights also argued that having too many "experts" in their camp at Kitty Hawk could result in a repeat of the lost time and disagreeable experience of Huffaker's presence during their 1901 trip to the Outer Banks. "On the other hand it was our experience last year that my brother and myself, while alone, or nearly so, could do more work in one week, than in two weeks after Mr. Huffaker's arrival."[24]

Chanute himself, his gliders notwithstanding, was always welcome in the Wright home and at Kitty Hawk. Wilbur and Orville were ever mindful to assure him so. Their welcome was also extended to one other member of the growing aeronautical community. This was George Spratt, the young enthusiast Chanute had sent to Kitty Hawk in 1901 who had been so helpful and pleasant, and who had provided the Wrights with a useful suggestion regarding their wind-tunnel drag balance. "Mr. Spratt, should he consent to come down in response to our invitation," Wilbur communicated to Chanute, "would be a very welcome addition to our camp at any time as we know him to be a willing worker and a most congenial companion."[25]

With all the matters regarding Chanute's machines and probable visitors at Kitty Hawk reasonably settled, Wilbur and Orville readied themselves and their own aircraft for the upcoming trip south.

8

"We Now Hold All Records!"

In addition to the seasonal increase in activity in the bicycle shop, there was another matter in the spring and summer of 1902 that distracted Wilbur and Orville from their aeronautical work. Although the Wright children never attended church, they tenaciously supported their father, Milton Wright, in his role as a bishop in the Church of the United Brethren in Christ. Milton began an active career as an itinerant minister in this midwestern Protestant sect in the 1850s. He rose quickly in the church, ascending to the level of bishop, and became editor of a number of the organization's newspapers and other publications. When it was discovered early in 1902 that the overseer of the church publishing business had misappropriated funds, Bishop Wright initiated a campaign for the culprit's removal and prosecution. Desiring to avoid a scandal, an opposing faction in the church attempted to cover up the misdeed and later launched an effort to oust the bishop. The Wright children eagerly rushed to the support of their father, as they always did on the numerous occasions when his position in the church was threatened.[1]

As the crisis intensified, Wilbur subordinated thoughts of flying to the defense of his father. "I returned last evening from Huntington, Ind.," he wrote Chanute, "where I had been all week attending to some matters for my father which have occupied much of my time and attention recently."[2] When the other church leaders began to take direct action against the bishop, the brothers' plans to go to the Outer Banks grew uncertain. In mid-July, Wilbur informed Chanute that "that church matter," as he referred to the trouble, "has taken on a phase which may possibly delay our departure for Kitty Hawk."[3]

To diffuse the attack on his father, Wilbur performed a thorough review of the church accounting records and demonstrated the discrepancies beyond a doubt. He followed up this effort by writing a scathing tract, skillfully outlining the legal aspects of the issue and denouncing the actions of the bishop's enemies. As the summer began to wane, he was still uncomfortable about leaving his father's aid and going off to fly airplanes. "Will and Orv . . . are talking of going [to Kitty Hawk] next Monday," Katharine informed her father in late August, "though sometimes Will thinks he would like to stay and see what happens at Huntington next week."[4] Despite these reservations, Wilbur and Orville decided they had done all they could to support their father's cause and delayed their plans no longer. They would head south on August 25.

The controversy involving Bishop Wright dragged on intermittently for three years. The matter finally was settled at a session of the church general conference in May of 1905. Wilbur's unyielding indignation and sense of injustice over the issue was quite apparent in a 1905 letter to Chanute reporting the outcome. "It was the decisive battle in the contest of which you have heretofore heard us speak. We won a complete victory; turned every one of the rascals out of office, and put friends of my father in their places."[5]

Unrelenting commitment to heartfelt points of view and personal convictions was a dominant Wright family trait. Be it religion, politics, or scientific principles, once the Wrights decided on their position, little could shake their belief that they were right. When it came to sticking with aeronautical ideas that ran counter to accepted wisdom, this resolute confidence in their own opinions was a great strength. However, concerning personal and business relationships with the world outside the Wright home, it at times proved to be a tremendous stumbling block. This was especially true with regard to their efforts to patent and market the airplane following their successful experimental flights. Many of the intense frustrations they experienced in these areas were partially attributable to a stubbornness on their part that sometimes could be described as siege mentality.[6]

The trying events of the spring and summer had taken a toll on the brothers. "They really ought to get away for a while," Katharine wrote their father. "Will is thin and nervous and so is Orv." The Wrights were drawn to the Outer Banks as much for therapeutic reasons as they were to test their aeronautical ideas. "They will be all right when they get down in the sand where the salt breezes blow, etc.," Katharine continued. "They think that life at Kitty Hawk cures all ills, you know."[7]

With their timetable set back a number of weeks, Wilbur and Orville feverishly prepared the parts for the new glider. "The flying machine is in the process of making now," Katharine reported to their father. "Will spins the sewing machine around the hour while Orv squats around marking the places to sew. There is no place in the house to live but I'll be lonesome enough by this time next week and wish that I could have some of their racket around."[8]

As in the two previous years, the Wrights began their journey to Kitty Hawk by taking a train from Dayton to Elizabeth City, North Carolina. Upon arrival they discovered a schooner, the *Lou Willis*, moored at the wharf across from the train station. The boat's skipper, Captain Franklin Midgett, was setting sail for Kitty Hawk at 4:00 A.M. the next morning. After arranging passage, the Wrights hurried back to the station before the depot closed for the evening to reclaim their trunks, baggage, and crates carrying the glider parts. Before leaving Elizabeth City, the brothers were also able to secure a small oven, a few cans of baking powder, and a barrel of gasoline.[9]

Slack winds stretched the trip across Albemarle Sound to an arduous day and a half. Bill Tate's half-brother, Dan Tate, met the brothers at Kitty Hawk and helped them ferry their belongings and equipment the four miles to the site of their old camp at Kill Devil Hills.[10]

The shed they had erected the year before to house the 1901 glider was badly dilapidated. "During the year the winds blew all the foundation, which consisted of sand, out from under the building and let the ends drop down two feet," Wilbur wrote Chanute, "thus giving the roof a shape like that of a dromedary's back."[11] With the assistance of Dan Tate, the Wrights placed foundation posts under the structure and remodeled and enlarged the building. They next windproofed the sides with battens and waterproofed the roof with tarpaper.[12] "The whole building . . . is much tighter and waterproof than before as well as sandproof." The brothers were intent upon living in greater comfort than they had during previous visits.[13]

Interior improvements included a burlap-upholstered dining table and chairs, a kitchen area with a complement of pans and dishes, and beds suspended from the rafters. A sixteen-foot well dug just outside rounded out the additions to their temporary home.[14] Wilbur boasted to his sister, "It is the best [water] in Kitty Hawk." Quite pleased with his and Orville's efforts, Wilbur continued humorously, "So far, in addition to cookery, etc., we have exercised ourselves in the trades of carpentering, furniture making, upholstering, well driving, and will add house moving next week."[15] They further eased the hardships of life on the Outer Banks by bringing a specially geared bicycle that could maneuver effectively on the sandy terrain, cutting down the roundtrip between Kill Devil Hills and Kitty Hawk to an hour.[16]

Things clearly were getting off to a far better start than they had during the rainy, depressing first week in 1901. Even the mosquitoes were cooperating. "We have not seen a dozen mosquitoes in the two weeks and a half we have been here."[17] In mid-September, Wilbur reported to George Spratt enthusiastically, "Everything is so much more favorable this year than last . . . , so we are having a splendid time."[18]

Work on the new glider began on September 8, but not before having to deal with some unwanted intruders. "Cleaned out building preparatory to beginning work on new machine," Orville wrote in his diary that evening. "Killed two mice, one with stick, the other with gun. Chased hungry razorbacks, and finally began work on machine at a little after 2 P.M."[19]

In a few days, the wings were assembled and the cloth covering was put on. Wilbur and Orville tested the efficiency of the individual surfaces by flying them as kites. Initial trials were very promising. "We have done a little experimenting with the finished surface and find that it lifts much better than our last year's surface and also has less drift. . . . it 'soared' on a slope of 7¾°, that is the cords attached to it were vertical."[20] The kiting tests also suggested that the finished glider would likely have good stability in pitch. "We find one thing about our new surface that is very fortunate. The center of pressure does not reverse till a very low angle [of attack]."[21] Their experience with the 1900 and 1901 machines showed that this characteristic would result in a smooth control response of the forward elevator.

Flying their gliders as kites is often pointed to in accounts of the Wrights' work. But its importance as a research technique in their inventive process is rarely emphasized. The 1899 kite, of course, afforded the Wrights a comparatively simple and inexpensive means of developing and testing their wing-warping control system, one of the most fundamental aspects of their invention.

Beyond this actual kite, flying their man-carrying aircraft as kites provided the brothers with a great deal of data upon which to evaluate and improve their designs. With this technique they could measure angles of attack in flight accurately. This enabled them to analyze with precision the efficiency of their lifting surfaces in accordance with their wind tunnel results and understand and track the movement of the center of pressure. Also, as with the small 1899 kite, the response of the control system on the full-size aircraft could be tested from the ground in safety. Finally, kiting the gliders with a pilot aboard offered the Wrights a valuable opportunity to familiarize themselves with the feel of the machine in the air before attempting free flight.

Wilbur and Orville continually returned to kiting to make initial tests of new machines and to analyze puzzling results observed in free glides. In many ways kiting was among the most crucial aspects of the Wrights' flight testing program. It allowed them to evaluate their theories and experimental data under actual flight conditions for extended periods of time. It also tempered the risks of launching oneself off a hill in a completely untried machine by providing them with some sense of the aircraft's flight characteristics before making untethered glides. According to Wilbur, "Testing a gliding machine as a kite on a suitable slope, . . . is one of the most satisfactory methods of determining its efficiency."[22]

By September 19, the 1902 glider was completed and ready for trial. The biplane wings spanned 32 feet with an area of 305 square feet. The fabric covering fit more smoothly than it had on the earlier gliders, owing to the spars being fitted into notched wing ribs rather than simply laid on top of the ribs as before. The struts supporting the planes of the 1901 glider were reused. The forward elevator was elliptical in outline and had an area of fifteen square feet. Similar to the shape of the wings, the new front rudder was much longer and narrower than earlier versions, reflecting the Wrights' recently acquired understanding of aspect ratio. On the new machine, Wilbur and Orville set up the control lever for the elevator reverse of what it had been in 1901. The fixed vertical tail that was added to deal with the lateral control problem consisted of two surfaces, side by side, totaling 11⅔ square feet in area. This structure was attached to the rear of the glider with hinged spars so that in the event it struck the ground during landing, it would spring upward, avoiding damage. The hip cradle developed in 1901 for actuating the wing warping was retained. The craft weighed just under 120 pounds.[23]

Although it maintained the continuity of design that was a hallmark of the brothers' aeronautical work, the 1902 glider was far more graceful and refined in appearance than its predecessors. In flight, with the wide-open stretches of pristine beach as a backdrop, it was truly a thing of beauty.

As was their pattern, the Wrights began flight testing by kiting the new machine.[24] Observing no problems, they continued with approximately twenty-five short, assisted, shallow glides that same day, September 19. At this point things were looking more promising than ever. The glider was able to sustain itself at fairly low angles of attack, meaning the lift was sufficient. "We . . . are convinced that [the] machine will glide on an angle of seven degrees or maybe less." Also, both the pitch and lateral control systems appeared sound. "The front rudder . . . gives abundant control with a change of not more than two or three degrees to either side of 0°." As for the wing warping, "The few trials . . . were not satisfactory as far as showing what effect the torsion had . . . , but we are convinced that the trouble with the 1901 machine is overcome by the vertical tail."[25] Feeling confident that their efforts of the past year were moving them in the right direction, Wilbur and Orville felt ready to attempt more ambitious, free glides from Big Hill, the largest of the three dunes that made up the group known as Kill Devil Hills.[26]

During the first two days of trials, the Wrights made about fifty glides with their latest machine. Most were short, under two hundred feet, with either the wing-warping or the forward-elevator control secured to give the brothers a chance to familiarize themselves with the habits of the new glider. Toward the end of the second day, Wilbur made the first glides with both controls free to operate.[27] On several of the longer ones, a new problem arose. "In several . . . glides there were disturbances of the [lateral] equilibrium more marked than we had been accustomed to experience with the former machines, and we are at a loss to know what the cause might be."[28]

Owing to its much longer wings, the new glider was more susceptible to crosswinds than the previous ones. The new behavior Wilbur was

46. In October 1902, Orville finally made his first free glides. Here, Wilbur and Dan Tate help him into the air.

experiencing was due simply to the effects of the stiff Kitty Hawk breezes on the new wing configuration. He ran into a bit of trouble on one flight when a crosswind tipped up the left wing of the glider while he was still getting used to the new arrangement of the elevator control. Orville recorded the episode in his diary.

The wind getting under the left wing from the side, . . . raised it higher & higher, when he [Wilbur] suddenly, by mistake, while attempting to alter the wing tips, turned the front rudder down at the rear, causing the machine to 'pierce the ethereal' to all appearances at an angle of over 45°. . . . the machine made a fast downward plunge directly toward the right wing.[29]

The Wrights addressed this new wrinkle by retrussing the wings such that the tips were approximately four inches lower than the center, giving the wings a noticeable droop. Kiting tests showed this to be an effective solution.[30] "We found that the trouble experienced heretofore with crosswind turning up the wing it first struck had been overcome. . . . The machine flew beautifully."[31]

After a day or so of rain, on September 23, the rerigged craft was taken out for further gliding.[32] In 1900, 1901, and thus far in 1902, Wilbur had made all the untethered glides. On this occasion, Orville was pilot, making his first free glides in a heavier-than-air flying machine. Most were with either the wing warping or the elevator tied off so that the younger Wright could gradually accustom himself to making untethered flights. About seventy-five flights were made that day, ranging in distance from 150 to 225 feet. After dinner, Orville attempted a few glides with both controls free. On his third or fourth flight, the right wing began to rise unexpectedly. He actuated the wing warping to correct the imbalance, but rather than leveling the wing it rose even further. Preoccupied with this surprising response, Orville neglected the attitude of the glider and unwittingly allowed it to pitch up sharply. Moments later the glider smashed into the sand from an altitude of thirty feet, leaving "a mass of fluttering wreckage."[33] "The result," as Orville put it, "was a heap of flying machine, cloth, and sticks in a heap, with me in the center without a bruise or scratch."[34]

Damage from the crash was severe enough to curtail experiments for a few days. Nevertheless, the brothers' spirits were high that evening. In only three days they had achieved more consistent flights of significant duration than in all the gliding of their two previous trips to the Outer Banks combined. They had sailed the 1902 glider down Kill Devil Hills nearly 125 times. Best of all, the efficiency of the machine and its stability and control in both pitch and lateral balance had fulfilled their expectations. "In spite of the sad catastrophe," Orville recorded in his diary, "we are tonight in a hilarious mood as a result of the encouraging performance of the machine both in control and angles of flight."[35]

This was the only accident with the glider that required any extensive repair during the entire 1902 stay at Kitty Hawk. The glider "was made as good as new by a few days' labor," Wilbur later boasted, "and was not again broken in any of the many hundred glides which we subsequently made with it."[36] The durability of the construction of the Wrights' aircraft is a factor in their success that should not go unnoticed. Their use of lightweight, resilient woods resulted in flexible structures that could withstand repeated poundings into the sand, as well as return to their original shape after being contorted in a crash. Their technique of applying the fabric covering on the bias to impart strength across the frame and still maintain the ability to twist the wings for lateral control also contributed to this characteristic. The basic airframe was essentially held together by the fabric, as the ribs and the spars were not rigidly attached to one another. These features produced an aircraft that was at once simple in design, structurally sound, and forgiving in a crash.

In interviews with builders and pilots of reproduction Wright aircraft, the flexibility and resiliency of the design is emphasized constantly. When recreating the brothers' experiments at Kitty Hawk, these modern-day pioneers of flight never cease to be amazed at how, after a bone-jarring, sand-spewing plunge into the dune, the glider typically only requires a few twists of the distorted structure to realign it and the shaking off of sand before making the next flight.[37]

This attribute of the Wrights' design is a somewhat subtle, but tremendously important, element of their experimental program. Many of their contemporaries, Lilienthal being the great exception, built flying machines that were structurally weak or made from unsuitable materials. Hiram Maxim's gargantuan steam-powered machine of 1894, Huffaker's paper-tube contraption taken to Kitty Hawk in 1901, and Samuel Langley's later man-carrying *Great Aerodrome*, which collapsed upon itself on two separate attempts in 1903, are a few notable examples. The structural shortcomings of these and other pioneer designs, aside from aerodynamic and control problems, prevented many experimenters from gaining the experience in the air that was necessary to achieve human flight. The Wright brothers demonstrated clearly that extensive flight testing and learning to fly were crucial to inventing the airplane. They made dozens of attempts before making even modestly successful glides and hundreds before resolving the basic problems of flight and mastering the art of piloting. The fact that they developed a structural design that enabled them to take many steps along the learning curve without losing their aircraft, not to mention their lives, was fundamental to their creation of the world's first airplane. Understanding this relationship between technical concepts and the process of testing and learning from intermediate stages of development was yet another mark of the brothers' fruitful inventive method.

Keeping the glider in one piece long enough to learn something from it was also important to the Wrights' approach to flight testing. They readily recognized the wisdom of comparatively mundane, incremental steps over bold, all-or-nothing attempts to fly. Wilbur eloquently expressed the brothers' view in an article published in 1903 by the Western Society of Engineers.

By long practice the management of a flying machine should become as instinctive as the balancing movements a man unconsciously employs with every step in walking, but in the early days it is easy to make blunders. For the purpose of reducing the danger to the lowest possible point we usually kept close to the ground. Often a glide of several hundred feet would be made at a height of a few feet or even a few inches sometimes. It was the aim to avoid unnecessary risk. While the high flights were more spectacular, the low ones were fully as valuable for training purposes. Skill comes by constant repetition of familiar feats rather than by a few overbold attempts at feats for which the performer is yet poorly prepared.[38]

After three days of repairs, the glider was "now ready for use at first favorable weather."[39] A few attempts were made over the next couple of days, but slack winds precluded extensive testing. The next day, September 29, the winds stiffened and the Wrights began nearly a week of uninterrupted gliding. They logged hundreds of flights during this period, averaging 150 to 200 feet in distance and eight to twelve seconds in duration, with some topping 300 feet. With increasing experience, the brothers began making gentle, swaying turns across the slopes. On October 2, three glides that covered over 500 feet were achieved.[40] That evening, Wilbur exuberantly reported the latest results in a letter to his father.

Our new machine is a very great improvement over anything we had built before and over anything anyone has built. . . . Yesterday I tried three glides from the top of the hill and made 506 ft., 504½ ft. and 550 ft. respectively. . . . Everything is so much more satisfactory that we now believe that the flying problem is really nearing its solution.[41]

Despite the Wrights' impressive performance and growing optimism, they were still plagued by one nagging problem concerning lateral balance. For the most part, the fixed vertical tail cured the control reversal that first appeared late in 1901. But on several of the many otherwise successful glides of the past week, the mysterious failure of the proven wing-warping system recurred. In fact, when this happened, the newly added tail seemed to make the untoward response even worse than with no tail.[42]

The current problem was actually slightly different from the behavior of the tailless 1901 machine. Before, when the wing warping failed, it was due to an imbalance in the forward speed of the wing tips. When the difference in drag on either side, owing to the oppositely warped wings, became too severe, usually because the airspeed dropped too low, the glider would pivot about the high-drag wing, swaying away from the intended direction of the turn. This response was a rotational motion, and under such circumstances the fixed vertical tail worked just as the Wrights had figured it would.

In 1902, when the lateral control system failed to respond, the glider was not rotating about the high-drag wing. Rather, it was "sliding" sideways out of control toward the low wing. When Orville explained this action to close friend and Wright biographer Fred Kelly in the 1940s, he said the glider behaved "just as a sled slides downhill or a ball rolls down an inclined plane."[43] When this happened, the glider fell out of the sky at a frightening rate, eventually planting the wing tip into the sand. The Wrights termed these episodes "well digging," referring to the small crater left in the sand that resulted from each bone-rattling meeting with the ground.[44]

This is precisely what happened to Orville in his crash of September 23. He neglected the forward elevator after becoming preoccupied with the glider's puzzling failure to respond to the wing warping. As the right wing rose, the glider began to drift sideways to the left. Under these circumstances, the fixed vertical tail contributed to the problem instead of relieving it. As the machine continued to fall off to the left, the pressure on the left face of the vertical tail increased. This forced the tail to the right, causing the glider to corkscrew around the low, left wing tip. If the airspeed had been sufficient, increased lift of the left wing owing to Orville's applying the wing warping would have prevented the glider from slipping to the left, averting the increase in pressure on the vertical tail. As it happened, pressure built up on the vertical tail because of sideslipping before the wing warping could take effect. In the 1902 machine's present configuration, if the pilot failed to apply the corrective wing warping soon enough, or the airspeed dropped so low that the glider began to fall off to one side, lateral control would be lost, and well digging would result.

The story of the Wright brothers' solution to this problem, now commonly referred to as a *tailspin,* is another case where the details concerning one of their central breakthroughs remain unclear. Like the twisted inner-tube box and the development of wing warping, our knowledge of how the cure for well digging came about stems largely from the Wrights' later recollections.[45]

Orville gave the following account to biographer Fred Kelly.[46] Enthusiastic discussion on the evening of October 2, the day of Wilbur's five-hundred-foot flights, led Orville to consume more than his usual amount of coffee. As he lay awake in bed that night, he pondered the well digging dilemma. The next morning he appeared at the breakfast table not only with an explanation of the brothers' latest puzzle, but a remedy. He suggested that if the vertical tail were movable, its position could be altered when a sideslip occurred to avoid the pressure buildup that caused the glider to pivot about the low wing. A movable tail would act like a ship's rudder, generating a torque in the opposite direction, which would allow the low wing to rise and sustain level flight.

After thinking over his younger brother's proposal for a few minutes, Wilbur concurred and contributed an idea of his own. Since the pilot already had his hands full with two separate controls, a third might be too much to manage. If the movable rudder were linked to the wing-warping control, Wilbur suggested, its positive effect could still be realized without adding to the demands on the pilot. With this refinement, the Wright system of control was perfected.

Wilbur's version of the event, expressed in a 1912 patent-infringement-suit deposition, is less melodramatic.[47] He indicated that the development of the movable rudder was simply another typical act of Wright collaboration that took place over a number of days. He relates no overnight revelations or breakfast-table solutions on Orville's part. The only surviving contemporary piece of evidence is a brief notation in Orville's diary for October 3, the day after his sleepless night. "While lying awake last night, I studied out a new vertical rudder."[48]

However it happened, this change to the control system was as fundamental to the invention of human flight as the wind tunnel experiments and the wing warping itself. The movable rudder transformed the Wrights' method of balancing their glider into a true three-dimensional system of control. The forward elevator controlled the machine in the pitch axis, the wing warping in the roll axis, and the new movable rudder in the third dimension, today referred to as *yaw* (see Figure 48). In its final form, the Wright brothers' 1902 glider was the first fully controllable aircraft. It was the realization of the Wrights' conceptual understanding that an aircraft operates in three dimensions and cannot rely solely on inherent stability for successful flight. Every air-

47. The Wrights resolved the persistent lateral control problems by making the vertical tail movable. The coordinated wing warping and rudder movement can be seen in this view.

plane following the Wrights' has used three-axis control to fly. It was the core claim of their later flying-machine patent and the principal reason the powered airplane that lifted off the beach at Kitty Hawk in December of 1903 is regarded as the world's first.

The unraveling of the lateral control problem and the conceptualization of a practical solution provide another instance of the presence of visual thinking in the Wrights' inventive method. As in the previous examples cited, the use of graphic imagery is not discussed overtly by the Wrights in their accounts of well digging and of the movable rudder. But it is readily apparent from what they do say that mentally picturing the forces involved and their effects was at the center of how they puzzled through the dilemma. Orville's use of the ball and inclined plane analogy to describe a sideslip in his account to Fred Kelly is perhaps the most obvious case. However, the brothers' descriptions of the

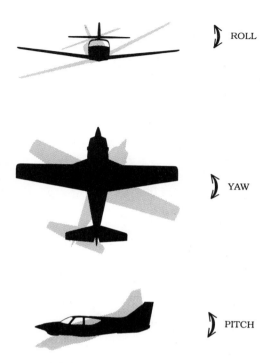

ROLL

YAW

PITCH

48. The three axes of motion about which an airplane is controlled.

low-drag wing surging ahead, the pressure buildup on the fixed vertical tail, and the corrective torque action of the movable surface also naturally cause the reader to imagine visually what is taking place. No doubt when the Wrights figured it out in their own minds they too pictured the various responses of the glider. Again, the primacy of visual thinking in their thought processes can only be inferred from the content of their verbal descriptions and, in some instances, from their sketches. While there are no direct references, the frequency with which such inferences can be drawn throughout the Wrights' technical work lends much substance to the idea.

Confident that a movable rudder would eliminate the well digging phenomenon, the Wrights began modifying the glider without delay. They hinged the vertical tail and ran control wires to the hip cradle to couple it with the wing warping action. The double tail of the fixed configuration was replaced with a single surface, halving the area to six square feet. By October 6, the changes were finished, and Wilbur and Orville were ready to resume gliding.[49]

The final adjustments to the 1902 glider were a complete success. The Wrights never again experienced well digging or any other unexpected behavior from the machine. Control in all axes was now smooth and responsive. "When properly applied," Wilbur reported, "the means of control proved to possess a mastery over the forces tending to disturb the equilibrium."[50] Orville enthusiastically recorded in his diary the precision with which the glider could now be flown.

> . . . he [Wilbur] came to a stop high in the air, turned with one wing up, and landed with the wind blowing directly from the side of the machine. . . . Will had no trouble in the control of the machine and made a difficult glide from the top of the second hill over a course of about 280 feet, in which the wind came at great angles from one side and then the other.[51]

The technical detail of the Wrights' aircraft, their flight testing program, even daily life at Kitty Hawk are all well documented in the brothers' voluminous correspondence, detailed diaries, and published articles. What is less apparent from the written record are some of the more mundane aspects of constructing and flying the gliders. The experiences of modern-day builders of reproduction Wright aircraft can help shed light on these less salient factors, factors that were as much a part of the invention of the airplane as the development of the control system or the design of an efficient wing surface.

I have already discussed how recreating the glider trials at Kitty Hawk has provided greater insight concerning the nature of the Wrights' structural design and its relationship to the longevity of the aircraft and their learning piloting skills. Flying a full-size reproduction Wright glider also illuminates a number of other experiences, even emotions, that the brothers voiced only sparingly.

Sailing down Big Hill on board the fully controllable 1902 glider for a long glide engendered a feeling of satisfaction beyond words. But paired with those few seconds of elation was the drudgery of hauling the machine back up the dune for another flight. Manhandling a hundred pounds of awkwardly shaped wood and fabric, in the sand, under the blistering August sun or in the face of chilly October evening winds, exacted a physical toll that is easily overlooked when reading the Wrights' accounts of those exciting pioneering glides in the comfortable environment of home or in the library. Wilbur mentioned on one occasion, "Whenever the breeze fell below six miles an hour, very hard running was required to get the machine started, and the task of carrying it back up the hill was real labor."[52] One can only attain a true sense of the energy expended in this activity by actually carrying such a machine up a hundred-foot ridge of sand several dozen times in an afternoon. Wilbur and Orville were as physically fit as they were mentally able.

Another subtle but impressive experience disclosed by experimenting with a reproduction glider is the power of the wind—not in terms of its velocity, but in the way in which wind imparts its energy to a glider. As the breeze flows over the wings and generates lift, there is a sense of the machine stirring to life. It becomes lighter in the handler's grasp as the wings begin to support it and starts to fly on its own as the forces of lift and drag take effect. It is as if the glider develops a mind and a personality. In flight, the operator merely directs its energies according to his or her will, in much the same way as a rider masters a spirited horse. Through this inanimate machine, the human pilot is able, to a degree, to embrace and transcend the forces of nature. There is a distinct feeling of power and control over the glider, yet at the same time there is a clear demand of respect by the machine for the forces it is harnessing. This interaction between pilot, aircraft, and environment is an experience that rarely fails to impress. It may in part explain the deeply personal feelings many pilots have for their aircraft and for the sensation of flight itself. Poring over the Wrights' records of distances and durations, angles of attack and airspeeds, constants and coefficients, the more sensory and emotional aspects of uncovering the secrets of flight can become lost. Building a glider and taking to the dunes yourself is one way of recapturing these less apparent elements of the Wright brothers' inventive experience.

Although performance of the perfected 1902 glider was now better than ever, the Wrights were limited in their practice over the middle two weeks of October by frequent spates of slack winds and bad weather.[53] They were also distracted during this period by the growing number of visitors in their camp.

Before leaving for Kitty Hawk, Wilbur and Orville had reluctantly agreed to help Chanute and his "experts" test his old multiple-wing glider of 1896 and the oscillating-wing machine he had recently contracted Charles Lamson to build. Chanute had hired Augustus Herring, his earlier collaborator on the multiple-wing glider, to pilot both this and the Lamson machine at the Outer Banks. In addition to Chanute and Herring, the Wrights also shared quarters with their older brother Lorin Wright and their well-liked acquaintance from the previous year, George Spratt.

Lorin and Spratt had reached camp on September 30, much to the Wrights' favor. During the course of their stay, they provided Wilbur and Orville with pleasurable companionship and an opportunity for unending aeronautical discussion while the brothers worked through the final problems with their glider. Lorin played a subtle, but important, behind-the-scenes role in the Wrights' 1902 experiments. He took many of the existing spectacular in-flight photographs of the glider, creating a rich visual record of the turning point in the brothers' flight testing program. Lorin also kept Katharine and their father informed of what was going on, freeing Wilbur and Orville from letter-writing chores to concentrate on flying.[54]

By October 5, things began to get a little crowded with the arrival of Chanute and Herring. "We erected the fifth cot 'upstairs,'" Orville noted in his diary, "and arranged camp so that the machine could be more easily stored." Chanute's multiple-wing glider had been sent ahead to Kitty Hawk two weeks earlier, and the Lamson machine would be there in a few days.[55]

While the Wrights' were making marvelous controlled glides with their perfected glider, Chanute was forced to witness the pathetic performance of his own machines. Herring barely got airborne with the multiple-wing glider: "After leaving the ground he alighted about 20 feet distant on the right wing and broke the main cross-span to the lower surface."[56] After making numerous measurements of the machine's lift and drag, kiting it with the Wrights' assistance, and attempting several more glides, Herring decided that it was "useless to make further experiments with the multi.-wing," Orville recorded in his diary. "Mr. Chanute seems much disappointed in the way it works," he added.[57]

The performance of the Lamson machine was equally discouraging. On October 13, the only day it was tried, the glider acquitted itself modestly when kited without a pilot, but the best Herring could manage gliding it was a flight of fifty feet. The next morning, the Wrights helped pull out the machine and ready it for another trial. The previously confident Herring, however, did not appear especially anxious to climb on board the rickety craft. After contemplating the situation briefly, "Mr. Herring soon decided to take it inside again to take its weight and ascertain its center of lift."[58] Nothing further was done with the Lamson machine. That afternoon, just ten days after arriving, Chanute and Herring departed abruptly. In light of the comparatively stunning performance of the Wrights' glider, Chanute no doubt left Kitty Hawk feeling rather embarrassed.[59]

To the brothers' amazement, Chanute continued to believe that some value could come from testing the Lamson oscillating-wing glider. Incredibly, after having just witnessed the world's first flights of an aircraft capable of full three-axis control, he still saw the oscillating wing principle as a viable alternative. True to his word of a few months before, Chanute insisted that Wilbur and Orville accept the Lamson and multiple-wing machines as presents. He was convinced that the brothers were interested in testing them further. Not wishing to humiliate their old friend, the Wrights graciously assumed custody of the gliders.[60]

Although the previous week and a half had been an utter disaster for Chanute, it was also a frustrating period for Wilbur and Orville. They had completed the movable rudder just as Chanute and Herring had arrived. Eager to practice with the latest refinement to their glider, they were reluctant to waste valuable time at Kitty Hawk on Chanute's antiquated designs. Unfortunately for them, during the relatively few opportunities when the winds were up and it was not raining, they were burdened with assisting their fellow experimenters. "We didn't have a bit of time while Chanute and Herring were in camp . . . ," Orville later lamented to Katharine.[61] Nevertheless, despite their personal frustration, it must have been more than a little painful for them to watch the respected elder statesman of aeronautics, and their loyal supporter, trying to coax his pitiful, dangerous, contraptions into the air.

Lorin had left the day before Chanute and Herring ignominiously departed. Spratt stayed another week, but the Wrights always considered his presence a help rather than a hindrance.[62]

The weather improved toward the end of October, and Wilbur and Orville, now alone in camp, finally had a chance to spend a significant amount of time in the air with their perfected glider. During the last week of their stay they made more than 375 glides, 250 in only two days. The Wrights were now consistently covering distances of three hundred feet, with five hundred feet being common, and occasionally making a flight of over six hundred feet. The total number of glides for the 1902 season was between seven hundred and one thousand. The single best was 622½ feet in twenty-six seconds.[63] Shortly before leaving, Orville wrote home enthusiastically of their success.

. . . we now hold all records! The largest machine we handled in any kind of weather, made the longest distance glide (American), the longest time in the air, the smallest angle of descent, and the highest wind!!! Well, I'll leave the rest of the "blow" till we get home.[64]

The control system was a particularly noteworthy achievement in their view. Wilbur, with some humility, later assessed it in comparison to his skills as a pilot.

With the method we have been using the capacity for control is evidently very great. The machine seems to have reached a higher state of development than the operators. As yet we consider ourselves little more than novices in management.[65]

Buoyant over the success, the Wrights wanted to stay in Kitty Hawk a few more weeks. But provisions were getting low, and Dan Tate, the only experienced hand at launching the glider still around, was about to take charge of a fishing expedition. They decided to leave for Dayton by the end of the month.[66]

The Wrights fully expected to return to Kitty Hawk in 1903. In fact, they had already begun designing their next aircraft, a powered machine, while still in camp. They decided to store the 1902 glider in their reinforced building over the winter so that it would be available for practicing with next season. Chanute's "magnanimous" gifts, the Lamson and multiple-wing gliders, were also left behind in the hangar but mercifully were never tested again. For years afterward, the Wrights politely deflected Chanute's periodic inquiries about them. Finally, in late 1907, a violent storm ripped the roof off the brothers' camp building at Kitty Hawk where the gliders had been stored all along, and they were destroyed.[67]

Early on the morning of October 28, the Wrights gathered up their gear and walked the four miles from Kill Devil Hills to Kitty Hawk in a cold, windblown rain. Unlike their departure in 1901, the unpleasant weather failed to diminish their spirits. For this year, Wilbur and Orville left the Outer Banks with all their expectations fulfilled.

9

The Dream Fulfilled

In many ways, the flights of the Wright brothers' 1902 glider in its final form marked the invention of the airplane. Of course, for sustained powered flight, an adequate propulsion system beyond mere gravity and the wind had to be developed. But in terms of the fundamental aerodynamic, control, and structural requirements, the 1902 glider represented the resolution of the problem of mechanical flight. In every meaningful sense, it flew just as a Boeing 747 airliner or a modern jet fighter flies, and it was the first machine ever to do so.[1] If invention can be defined as creating a workable piece of hardware that incorporates all the original and genuinely innovative thinking and solutions necessary for accomplishing a given technical challenge, then the Wrights had invented the airplane by the fall of 1902.

Many difficult tasks remained before the brothers would be winging their way effortlessly through the sky in a powered flying machine. Indeed, the Wrights had to build two aircraft beyond their first successful powered machine of 1903 before finally accomplishing that reality in 1905. However, despite the considerable amount of labor that still lay ahead, these later aircraft were in large measure only refined versions of the basic 1902 design. There was little about them, or the manner in which the Wrights developed them, that paralleled the truly original breakthroughs of the earlier period. Wilbur and Orville often resolved the remaining technical problems of engineering the world's first powered airplane with great imagination and cleverness. But these accomplishments were dominated for the most part by problem-solving techniques that took advantage of engineering data and practices that had become standard by 1903. These achievements were of a different character from the initial design stages of the gliders, the wind tunnel experiments, or the perfection of the control system. The truly creative and original aspects of their inventive work, the principal focus of this study, were thus largely completed by late 1902. The propellers of the 1903 airplane were a notable exception, but even they were rooted in the wind tunnel research.

It is apparent that Wilbur and Orville realized they had reached the turning point in the long human quest for wings with the successful flights of 1902. On December 11, in response to Chanute's urging them to patent their ideas, Wilbur informed him promptly that the process was already well under way. "We have our patent specifications about complete and hope to have them filed soon."[2] Many others had filed patents on various aspects of flying machines during the nineteenth century, and more than a few had been granted.[3] But none had the credibility of hundreds of actual flights to back them up. The Wrights recognized that they had achieved the core of the invention of the airplane and now began to take steps to protect their interests.

The brothers' initial patent application was turned down for lack of clarity. After they secured the aid of a patent lawyer to help them properly prepare the application, their basic flying machine patent was finally granted in May of 1906. This was two-and-a-half years after their first successful powered flights in December 1903. Nevertheless, the patent still covered only the principles embodied in the 1902 glider. No mention of power is made in the claims. The Wrights understood that the truly innovative elements of their airplane were the basic aerodynamics and the control system, and they chose not to confuse matters by introducing the comparatively unoriginal aspect of mating power to the airframe.[4] Other prominent experimenters, learning of the Wrights' latest developments largely from Chanute, began to take notice of how far the brothers had come. Samuel Langley, in the midst of building his ill-fated, man-carrying *Great Aerodrome*, extended an invitation to the Wrights in late 1902 through Chanute to "visit Washington at my expense, to get some of their ideas on the subject, if they are willing to communicate them."[5] By this point, Wilbur and Orville had no intention of giving their ideas to anyone, and they politely declined the invitation. Being so close to actually flying a powered airplane, they felt they could no longer afford the attitude of open exchange that had characterized their dealings with fellow experimenters up until now.[6]

49. U.S. Patent 821,393, granted May 22, 1906, to Wilbur and Orville Wright for "new and useful improvement in Flying Machines."

This change in outlook would soon lead to conflict with their old friend from Chicago and ultimately cause an irreparable rift in their relationship. Chanute believed fervently that the brothers should worry less about ensuring personal credit and continue to share their discoveries with the rest of the aeronautical community. The first of many disputes over this issue erupted in the summer of 1903. In this instance, the flap was over an article disclosing the details of the Wrights' 1902 glider that Chanute planned to publish in a French scientific journal. Wilbur's lean, somewhat cold, response to Chanute's persistent inquiry regarding the operation of the movable rudder expresses his frustration with the elder experimenter's intention to release this critical piece of information while their patent application was still pending. "I only see three methods of dealing with this matter," Wilbur wrote. "(1) Tell the truth. (2) Tell nothing specific. (3) Tell something not true. I really cannot advise either the first or the third course."[7] Chanute quickly got the message. "I was puzzled by the way you put things in your former letters. You were sarcastic and I did not catch the idea that you feared that the description might forestall a patent. Now that I know it, I take pleasure in suppressing the passage altogether." Nevertheless, Chanute still did not seem to grasp what the concern was about. He continued, "I believe however that it would have proved quite harmless [to describe the rudder] as the construction is ancient and well known."[8]

This was an especially telling example of Chanute's growing inability to keep pace with the brothers' aeronautical advances. To refer to the perfection of three-axis control, the very thing that opened the final door to human flight, as something "ancient and well known" showed almost unfathomable ignorance on the part of Chanute, and undoubtedly exasperated Wilbur and Orville to no end. Setting their understandable displeasure aside, the brothers closed the incident with a conciliatory note to Chanute thanking him for striking the passage regarding the movable rudder from his article. For the moment at least, they decided to keep their annoyance with Chanute in check, and their friendship and regular correspondence with him continued.[9]

The Wrights' immediate move to file for a patent upon returning from Kitty Hawk, and their changing attitude toward sharing what they had done, reveal that they had comprehended the significance of the 1902 flights. It is clear that by this point the brothers recognized that they would be the inventors of the airplane.

In the same December 11 letter in which the Wrights told Chanute of their patent application and asked him to give Langley their regrets, they also shared their plans for the coming year.

It is our intention next year to build a machine much larger and about twice as heavy as our present machine. With it we will work out the problems relating to starting and handling heavy weight machines, and if we find it under satisfactory control in flight, we will proceed to mount a motor. [10]

In designing the 1903 powered airplane, which the Wrights would later refer to simply as "the Flyer," they returned once again to the basic equations upon which their earlier gliders had been based. [11] In order to carry the extra weight of an engine, propellers, and added structural reinforcement of a powered aircraft, they decided they would have to increase significantly the 305-square-foot wing area of the 1902 machine to approximately 500 square feet. Based on their experience with the gliders, Wilbur and Orville estimated that a completed airplane of this size, allowing 200 pounds for the engine and propellers, would weigh 625 pounds with pilot.

Beginning with these estimates for the size of their airplane, the Wrights were then able to calculate the velocity, drag, thrust, and power requirements. As with the gliders, they began by considering the minimum case condition of the lift being equal to the flying weight of the aircraft. In terms of the lift equation, this was expressed as

$$L = W = kV^2SC_L$$

where L is the minimum lift required to sustain flight, W is the estimated weight of 625 pounds, k is the Wrights' adjusted pressure coefficient of 0.0033, V is the minimum velocity necessary to fly, S is the wing area of five hundred square feet, and C_L is the coefficient of lift for the particular surface chosen at the desired angle of attack. The value for C_L was of course taken from the tables the Wrights prepared using their wind tunnel data.

From here it was a matter of simple algebra to solve for the velocity V to determine the airspeed that must be attained. Within the range of angles of attack at which the Wrights planned to fly, they calculated that a minimum velocity of twenty-three miles per hour had to be achieved.

Knowing the velocity, it was now possible to compute the drag. This becomes far more important when designing a powered airplane than a glider because the variable of thrust is involved. Drag and thrust exert forces in opposite directions. Under minimum case conditions, the propellers must generate at least as much thrust as there is drag. Therefore, in order to know how much thrust is necessary, it is crucial to be able to calculate the total drag on the airplane. *Total drag* is the sum of the aerodynamic and the parasitic drag. *Aerodynamic drag* is that which is generated by the airflow over the wing surface as lift is being produced, and *parasitic drag* refers to the resistance caused by the frontal area of the craft exposed to the wind.

It was here that the drag equation and the coefficients of drag collected with the wind tunnel become extremely important. The Wrights substituted the known terms into the drag equation

$$D = kV^2SC_D$$

To obtain the aerodynamic drag, the equation was solved for D using the proposed wing area of five hundred square feet for S. The velocity was known from the previous calculation, and C_D was taken from the wind tunnel tables. To find the parasitic drag, the Wrights performed the operation a second time. Now the frontal area of the airplane was used for S; i.e., the exposed surface of the struts, the wing leading edges, the engine, the pilot, and any other nonaerodynamic piece of the structure. They estimated this to be twenty square feet. The two results for D were then added to arrive at the total drag. Wilbur and Orville estimated that the drag on a five-hundred-square-foot airplane of the type they planned to build would be ninety pounds. This meant that they would need to generate a minimum of ninety pounds of thrust to leave the ground.

The drag value was also used to determine the amount of horsepower that would be required using the simple relationship

$$P = DV$$

where D is drag and V is velocity as in the other equations, and P is equal to the power required. Continuing with the minimum case condition, the brothers calculated that they would need an engine of at least eight horsepower to sustain their 625-pound machine at the minimum airspeed of 23 miles per hour. (To calculate the actual value for the horsepower, a third multiplying factor to make the units correlate must also be applied.)

In this fashion, the Wrights methodically went through each of the basic design variables and came up with a set of estimates upon which to base their first powered airplane. To sustain flight in their five-hundred-square-foot, 625-pound aircraft, they would require an eight horsepower engine, generating ninety pounds of thrust, to achieve a minimum airspeed of twenty-three miles per hour.

This was the same procedure the Wrights had used all along to build their gliders; however, with the powered machine they expanded the range of factors to be addressed. Every element of design from propulsion to materials was investigated before beginning construction. In light of these additional concerns, the pivotal role of the wind tunnel data is even more apparent. As we have seen, Wilbur and Orville cleverly used their tables of C_L and C_D in conjunction with the lift and drag equations to determine the velocity, drag, thrust, and power requirements for their aircraft. This illustrates yet again how integral a part of the invention of the airplane the wind tunnel experiments were.

Beyond the original data they derived, the Wrights also referred to engineering handbooks of the day to estimate the structural loadings on the wing spars and struts and to figure the sizing of individual parts. There was no component of the 1903 Wright Flyer that was not based on prior calculation or thorough planning. Unlike every flying machine that had preceded it, this airplane was engineered in the strictest sense of the word.

The last fundamental obstacle to powered flight Wilbur and Orville had to overcome was the propulsion system. Their work in this area was the one significant element of the 1903 Flyer that represented a conceptual breakthrough comparable to wing warping or displayed creativity as imaginative as the design of the wind tunnel balances. The term *propulsion system* is important. On an airplane, not only must there be an engine of some kind to generate power, but also a means of transforming that power into thrust to drive the airplane forward. The Wrights astutely recognized that developing an effective propeller, as well as an efficient transmission linkage from the power plant, was just as crucial as coming up with a suitable engine. Most of their predecessors failed to see this. Maxim and Langley, for example, built extremely powerful, lightweight engines, but they equipped them with terribly inefficient, flat-bladed propellers. The result was a very low output of thrust despite the high horsepower delivered by these fine engines.[12]

From the beginning of their experiments, the Wrights had always considered propulsion the least of their problems. In light of the significant advances in both steam and gasoline engine technology toward the close of the nineteenth century, they assumed that when the time came they would be able to purchase a suitable engine with little difficulty. Similarly, by the time the brothers began their aeronautical investigations, the propeller had become established as the most viable means of generating thrust. A few fringe experimenters still clung to the ornithopter or the flappers for propulsion, but by 1903 these were ideas whose time had long since passed. Several decades of marine use of propellers led Wilbur and Orville to believe that the operation of these devices was largely understood, and that it would be a simple matter to adapt known theories to aircraft propulsion. Much to their surprise, they found these assumptions to be premature.

Despite several encouraging examples, steam engines for aircraft use were always plagued by poor power-to-weight ratios owing to the necessary boilers and water that had to be carried. However, beginning with Nicolaus Otto's first practical four-cycle internal combustion gasoline engine of 1876, the development of this type of power plant during the last quarter of the century opened a whole new avenue for the evolution of lightweight propulsion.[13]

By the time the Wrights were ready to mount a motor on their flying machine, there were dozens of firms manufacturing gasoline engines. In December of 1902, the brothers contacted a number of them concerning the possibility of obtaining an engine capable of delivering eight or nine horsepower at a weight of no more than 180 pounds. Ten firms responded, but none could meet the specifications or do so at a reasonable price. Undeterred, Wilbur and Orville decided to build their own.[14]

Charlie Taylor, the mechanic they had hired in 1901 to give themselves more time to experiment, played an important role in this phase of their aeronautical work. He assisted in designing the engine and did virtually all the machine work. "We didn't make any drawings," Taylor later recalled. "One of us would sketch out the part we were talking about on a piece of scratch paper and I'd spike the sketch over my bench."[15] The engine was the one aspect of the Wrights' invention of the airplane that someone else had a significant hand in creating.

The engine was a bit crude, even by the standards of these early days of the technology, but it did the job.[16] A rudimentary version of a contemporary automobile engine, it had four water-cooled, horizontal, in-

50. The twelve-horsepower engine built by Charlie Taylor that powered the 1903 Wright Flyer. It is displayed here tipped up to show the underside of the motor.

line cylinders. The four-inch bore, four-inch stroke cast-iron cylinders were fitted into a single-piece cast-aluminum crankcase that extended outward to form a water jacket around the cylinder barrels. Cooling water was supplied by a narrow vertical trough mounted to one of the forward center-section struts. It was not a radiator in the typical sense. There was no water pump, and the fluid did not circulate. The device simply replenished the water jacket as the coolant evaporated. With such a crude arrangement, the engine could be run only for a few minutes before overheating. The crankshaft was rough cut from a slab of high-carbon steel and lathe turned to precise size and smoothness. The brothers had the crankcase cast by a local foundry, but Charlie Taylor machined every other component in the bike shop.

The Wright engine had no fuel pump, carburetor, or spark plugs. Gasoline was gravity fed from a small quart-and-a-half capacity tank mounted to a forward strut just below the upper wing. There were two valves in the copper fuel line, one for metering the flow, and a second shutoff valve for stopping the engine. Raw gasoline entered a shallow chamber next to the cylinders, mixing with the incoming air. The heat from the engine crankcase then vaporized the fuel/air mixture, causing it to pass into the intake manifold and on into the cylinders. Ignition was produced by opening and closing two contact breaker points inside the combustion chamber of each cylinder via a camshaft. The initial spark for starting was generated with a coil and four dry-cell batteries, not carried on the airplane. A low-tension magneto driven by a twenty-six-pound flywheel supplied the current while the engine was running. The speed could be regulated slightly by retarding or advancing the timing of the spark; however, this was possible only while on the ground.

Taylor completed the basic engine in only six weeks. It was given its first test run on February 12, 1903. The next day, however, the crankcase was fractured when dripping gasoline caused the bearings to freeze. "The boys broke their little gas motor in the afternoon," Bishop Wright recorded laconically in his diary that evening.[17] By April, a new casting was received and testing resumed. After replacing a number of parts and making a few adjustments, the brothers had the engine running successfully. Upon starting, it delivered sixteen horsepower, but after turning over for a minute or two, the preheated air entering the cylinders expanded so greatly that output typically dropped to about twelve horsepower. Despite the twenty-five percent reduction in power after warming up, and the rather short running time because of the inadequate cooling system, the Wrights were satisfied with their homemade engine. Even at twelve horsepower, they had a significant margin above the anticipated eight horsepower. They took advantage of the extra power, which meant they could afford an increase in weight, by adding further structural reinforcement to the airframe. Equally encouraging, the weight of the engine was within their target specification of 180 pounds. Depending on the source and on what components they were including, the Wrights quoted a number of different figures ranging between 140 and 179 pounds. At the time the airplane flew, the completed propulsion system, including propellers and transmission system, added up to about 200 pounds. This was precisely in line with their initial design estimates for a total weight of the Flyer of 625 pounds.

Although the Wrights' first aircraft engine was not intrinsically remarkable, the nature of its design does tell us something important about their thought process. Wilbur and Orville had no prior experience with gasoline engines beyond the small, one-cylinder example they had built to power their shop machinery in 1901. But this mattered little to them, since they were after only a relatively modest eight horsepower. Because they engineered the 1903 airplane as a complete technological system capable of flight, they did not need to concern themselves with creating a highly efficient, sophisticated engine. Unlike so many of their predecessors, who had focused on the propulsion problem separately, the Wrights considered power requirements in terms of the aerodynamic qualities of their aircraft and the estimated thrust of their propellers. The output of their engine was calculated expressly as a function of the lift, the drag, and the projected velocity of their airframe. As such, they knew ahead of time how good their engine needed to be and designed it accordingly. One of the great strengths of the Wrights' inventive method in building the gliders was their consistent attention to the concept of the airplane as an amalgamation of interdependent component parts, no one more or less vital to the success of the machine than any other. Their approach to the engine continued to reflect this view. It did not have to be exceptional, merely good enough. Moreover, this conclusion was based on careful planning that was anything but merely good enough. When looking at the engine from the perspective of the thought processes that led to the brothers' overall invention, one might argue that the Wright engine was somewhat crude specifically because the design of their airplane as a whole was so incredibly precise.

This is not to say that the Wright engine was not an impressive achievement; it was, especially in light of the limited resources and conditions under which it was built. The point is that, compared to other contemporary examples of the technology, both automotive and aeronautical, it was not particularly sophisticated in design or operation. As a frame of reference, consider Langley's engine in the *Great Aerodrome* of 1903. Admittedly the best of its day, it delivered fifty-two horsepower and weighed only 124 pounds. Further, the Wrights' engine was nowhere near as groundbreaking as the other elements of their airplane. It is noteworthy only when viewed in conjunction with other aspects of the entire machine.

As work on the engine progressed, the Wrights also gave consider-able attention to developing a propeller that would transform the esti-mated eight horsepower into ninety pounds of thrust.[18] They began by pursuing their usual course of first determining what had been done previously. A quick study of marine use of propellers, however, proved disappointing. ". . . so far as we could learn, marine engineers pos-sessed only empirical formulas, and the exact action of the screw-propeller, after a century of use, was still very obscure."[19] Upon em-barking on their own research into the subject, the brothers began to see why so little usable theory on propellers existed. "We have recently done a little experimenting with screws," Wilbur wrote to Spratt in late 1902, "and are trying to get a clear understanding of just how they work and why. It is a very perplexing problem indeed."[20] In an article published in 1908, the Wrights candidly recalled their initial frustrations.

What at first seemed a simple problem became more complex the longer we studied it. With the machine moving forward, the air flying backward, the pro-pellers turning sidewise, and nothing standing still, it seemed impossible to find a starting point from which to trace the various simultaneous reactions. Contem-plation of it was confusing. After long arguments, we often found ourselves in the ludicrous position of each having been converted to the other's side, with no more agreement than when the discussion began.[21]

After months of thought, experimentation, and discussion, Wilbur and Orville finally hit upon the answer. They decided to treat the pro-peller as if it were a rotary wing. They reasoned that the same physics that generated an upward lifting force when a curved wing surface was placed in an airstream would also produce a horizontally oriented thrust when such a surface was positioned vertically and rotated to create the airflow. Unlike a marine propeller, which pushes a ship forward by dis-placing a volume of the water through which it is passing, similar to the advance of a screw through a board, the Wright aircraft propeller generated thrust aerodynamically. Working from this premise, the brothers could once again take advantage of their fruitful wind tunnel experiments to select an appropriate airfoil for the blades of their pro-peller.

It was apparent that a propeller was simply an aeroplane [a wing] traveling in a spiral course. As we could calculate the effect of an aeroplane [a wing] traveling in a straight course, why should we not be able to calculate the effect of one traveling in a spiral course?[22]

Here again, the Wrights overcame a daunting technical problem by approaching it from a new and uniquely different perspective. Similar to the manner in which they had arrived at the recognition of the reversal of the center of pressure on a wing surface, the principle of wing warping, and three-axis control, the brothers dealt with the question of generating adequate thrust for their airplane by looking at the basic problem in an original way that resulted in yet another imaginative solution. As with so many aspects of their aeronautical work, before the Wright propeller there were none like it, and after it there were none that were different. Wilbur and Orville not only designed an effective device to meet their own propulsion needs, but laid another key building block on the foundation of aeronautical engineering.

Once this fundamental idea was understood, the Wrights moved ahead confidently with the process of creating an efficient aerial propeller. "Our tables made the designing of the wings an easy matter; and as screw propellers are simply wings traveling in a spiral course, we anticipated no trouble from this source."[23] Like the rest of the airplane, extensive planning and calculation preceded carving the actual propellers. Wilbur and Orville filled no less than five notebooks with formulas, sketches, tables of data, and computations.[24]

As we were not in a position to undertake a long series of practical experiments to discover a suitable propeller . . . , it seemed necessary to obtain such a thorough understanding of the theory of its reactions as would enable us to design them from calculation alone.[25]

The basic design procedure of the propellers followed the pattern employed for the aircraft's wings. Using the lift and drag equations and the wind tunnel data, the Wrights determined the most efficient curvature for the airfoil of the blades given their estimated area, rotational velocity, and angle of attack. Because of the added variables in computing the forces acting on a curved surface moving in a spiral course, they also had to consider factors such as torque, thrust, blade width and planform, and *slip*, a term that refers to the difference in the forward velocity of the propeller and the forward velocity of the airplane relative to the airflow.[26]

The actual calculations encompassing all these variables and deter-mining the efficiency of the final design were extremely complex, far more so than what was done for the lifting surfaces. But the effort paid off. By June of 1903, the Wrights had designed and built a pair of highly efficient propellers that were based entirely on a well-conceived theory of operation and thorough calculation. In a letter to George Spratt, Orville shared the latest developments with a clever turn of phrase that succinctly illustrates the brothers' typical method of approaching a problem, as well as their burgeoning self-confidence concerning even-tual success.

We had been unable to find anything of value in any of the works to which we had access, so that we worked out a theory of our own on the subject, and soon discovered, as we usually do, that all the propellers built heretofore are *all wrong*, and then built a pair of propellers . . . , based on our theory, which are *all right*! (till we have a chance to test them down at Kitty Hawk and find out differently). Isn't it astonishing that all these secrets have been preserved for so many years just so that we could discover them!![27]

The Wrights decided to use two propellers to maximize the volume of air acted upon. This arrangement had the additional benefit of allow-ing for a greater pitch angle, or *twist*, of the blades than with a single propeller. Also, two propellers could be spun in opposite directions, thereby neutralizing the gyroscopic effects of the large, whirling blades. Each one was 8½ feet in diameter and made of three laminations of 1⅛-inch spruce, shaped with a hatchet and a drawknife. The tips were covered with fabric and varnish to prevent splitting. The propellers were located behind the wings to prevent any disturbance of the airflow over the lifting surfaces.

The transmission linkage that mated the propellers to the engine completed the Wright propulsion system. The brothers settled upon an arrangement of sprockets and chains running from the engine crank-shaft to a pair of steel-tube propeller shafts mounted to each side of the aircraft's center section. The chains were encased in metal tubes to reduce vibration. The engine resided on the lower wing immediately to the right of the pilot's hip cradle. Counter-rotation of the propellers was achieved by simply twisting the chain leading to one of the propel-ler shafts in a figure eight to reverse the direction that the sprocket turned.[28]

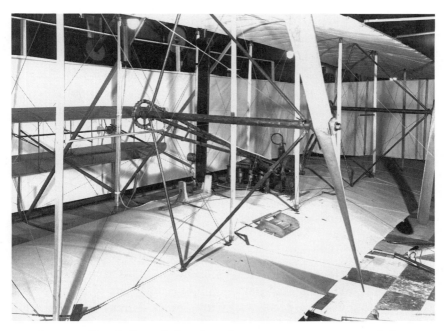

51. The propeller shafts and the chain-drive transmission system of the 1903 Flyer. The transference of bicycle technology is unmistakable.

The chain-driven transmission system had two advantages. First, it was in common use in automobiles and bicycles at the time, so parts were readily available in varied sizes, and the operation of the mechanism was very familiar. Second, and perhaps more importantly, this system offered flexibility in changing engine/propeller speed ratios, not possible with a propeller mounted directly to the engine. Regardless of how accurately the Wrights designed their propellers, they could not predict with certainty how much of a loss of efficiency there would be in actual practice. A change in the diameter of the sprockets would enable them to adjust output easily on the completed airplane. Also with this system, the engine could be geared down to allow the Wrights to turn their large-diameter propellers without overloading it. On the 1903 Flyer, they used a transmission ratio of twenty-three to eight, which meant that for every twenty-three revolutions of the engine crankshaft, there were eight rotations of the propellers.[29]

The Wrights' development of their propulsion system is illustrative in that it incorporated many of the various aspects of their inventive method that have been defined and traced throughout this study. Their conceiving the propeller as a rotary wing again demonstrates the brothers' ability to realize effective solutions to fundamental problems by creating conceptual models of the forces involved, which could then be turned into practical hardware. The critical role of mental imagery is also readily apparent. One literally has to "see" the propeller as a wing moving in a spiral course to make this intellectual leap. Even the Wrights' own language—"It was apparent that a propeller was simply an aeroplane traveling in spiral course"—suggests that this was in fact an encompassing visual realization.

Further examples of the Wrights' method are also present in the propulsion work. The preliminary literature search, strict engineering technique, and thorough calculation employed to create the propellers were all pertinent aspects of their approach, apparent in every phase of their invention of the airplane. Thinking in terms of technological systems and transferring technology from other sources were two other keys to the design of the Wrights' means of propulsion. Their insight into the relationship between estimating horsepower and thrust and their adaptation of the sprocket-and-chain-drive transmission system reflect both of these elements. And, of course, the sprocket-and-chain transmission was certainly the most visible, though not the most important, manifestation of the bicycle on the Wright Flyer.

As we have seen, these approaches to problem solving, innate skills, and techniques appear over and over again in all of the Wrights' aeronautical research and experimentation. They comprise a definable inventive method that undergirded their entire effort. Tracing the development of the final major component of the Flyer, the propulsion system, allows us to see with great clarity how these elements coalesced to enable the Wright brothers to produce an object of incredible technical creativity.

By midsummer 1903, Wilbur and Orville had completed the design phase of their powered airplane, had built the engine and the propellers, and were busy fabricating the airframe. They stuck with their proven canard biplane configuration. The final dimensions of the wings were forty feet four inches in span with a 6½-foot chord. This gave the finished Flyer a wing area of 510 square feet, 10 more than estimated. To compensate for the engine being heavier than the pilot and being

52. The 1903 Flyer wing with the top layer of fabric covering removed during the 1985 restoration of the aircraft at the National Air and Space Museum. Note the rib pockets and the bias seams of the lower layer of covering. These design features contributed immeasurably to the strength and flexibility of the wing structure.

offset slightly to the right of the hip cradle, the right wing panels were four inches longer to provide the necessary extra lift on that side to balance the aircraft. Like the 1902 glider, the wings were rigged with a slight droop to reduce the effects of crosswinds.

Unlike the solid, steam-bent wing ribs of the earlier gliders, the ribs on the 1903 machine were built up from two thin strips of ash with small blocks in between. The joints were reinforced with glued paper.[30] A further refinement was the addition of a layer of fabric covering to the bottom of the wing surfaces. The gliders had fabric only on the top surface; the rib pockets below were exposed. The double layer covering on the 1903 wings resulted in a much smoother lifting surface that enhanced efficiency. The powered airplane was covered with the same Pride of the West muslin used on the 1901 and 1902 gliders and was again left unsealed to save weight. The Wrights continued to apply the fabric with the weave on the bias to enhance the stiffness of the wings without any additional internal structure.[31]

Despite the fine performance of the 1902 glider when its wings were rigged with a camber close to 1 in 30, the Wrights felt that a deeper curvature of 1 in 20 would provide better lift for the larger, heavier powered machine. Unfortunately, they never say precisely why they believed this. Like the decision to use an airfoil different from any tested in the wind tunnel on the 1902 glider, this appears to have been an intuitive judgment based on their glider experience and aerodynamic research.[32]

A possible explanation for the change beyond gut instinct may have to do with the Wrights' recognition of the phenomenon now referred to as *Reynolds number*. This relates to the changes in aerodynamic properties of lifting surfaces when extrapolating data from small wind tunnel test models to full-size wings. In a 1939 interview, Orville expressed that he and Wilbur were concerned about relying too heavily on the tiny model surfaces and explained that the actual lift and drag measurements taken on the full-size 1902 glider were used to calibrate the data collected on all the wind tunnel test wings. This provided them with a more accurate sense of how the various curves tested would perform in full scale. Orville did not indicate so, but perhaps this accounting for Reynolds number by calibration with the 1902 glider data, in part, led the brothers to choose the more deeply cambered 1 in 20 airfoil for the 1903 Flyer.[33]

The elevator on the new machine was a biplane version of the graceful, elliptical surface used on the 1902 glider. It was mounted in front as before, but on a more substantial spruce framework that also protruded below the wings to serve as landing skids for the larger, much heavier Flyer. The movable vertical rudder was also a double surface, similar to the initial fixed tail of the 1902 machine.

The Wrights' attention to detail even extended to the aerodynamic resistance of the struts that supported the wings. Early in 1903, the brothers conducted wind tunnel tests on a series of potential shapes for the uprights. Much to their surprise, they found that rectangular cross-sections with the corners merely rounded off slightly offered noticeably less resistance than the traditional teardrop streamlined form. Despite Chanute's serious doubts about the accuracy of their measurements, the Wrights carved the Flyer's struts according to what their data told them.[34] "We have . . . made some experiments on the best shapes for the uprights of our machine," Orville informed Spratt boastfully, "and

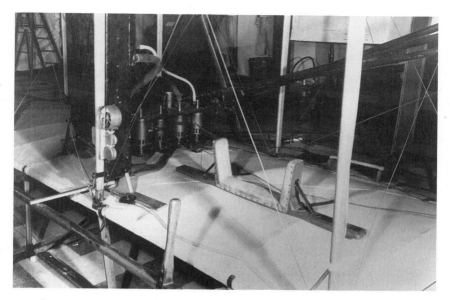

53. The "cockpit" of the 1903 Wright Flyer. The pilot laid prone next to the engine in the hip cradle, which controlled both the wing warping and the movable rudder. The lever to the pilot's left controlled the forward elevator. The thin horizontal lever on the opposite side shut off the engine and the flight-data recording instruments at the conclusion of the flight. The instrument package visible on the forward strut included a Richard anemometer and a stopwatch.

again found out that everybody but ourselves are very badly mistaken!!!"[35]

There was another subtle, but extremely important, design decision related to the struts that again demonstrates how carefully and ingeniously the 1903 Wright Flyer was engineered. Close examination of the airplane reveals a thin wire running the length of the wings that passes through the midpoint of all the vertical uprights and is secured on both sides of each one. The function of this wire was to stabilize the struts against lateral deflection under flight loads. The wire effectively halved the length of the struts, which in turn increased significantly the buckling load of these critical structural members. This was an incredibly clever, yet simple, means of adequately supporting the wing surfaces without using excessively broad, and therefore heavy, struts.[36]

The basic controls on the Flyer were essentially like those on the

1902 glider. A hip cradle, now padded, actuated the wing warping and the coupled rudder, and a simple wooden lever that the pilot operated with his left hand controlled the elevator. There was also a small complement of instruments on the powered airplane to collect flight data. A handheld Richard anemometer of the type the Wrights had been using to measure wind speeds was mounted on the forward strut just to the right of the pilot. The device was calibrated to display in meters the distance the airplane traveled through the air. Below it was a stopwatch for timing the flights. By combining the distance and duration readings, the brothers could later easily calculate the machine's average airspeed. In addition, a Veedor revolution counter was mounted at the base of the engine crankshaft to record engine and propeller RPM. The instruments were arranged so that all could be turned off the instant the flight was over. With a single movement of a wooden lever on the lower wing, the pilot simultaneously stopped the watch and tripped the fuel shutoff valve to cut the engine, which automatically halted the revolution counter and the anemometer.[37]

By September of 1903, in what was becoming an annual late summer, early fall ritual, the Wrights again prepared to go to Kitty Hawk. They had approached each of the previous trips as stimulating opportunities to experiment in an exciting new field, as well as a welcome chance to escape from their daily routine and relax for a while. Through 1902, their goal was to contribute what they could to the general knowledge of aeronautics and have some fun in the process. In 1903, things were different. This year they did not intend to merely add to the growing body of information on human flight; they were going to fly an airplane.

The story of what took place at Kitty Hawk in the fall of 1903 has been told and retold in countless articles and books.[38] It does not bear repeating at great length yet again. There was the usual long, and at times arduous, trip to Elizabeth City and across Albemarle Sound. However, with all the extra equipment and supplies they brought for the 1903 trip, not to mention over six hundred pounds of airplane, logistics were a bigger problem than ever before. Weather continued to be a major factor. The rains and cold were especially fierce this time around. And, of course, the omnipresent hoards of mosquitoes were on hand to welcome the brothers. Chanute and Spratt were in camp again this year, along with the Tates and other local helpers, but the

Wrights were careful to avoid the presence of anyone like Huffaker or Herring. As they assembled the powered machine, they took advantage of breaks in the storms to practice their piloting skills with the 1902 glider.[39]

Over the course of the three months from their arrival to the successful first flights in December, the Wrights' spirits and confidence followed an unsettling course of upswings and downturns. Between the bad weather and technical problems with the airplane, they at times began to wonder if their self-assured intentions of flying a powered airplane in 1903 were premature.

About a month into their stay, when a particularly severe storm threatened to tear the roof off their shelter one evening, the brothers went out in the windblown torrent and hastily added further bracing to the building. Although they had stemmed the forces of nature for the moment, they were beginning to feel a bit defeated. Wilbur reported to his sister Katharine that the incident prompted them to take the advice offered by the Oberlin College football coach when things got rough: "Cheer up, boys, there is no hope."[40]

Fortunately, the discouraging circumstances did not last much longer. When the storm subsided in a few days, the Wrights' enthusiasm returned. "The 'whopper flying machine' is coming on all right and will probably be done about Nov. 1st.," Wilbur informed home.[41]

As the results of their efforts during the next few weeks alternated between problems and progress, they used the entertaining metaphor of the vicissitudes of the stock market to chart their headway and attitudes. After a number of puzzlingly poor flights during practice with the 1902 glider, Orville sent the following message to Charlie Taylor:

Flying machine market has been very unsteady the past two days. Opened yesterday morning at about 208 (100% means even chance of success) but by noon had dropped to 110. These fluctuations would have produced a panic, I think, in Wall Street, but in this quiet place it only put us to thinking and figuring a little. It gradually improved during rest of yesterday and today and is now almost back to its old mark.[42]

As fall began to slip into winter, the storms became less frequent, but the cold became a major hindrance to the work. On several occasions it was simply too cold to do anything on the airplane at all.[43] Beyond the weather, the Wrights were facing an even bigger problem,

54. In 1903, the Wrights added a second building to their camp at Kitty Hawk. The completed 1903 powered Flyer sits outside its hangar, with Wilbur looking on.

one that was wreaking havoc with all their careful planning and designing. As the brothers were completing the final assembly of the Flyer, they were disturbed to realize that their estimated total weight for the aircraft of 625 pounds had risen unnervingly to over 700 pounds. Despite the few extra horsepower they had available, the Wrights were worried that they did not have enough power to get off the ground.

The weight of our machine complete with a man will be a little over 700 lbs. and we are now quite in doubt as to whether the engine will be able to pull it at all with the present gears.[44]

Upon evaluating the situation, Orville entered in his diary, "After figuring a while, stock in flying machine began dropping rapidly till it was worth very little!"[45]

In addition to the unexpectedly high weight, which of course threw off the other design estimates, the Wrights were experiencing frustrating difficulties with the engine and propeller shafts. Misfiring of the engine and the resulting vibration placed enormous strains on the shafts. The problem was compounded by continual loosening of the sprockets.

During initial runups of the engine, the jerking of the unsteady rotation of the propellers twisted the shafts and ripped them from their mountings. The damaged propeller shafts could not be repaired on the spot and had to be returned to Charlie Taylor in Dayton. This latest turn of events caused the Wrights' earlier high hopes for making an attempt at powered flight in 1903 to grow dim.

> While the shafts were away we had lots of time for thinking, and the more we thought, the harder our machine got to running and the less the power of the engine became, until stock got down to a very low figure.[46]

The repaired shafts arrived back in Kitty Hawk on November 20, and the brothers quickly set up the machine for another test. The engine continued to run poorly, causing the sprockets to loosen immediately. No matter what they did, the sprockets failed to stay secure, exasperating Wilbur and Orville to no end.

> We used a chain and six-foot 2 x 4 to tighten them and the nuts, but ten seconds' more run and they were loose again. We kept that up all Friday afternoon, and by evening stock had gone still lower, in fact just about as low as it could get, about 100 percent below par.[47]

As a last resort, the Wrights locked the sprocket nuts in place with bicycle tire cement, and at last the problem was solved. "The next morning," Orville reported to Charlie Taylor, "thanks to Arnstein's hard cement, which will fix anything from a stop watch to a thrashing machine, we stuck those sprockets so tight I doubt whether they will ever come loose again."[48]

Things finally seemed to be going in their favor. In addition to curing the loosening sprocket problem, the higher than expected weight of the Flyer ceased to be a concern when the brothers found the thrust delivered by their propellers to be fifty percent more than the ninety pounds they had estimated.

> After a few minutes' run to get the adjustments, . . . the engine speeded the propellers up to 351 rev. per min. with a thrust of 132 pounds.[49]

With their two principal problems solved, the Wrights' confidence soared. "Stock went up like a sky rocket, and is now at the highest figure in history," Orville wrote Taylor enthusiastically, "We will not be ready for trial for several days yet on account of having decided on some changes in the machine. Unless something breaks in the meantime we feel confident of success."[50]

This last statement proved prophetic. Just as everything seemed ready, one of the propeller shafts cracked during a test run on November 28. The Wrights decided to waste no more time with the unreliable steel-tube shafts. Orville left for Dayton two days later to make a new pair out of more durable solid-spring steel. He returned with the new shafts on December 11, and three days later the Wrights were, at last, prepared to make an attempt at powered flight.[51]

Owing to its size and weight, the powered Flyer could not be hand launched in the manner of the gliders. To accommodate the heavier craft, a simple sixty-foot launching rail to support the airplane during its takeoff run was built from four fifteen-foot 2' x 4's laid end to end, sheathed with a thin metal strip. The Flyer rode down this track on a small wheeled dolly, or "truck" as the Wrights called it. A helper was positioned at each wing tip to steady the machine until it gained flying speed. Beyond its practical necessity, this launching method would also make it clear that the takeoff had been unassisted, allaying any possible doubts that the Flyer had made a true flight. The brothers humorously referred to the track as "the Grand Junction Railroad."

The Wrights made their first attempt to fly on December 14. To compensate for the light wind that day, the starting track was set up on a gentle nine-degree slope to aid in generating the necessary flying speed for takeoff. To ensure witnesses to what they were aware would be an historic event, the brothers alerted the crew of the lifesaving station and the other villagers that they were ready to go by raising a prearranged signal flag. The Flyer was positioned on the launching rail and the engine warmed up. Wilbur won the toss of a coin to determine who would have the honor of making the first flight and then climbed into the hip cradle while Orville made a last-minute adjustment to the motor.

When he was ready, Wilbur tried to release the restraining line that held the Flyer in place before takeoff, but the thrust of the propellers was so great that he was unable to free it. Orville and the other assistants had to push the airplane back a little to loosen the rope. As the Flyer began its run, Orville ran alongside to steady the wings, carrying a second stopwatch he would start the instant the machine broke ground. About forty feet down the launching rail, the Flyer rose into

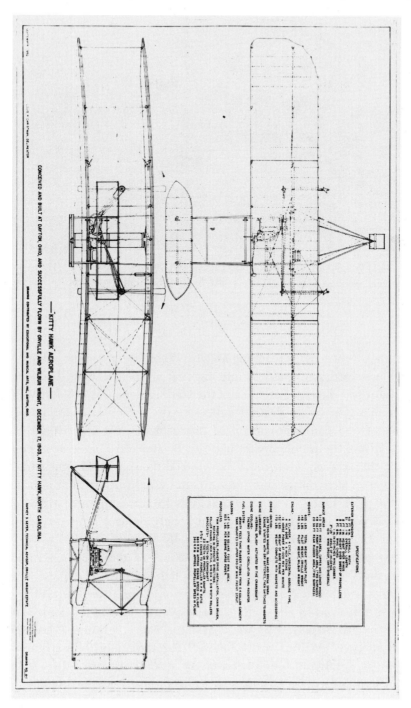

55. The 1903 Wright Flyer.

56. The Wright Flyer rests atop "the Grand Junction Railroad," the Wrights' sixty-foot wooden launching rail, ready for flight. Members of the lifesaving station crew stand by.

the air sharply. After reaching an altitude of fifteen feet, it stalled, settled backward, and smashed into the sand on the left wing. The forward elevator was damaged and one of the landing skids was broken. Wilbur, unhurt in the crash, did not anticipate the extreme sensitivity of the elevator and had over-controlled the airplane as it was lifting off the rail. Part of the problem was that the elevator was hinged at its center. With this arrangement, the airflow forced the surface to sharply deflect on its own after only a slight movement away from the neutral position by the pilot. Once the elevator got away from the operator in this manner, it was very difficult to regain steady control, and the airplane would begin to pitch up and down wildly.[52]

Even though the Flyer covered a distance of more than one hundred feet, the Wrights did not consider this hair-raising, 3½-second first attempt a true flight. Nevertheless, their confidence was bolstered by the power delivered by the engine, the responsiveness of the controls, and the strength displayed by the airframe. "There is now no question of final success," Wilbur wrote home.[53] The events of the 14th and the brothers' confident anticipation of the next trial were expressed succinctly in a telegram Orville sent to his father the following day.

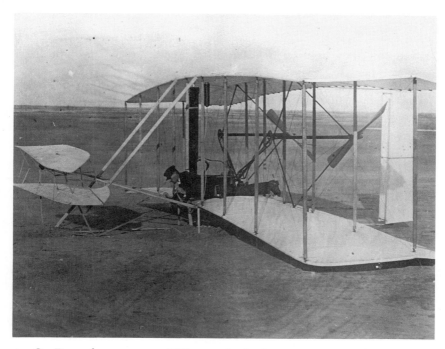

57. On December 14, 1903, Wilbur made the first attempt. Unfamiliar with the sensitive elevator control, he stalled on takeoff and slightly damaged the forward elevator.

Misjudgment at start reduced flight to hundred and twelve. Power and control ample. Rudder only injured. Success assured. Keep quiet.[54]

The next couple of days were spent repairing the Flyer and waiting for suitable weather.[55] On the morning of December 17, the brothers woke up to freezing temperatures and a twenty-seven-mile-per-hour wind. Conditions were far from perfect, but they decided to make a trial nevertheless. They were running out of time, as the harsh Kitty Hawk winter was descending quickly.

At about 10:00 A.M. they put out the signal flag and began to set up the launching rail on a level stretch near their camp building. Because of the stiff wind, there was no need to lay the track on a slope this time. By 10:30, everything was ready and the engine was started. As it warmed up, Wilbur and Orville shared some final words and shook hands. A witness later recalled the scene, saying that "we couldn't help notice how they held on to each other's hand, sort o'like they hated to let go; like two folks parting who weren't sure they'd ever see each other again."[56]

It was now Orville's turn at the controls. Wilbur took his position at the right wing tip, and John Daniels, a member of the lifesaving station crew, manned a camera that Orville had aimed carefully at the end of the launching rail. At 10:35 A.M., Orville tripped the release and the Flyer began to trundle slowly forward. Owing to the high wind, the speed of the airplane over the ground was only seven or eight miles per hour; airspeed was close to thirty miles per hour. Again, the Flyer left the launching rail about forty feet into its run. Like Wilbur, Orville found the elevator very sensitive. As a result, the airplane darted up and down as it sailed slowly over the sand, finally coming to rest with a thud 120 feet from where it had taken off. The duration of the flight had to be estimated, as the on-board stopwatch zeroed itself with the shock of the landing, and Wilbur, in his excitement, neglected to start the one he was carrying. They judged the time to be about twelve seconds. It had been a brief and relatively short flight, but a true flight nevertheless. As Orville put it,

This flight lasted only 12 seconds, but it was nevertheless the first in the history of the world in which a machine carrying a man had raised itself by its own power into the air in full flight, had sailed forward without reduction of speed, and had finally landed at a point as high as that from which it started.[57]

Although Wilbur forgot to click his stopwatch, John Daniels snapped the camera shutter at the perfect instant. A short time later, when the photograph was developed, a beautifully composed and balanced image of Orville being carried into the air on board the Flyer and Wilbur trailing alongside was revealed. Capturing the moment of invention forever, the picture reflected the precision that had characterized the Wrights' entire inventive effort.

Three more flights were made on that chilly wind-swept December morning. Wilbur took his turn on the second flight, covering 175 feet in a similar up-and-down course. Orville then put in a third flight on the airplane that lasted fifteen seconds and measured a little over two hundred feet. With Wilbur back at the controls, the final and most sig-

58. The "moment" of invention. Three days after Wilbur's abortive first trial, the Wright Flyer lifts off the launching rail at 10:35 A.M. on December 17, 1903, with Orville as pilot and Wilbur trailing behind. Lifesaving crew member John Daniels snapped the shutter of Orville's camera just as the airplane left the rail, resulting in one of the most famous photographs ever taken.

nificant flight of the day was logged. After another erratic start, Wilbur managed to steady the Flyer and hugged the contour of the beach for several hundred feet before the overly sensitive pitch control caused the machine to start an oscillating path once again, ending the flight with a dart into the sand. The Flyer had traveled an impressive 852 feet and had been airborne for fifty-nine seconds.

With this last flight, the Wrights showed beyond any doubt that they had invented the airplane. Without it, skeptics may have debated the credibility of the success of the relatively short initial flights. But there was no question that the fourth effort was a fully controlled, sustained heavier-than-air flight. Seven years after Lilienthal's fatal crash, four-and-a-half years after Wilbur's eloquent inquiry to the Smithsonian Institution, the Wright brothers had achieved the timeless dream of human flight.

The forward elevator was again damaged slightly in the hard landing of Wilbur's long, fourth flight. As the Wrights and others present dis-

59. The Wright Flyer comes to rest 852 feet from the launching rail after its fourth and final flight. This fifty-nine-second effort clearly demonstrated that the Wrights had truly flown.

cussed the latest trial, a strong gust of wind overturned the airplane and sent it tumbling across the sand. There would be no more flights of the 1903 Wright Flyer. Nearly all the wing ribs were broken, one spar and several struts had snapped, the engine crankcase was fractured, and the chain guides were badly bent. The experiments for 1903 were over, but not before the Wrights had accomplished what they set out do to.

After a break for lunch, Wilbur and Orville walked the four miles from Kill Devil Hills to Kitty Hawk to send a telegram to their father confirming the hopeful message sent forty-eight hours earlier.

Success four flights Thursday morning   all against twenty-one mile wind started from level with engine power alone   average speed through air thirty-one miles   longest 57* seconds   inform press   home Christmas.[58]

---

*The telegram incorrectly stated the duration as fifty-seven rather than fifty-nine seconds. Also, the wind speed given was an average for the morning the flights were made.

10

The Meaning of Invention

Three weeks after the successful first flights at Kitty Hawk, the Wrights prepared a statement for the Associated Press in response to several wildly exaggerated reports that had appeared shortly after December 17. The brothers provided an accurate account of the events, and then, in closing, affirmed that their primary goal had been achieved. " . . . we . . . packed our goods and returned home, knowing that the age of the flying machine had come at last."[1]

The 1903 Wright Flyer did indeed make the world's first powered, controlled flights in a heavier-than-air man-carrying craft. But before the airplane could be considered a practical, useful device, the Wrights had to prove that their design was capable of more than short, marginal, straight-line jaunts. Before marketing their invention was possible, they would have to be able to make turns and operate over more commonplace terrains than the sandy open spaces of the Outer Banks. Like any prototype invention, the Flyer would have to be perfected if it was to have an impact beyond a small community of aeronautical enthusiasts. In 1904 and 1905, Wilbur and Orville built two more powered aircraft with this intention in mind.

To enhance their opportunities for experiment and practice, and to avoid the tedious journey to Kitty Hawk, the brothers obtained permission to fly off a local cow pasture eight miles outside Dayton, known as Huffman Prairie. The principal problems experienced with the 1903 machine were pitch instability and the overly sensitive elevator. Loss of steady control in this axis put an abrupt end to all the Kitty Hawk flights. In time, the Wrights ameliorated these undesirable characteristics of the 1903 design. They accomplished this on the 1904 and 1905

60. Orville (left) and Wilbur stand before their second powered airplane in 1904. Following their triumph at Kitty Hawk, the brothers continued their experiments closer to home at a cow pasture a few miles outside Dayton, known as Huffman Prairie.

airplanes by adding weight to the front of the machines to shift the center of gravity forward, and by mounting the elevator further ahead of the wings. These changes dampened the control response of the elevator, thereby reducing the tendency of the airplane to dart up and down when the pilot attempted to climb or descend.[2]

Improvement came slowly, however. The Wrights did not match their fifty-nine-second 1903 effort until September 15, 1904, with the *forty-ninth* flight of their second powered machine. Five days later, after a frustrating summer of limited success, the brothers finally made their first complete circle. The flight lasted one minute thirty-six seconds, and covered 4,080 feet. By the fall of 1905, with their third airplane, the Wrights at last began to overcome the stability problems that had plagued them since Kitty Hawk. They were now making flights of several minutes routinely. On October 5, 1905, Wilbur made a spectacular flight in which he circled the field thirty times in thirty-nine minutes for a total distance of 24½ miles.[3]

The modifications made during 1904 and 1905 did not actually cure

61. The 1904 Flyer over Huffman Prairie. The Wrights made their first complete circle with this machine on September 20, 1904.

the stability problem. However, they did reduce the severity of it to the point where the aircraft could be flown with reasonable control and consistency for indefinite periods. The Wright machine remained tricky to fly. But in the hands of a trained pilot, the 1905 airplane could maneuver responsively and stay aloft as long as the fuel supply lasted. By any definition, the Wright brothers now possessed a practical flying machine. The experimental phase of their aeronautical work was completed.

In light of the further experimental work performed during 1904 and 1905, a reasonable characterization of the Wrights' invention of the airplane would be to point to the 1903 Flyer as the breakthrough machine, and to identify the practical Flyer of 1905 as the culmination of their creative work. From this perspective, the refinements made during the two years after Kitty Hawk must be considered an essential phase of the Wrights' invention of the flying machine and can therefore be seen as an indistinguishable part of the process that produced the world's first airplane.

62. The 1905 Wright Flyer, the world's first truly practical flying machine. Wilbur stayed aloft in this airplane for thirty-nine minutes on October 5, 1905.

On one level this is true. The 1903 machine was the first powered airplane to fly. But it was not until 1905 that the Wrights' invention reached a stage of development where it could do what aeronautical experimenters ultimately were striving for, namely, to fly to a predetermined destination under the full control of the pilot.

On another level, however, it can be argued that the Wrights' true inventive work was finished even before they left for Kitty Hawk in 1903. This study has focused on the creative process that resulted in mechanical flight. It has illustrated a definable inventive method with which the Wrights produced each of the necessary elements of the airplane and incorporated them into a workable technological system capable of flight. If the Wright brothers are to be cited as the inventors of the airplane based on their having resolved all the fundamental problems of mechanical flight, then it is not necessary to look beyond the 1902 glider and the propeller research to support this claim. As impressive as the design work of the 1903 Flyer was, and as important as the refinements of 1904 and 1905 were, these achievements did not represent the type of genuinely original thinking and innovative solutions that were at the heart of the earlier work. This is not to say that original ideas were absent from the 1903 airplane. The point is simply that what was innovative about the Flyer was present in the earlier 1902 glider. Of course, the validity of these original ideas had to be demonstrated with successful powered flights before the Wrights could take credit for giving humans their wings. But from the perspective of inventive creativity, the 1903 machine was only the realization of the basic elements of mechanical flight in powered form.

Moreover, these later accomplishments were not a product of the inventive method illustrated in this study. In the case of the 1903 airplane, the Wrights took advantage of established, turn-of-the-century engineering data and techniques throughout. Granted, they did so in clever and ingenious ways, but, with the exception of the propellers, there was nothing fundamentally original about the way in which 1903 machine was designed.

The work of 1904 and 1905 is even less relevant to the issues discussed in this study. The refinements incorporated in the basic Wright design that finally resulted in a practical flying machine were largely trial and error. The changes made to reduce the severity of the pitch instability were not based on careful mathematical or theoretical analysis. There were no wind tunnel tests or other empirical experiments underlying these modifications. Indeed, the last few steps to the door of practical flight were taken in the dark.

The Wright brothers are not credited with having invented the airplane simply because they got a machine into the air before anyone else. They are so recognized because they invented a fundamentally new technology, one that could evolve and be developed to meet challenges that were unimaginable in 1903. Their invention lies less in the hardware that carried the Wrights aloft for the first time on December 17, 1903, than in their comprehension of the essential barriers to mechanical flight and their design solutions to overcome them. It is therefore in this phase of their work that we have searched out the answer to the question posed at the outset of this study: How did these two men, essentially alone, accomplish so quickly, and with such sophistication, what had eluded a great many others for so long? In short, the Wright brothers were the inventors of the airplane because they approached the problem with an effective methodology that was under-girded by a number of innate talents and personality traits that were especially conducive to technical creativity.

The Wright brothers went on to market their flying machine success-fully in 1908 and 1909 with sales and licensing agreements in the United States and Europe. By 1910, they were world celebrities and well on their way to becoming very wealthy men. But, ironically, just as the Wrights began to reap the full fruit of their years of labor, the rest of the aeronautical world was passing them by. The technology that they created almost single-handedly had been embraced by other talented enthusiasts of flight and quickly brought to a level that made Wright aircraft appear primitive even in their own day. The brothers never car-ried the development of their invention beyond the 1905 airplane in any meaningful way. When Wilbur died suddenly in 1912 from typhoid fever, it was the closing episode in a period of the Wrights' career that had seen their influence wane dramatically. Nevertheless, it is unfair to criticize Wilbur and Orville for failing to keep pace with the technol-ogy to which they had given birth. They had done enough.

Epilogue:
A Final Accounting

The Machines

The 1899 kite does not exist, nor are there any photographs of it. The kite was kept in the bicycle shop for several years and used while performing experiments with an automatic stabilizer. It was broken during one of these experiments and destroyed about 1905. The only surviving visual representation of the craft is a sketch Orville made in 1920 as part of a biographical deposition he filed while serving as a witness in connection with an airplane patent-infringement suit.

The Wright gliders were all simply left behind at Kitty Hawk when the brothers had finished experimenting with them. Even the breakthrough 1902 machine was left in the Wrights' hangar after the 1903 season, and, like the building itself, was ravaged by the harsh Kitty Hawk climate not long after. The French sateen fabric used to cover the 1900 glider was salvaged by Bill Tate's wife and made into dresses for their two young daughters, Pauline and Irene. The garments no longer exist, however. All that survives of the Wrights' three experimental gliders is one wing tip from the 1902 machine, which is in the collection of the National Air and Space Museum.

The 1903 Wright Flyer, unlike the previous machines, was saved by the brothers. Even so, the Wrights' indifferent treatment of the world's first airplane suggests that they did not consider the Flyer a national treasure until quite some time after the flights.

After the airplane made its destructive tumble across the sand following its fourth and final flight on December 17, 1903, the brothers crated it and shipped it back to Dayton along with their other equipment. It was stored in a shed behind their bike shop and lay untouched for the next ten years. In March 1913, Dayton was hit by a tremendous flood, during which the boxes containing the airplane were submerged for several weeks in eleven feet of water and mud. Shortly thereafter, the shed was torn down and the 1903 machine, still in the same Kitty Hawk shipping crates, was moved to a barn located at 15 N. Broadway in Dayton.

The Flyer finally was uncrated for the first time since Kitty Hawk in the summer of 1916, when Orville repaired and reassembled it for a brief exhibition at the Massachusetts Institute of Technology. The forward elevator and the rudder had to be almost entirely rebuilt. The broken ribs and spars were repaired, and the center section of both wings was re-covered with new fabric. Orville resurrected the engine as best he could. Unfortunately, some parts had either been damaged in 1903, used on subsequent engines, or lost over the years. The original propellers still exist, but they were badly damaged in 1903 and therefore have never been on the airplane since it flew. The Flyer was displayed briefly on several other occasions shortly after MIT, including at the National Air Races in Dayton in 1924.

By this time, Orville had replaced the barn at 15 N. Broadway with a more substantial brick building, which became his personal laboratory. The 1903 machine was stored there until it was sent to England for exhibition at the Science Museum in London in 1928. Before shipping it, Orville refurbished the airplane again, this time re-covering the machine with new fabric completely. The remaining covering from 1903 was saved, and portions of it still exist today in various places. The Flyer was returned to the United States twenty years later in 1948.

The story behind Orville's decision to exhibit the airplane in London for an extended period is an interesting one. It centers on what had been a long-standing dispute between the Wrights and the Smithsonian Institution over misleading claims the Smithsonian had advanced regarding the performance of the man-carrying aircraft Samuel P. Langley had attempted to fly shortly before the brothers' successful flights in 1903. Orville sent the Flyer out of the country as a gesture of protest in response to the Smithsonian's slow and ambivalent recognition of the brothers' achievement. The matter was finally settled in 1942 when the Smithsonian published in the Institution's annual report an unequivocal statement crediting the Wrights with having invented the airplane. Because of the war in Europe and other factors, however, transport of the airplane back to the United States did not take place until 1948. The most complete and accurate account of the controversy is Tom D. Crouch, "Capable of Flight: The Feud Between the Wright Brothers & the Smithsonian," *American Heritage of Invention and Technology* (Summer 1987). The story is also well told in Tom D. Crouch, *The Bishop's Boys: A Life of Wilbur and Orville Wright*; Fred Howard, *Wilbur and Orville: A Biography of the Wright Brothers*; and Fred C. Kelly, *The Wright Brothers*.

The 1903 Wright Flyer was donated formally to the Smithsonian Institution in an elaborate ceremony on December 17, 1948, the forty-fifth anniversary of the flights, and it has been on display there ever since. The airplane received some minor repairs and cleaning in 1976 just prior to being moved into the Smithsonian's then new National Air and Space Museum building. In 1985, the Flyer was given its third major refurbishment. It was completely disassembled, the parts thoroughly cleaned and preserved, and all new fabric covering applied. The aircraft was in amazingly good shape. Nothing other than the fabric was replaced. The fabric removed in 1985 was the material put on before the Flyer went to England in 1928, which of course was not original to the 1903 flights. The 1928 fabric, along with a large section of the wing covering from 1903, is in the National Air and Space Museum collection.

The 1904 Wright Flyer was not saved by the Wrights. The second powered Wright airplane had been battered by the many minor accidents and prangs during the difficult 1904 flying season at Huffman Prairie. The Wrights salvaged the engine, the propellers, and other hardware for use in a new machine they were building to continue their work in 1905. Early in 1905, they burned the wings of the 1904 airplane to make room in their shop to assemble the new machine.

The 1905 Wright Flyer, the brothers' third powered airplane and first truly practical flying machine, was retained by the Wrights only for a short period. After the spectacular long flights at Huffman Prairie in the fall of 1905, the brothers stored the 1905 machine until 1908. At that time, after making modifications for upright seating for both the pilot and a passenger, they took the 1905 airplane down to Kitty Hawk to do some practice flying. They were getting ready for a series of demonstrations of another new machine before the U.S. Army Signal Corps later that year. When the flying was completed, the Wrights removed the engine and other useful parts and, like the 1902 glider, left the airframe of the modified 1905 airplane in their camp building.

As before, storms and windblown sand took their toll on the Wrights' hangar and the aircraft inside. When they returned to Kitty Hawk for the last time in 1911, the brothers found the pieces of the 1905 machine strewn throughout the ruins of their old camp building. They gave some thought to gathering up the fragments but in the end felt that the pieces were too badly deteriorated to be worth preserving. In 1912, a wealthy Massachusetts paper manufacturer named Zenas Crane made arrangements to salvage the remains of the 1905 airplane with the hope of restoring it for display in a museum he had established recently in Pittsfield, Massachusetts.

Even with the parts in hand, however, Crane still needed advice from the original builder to piece it back together accurately. Despite numerous pleas for assistance, he was unable to secure Orville's help. Orville refused Crane's requests because he felt that the airplane was too far gone, making the endeavor pointless. As a result, the parts sat in storage for over three decades.

Finally, in 1946, in connection with a project sponsored by the National Cash Register Company to build a park in Dayton commemorating the development of industry and transportation, the parts of the 1905 Flyer were reclaimed by Orville and a restoration was begun. The engine, propellers, chain guides, sprockets, and shafts were still on hand in Orville's laboratory. The restoration was not completed until 1950, two years after Orville's death. The airplane has been on display at Carrillon Park in Dayton, Ohio, since that time. In its present state, the 1905 Flyer is approximately sixty percent original.

Other extant original Wright aircraft include a 1908 Wright Model A, located in the Deutsches Museum, Munich, West Germany; the 1909 Wright Military Flyer, the world's first military airplane, in the collection of the National Air and Space Museum, Washington, D.C.; a 1910 Wright Model B, belonging to the Franklin Institute, Philadelphia,

Pennsylvania; a modified Model B with ailerons at the U.S. Air Force Museum, Dayton, Ohio; a 1910 Wright Baby Grand Racer in the possession of the Musée de l'Air et de l'Espace in Paris; and the 1911 Wright EX *Vin Fiz*, the airplane flown by Calbraith Perry Rodgers to make the first U.S. transcontinental flight in 1911, also in the National Air and Space Museum. These six aircraft, along with the 1903 Wright Flyer and the 1905 airplane, are the sum total of extant original Wright brothers flying machines.

The Wright brothers' wind tunnel is not in existence. Exactly what happened to it is unknown. Considering that the tunnel was simply a crude wooden box that was bulky and took up valuable space in the shop, it was likely broken up and discarded by the brothers shortly after they concluded their experiments.

The wind tunnel balances have survived. In 1916, during a move of equipment from the old bike shop to his new laboratory at 15 N. Broadway, Orville had his older brother Lorin hand carry the balances to the lab because he did not trust the movers with them. Thirty years later, on December 9, 1947, Orville was cleaning some junk out of the attic in the lab. As he was about to toss out an old typewriter case, he shook it to see if there was anything inside. The box rattled, and when Orville opened it he found the original lift and drag balances. They were a bit rusty and a little worse for wear, as they too had been through the 1913 Dayton flood. Just as with the aircraft, the Wrights saw the balances as nothing more than research tools, and therefore took no special care to preserve the instruments after they had served their purpose. The Wright wind tunnel balances are now in the collection of the Franklin Institute in Philadelphia, Pennsylvania.

The Places
The Wright bicycle shop was vacated by Orville in 1916 when he moved into his new laboratory at 15 N. Broadway. The shop was purchased by Henry Ford in 1936 for thirteen thousand dollars and moved in 1937 to Greenfield Village, Ford's monument to American ingenuity and industrial achievement, located in Dearborn, Michigan.

Beginning in the late 1920s, Ford relocated homes and structures belonging or related to people he considered heroic Americans to an empty field near his huge River Rouge automobile plant. The complex of historic buildings includes, for example, Thomas Edison's Menlo Park laboratory, Noah Webster's home, and Charles Steinmetz's camp, along with an assorted collection of typical mills and machine shops representing what Ford saw as the golden age of American industrial growth. The Wright brothers' bicycle shop fit perfectly into Ford's idyllic presentation of the towering figures and achievements of nineteenth-century American industrial and business life.

The Wright home at 7 Hawthorn Street, the site of much of the thinking and planning that produced the world's first airplane, was also purchased by Henry Ford and transported to Greenfield Village in 1937. Both the bicycle shop and the Wright home are still maintained at Greenfield Village and are open to the public.

Kitty Hawk, North Carolina, the little fishing hamlet where humans first took wing, has lost much of its primitive, desolate character in the decades since Wilbur and Orville experimented there. The route to their old camp is lined with motels, restaurants, gift shops, and private beach houses. Neon signs to attract the tourist trade abound, and the shoreline is no longer visible from where the brothers made their flights. The year-round residents still maintain a fair degree of their traditional clannish suspicion of outsiders, but the look of the place has changed dramatically.

Most of this development took place following the construction of the Wright Brothers National Memorial. On March 2, 1927, President Calvin Coolidge signed into law a $50,000 appropriation bill for the creation of a permanent national monument to the Wrights and their achievement at Kill Devil Hills. After stabilizing the largest of the great sand dunes with artificial topsoil and hardy imported grasses, a beautiful, sixty-foot granite shaft with feathered wings sculpted into the sides was erected upon a five-point star base. An aeronautical beacon was placed on top, which can be seen for miles in every direction at night. The structure was completed in 1932.

In later years, further tributes to the Wrights' work were added to the site. Nestled below the monument are reconstructions of the brothers' camp buildings and a visitors center that tells the Wright story. Just outside are four markers showing the distance of each powered flight made on December 17, 1903.

The Wright Memorial is the only one of America's great national monuments that was dedicated to a person still living. Wilbur had long since passed away, but Orville survived to receive this great honor for both of them. Carved into the lower section of the granite shaft is the following inscription:

In commemoration of the conquest of the air by the brothers Wilbur and Orville Wright. Conceived by genius, achieved by dauntless resolution and unconquerable faith.

The People

Wilbur Wright died at age forty-five on May 30, 1912, after a four-week battle with typhoid fever, ironically the same illness that had nearly claimed Orville's life in 1896. Years of frustration trying to market their invention after 1905 culminated in dramatic flying demonstrations in Europe and the United States in 1908 and 1909, making the Wrights world celebrities. By 1910, the brothers had established their own company for the manufacture and sale of aircraft, exhibition flying, and the training of pilots. During the last two years of his life, Wilbur left much of the responsibility for running the company to Orville and spent most of his time and energy fighting several bitter patent-infringement suits. Drained by the strain and pressures of court battles and affirming the Wrights' priority of invention, Wilbur succumbed rapidly when his illness struck. His father, Bishop Milton Wright, summed up his famous son's life with this succinct diary entry:

This morning at 3:15, Wilbur passed away, aged 45 years, 1 month and 14 days. A short life, full of consequences. An unfailing intellect, imperturbable temper, great self-reliance and as great modesty, seeing the right clearly, pursuing it steadfastly, he lived and died.

Orville Wright carried on the patent fights after his brother's death. Although a few cases dragged on for years, the principal issues were resolved to his satisfaction by 1914. In 1915, he sold out his aeronautical interests and retired from the airplane business a wealthy man. Being painfully shy in the presence of anyone outside his immediate family, it became extremely difficult for him to carry on a public persona without Wilbur. Throughout the rest of his life, he was a consultant to many corporations and government programs and agencies on aeronautical matters, and as the elder statesman of aviation, his presence was always felt. But he never took a leadership role in any of these activities, and his contributions rarely made any significant impact.

In 1908, during the demonstrations before the U.S. Army Signal Corps, Orville crashed and was severely injured. His passenger, Lieutenant Thomas E. Selfridge, was killed, the first fatality in a powered airplane. Orville recovered and finished the demonstrations the following year, which ended in the sale of the airplane to the U.S. government for thirty thousand dollars. As a result of injuries sustained in the crash, he was plagued with sciatica for the rest of his life.

In 1913, Orville, Katharine, and their aging father moved into a lavish home the Wrights had built for them on the outskirts of Dayton. The mansion, called Hawthorn Hill, became Orville's fortress, shielding him from the outside world. He outfitted it with all sorts of strange contrivances such as a heating system that could only be controlled from *his* bedroom and a vacuum cleaner system built into the walls with hose outlets in all the rooms. He spent a great deal of time during the remaining thirty-five years of his life tinkering with the unique, and usually temperamental, plumbing, heating, and wiring systems he had installed in the house. On the morning of January 27, 1948, Orville was again fixing something at Hawthorn Hill; this time it was a doorbell. Later that day, he suffered his second heart attack in less than four months. He died three days later in a Dayton hospital at the age of seventy-seven.

Katharine Wright lived with Orville in the Wright family home until 1926, when she married at age fifty-two. All the Wright family members had been extremely close, Katharine and Orville in particular. When she married and moved to Kansas City with her husband Henry J. Haskell, Orville felt betrayed and turned his back on her. Katharine was desperate for a reconciliation, but her brother remained resolute in his conviction that she had violated some sort of unspoken family pact to never let an outsider come between the members of the Wright household. Sadly, Katharine died of pneumonia in 1929 only two-and-a-half years after her marriage, never having regained Orville's trust or affection.

Bishop Milton Wright lived a very long, eventful life, passing away in 1917 at age eighty-eight. The bishop was generally too preoccupied with church matters during the experimental years of 1900 and 1905 to pay much attention to the aeronautical activities of his boys. However, with their success and resulting notoriety, Milton could not help but be drawn into the world of his increasingly famous sons. On May 25, 1910, when the brothers were at the pinnacle of their aeronautical career, Orville took his father up for his first ride in an airplane. Concerned over how his father might react to being in the air, Orville maintained an altitude of no more than 350 feet. Throughout the near seven-minute flight the eighty-one-year old Wright patriarch made only one comment: "Higher, Orville, higher!"

There was another noteworthy flight that day. For the first and only time in their lives, the Wright brothers flew together. With Orville as pilot and Wilbur as passenger, the brothers circled Huffman Prairie for six-and-a-half minutes. Previously they had always observed a strict rule never to be in the air together. They had promised their father that they would always avoid the risk of his losing both his sons in the event of a fatal crash. Also, by never flying together, there would always be one brother left to carry their experiments to completion if an accident should occur. Just this once, however, they decided to set caution aside and share the exhilaration of flight together.

Octave Chanute, the long-time friend and confidant of the Wrights, grew increasingly frustrated with the brothers' refusal to publicly demonstrate their airplane and share their secrets with the world after 1905. As early as 1902, Chanute began to give speeches and publish papers in America and abroad on their work, much to the annoyance of Wilbur and Orville. The enthusiasm for flight that had waned in Europe following the death of Lilienthal was reinvigorated by Chanute's dissemination of information about the Wrights' aircraft. Most European machines of this period incorporated numerous aspects of Wright technology, garnered largely from Chanute's writings and speeches. The Wrights felt that their friend had no right to give away the answers to the problem of human flight they had labored so long and hard to acquire. Chanute believed that the brothers were growing increasingly obsessed with becoming famous and wealthy. After 1905, the once warm and frequent communication between the friends diminished to only occasional contacts tinged with acrimony. They eventually began to reconcile their differences, but with Chanute's death in 1910, the long series of letters bearing the story of the invention of the airplane finally came to an end.

Charlie Taylor, the Wrights' mechanic and principal creator of the world's first successful airplane engine, continued to work for the brothers after 1903. He left the Wrights' employ in 1911 to serve as mechanic for Calbraith Perry Rodgers during his 1911 U.S. transcontinental flight. Following his association with Rodgers, he held jobs in various machine shops. After being laid off during the Depression, he lost his life's savings in a real estate venture. He was working for North American Aviation in Los Angeles at 37½ cents an hour when Henry Ford found him and hired him to man the Wright bicycle shop he had recently moved to Greenfield Village. He left there in 1941 to take a wartime job in California. Four years later he suffered a heart attack that forced him to retire. Orville never forgot his old employee. Every December 17, on the anniversary of the first flight, Charlie received a letter from him. When Taylor died in 1956 at age eighty-eight, his only income beyond Social Security was an eight hundred dollar annuity from a fund left by Orville.

Bill Tate, the Wrights' host and assistant at Kitty Hawk, was not present for the flights on December 17, 1903. He thought it was too windy for flying that morning and stayed home. Having been with the Wrights through so many of their experiments and frustrations, he always regretted missing their historic moment of success. He continued his warm friendship with them in future years and was often on hand for the periodic ceremonies commemorating the achievement of his two good friends from Dayton. Tate sorely wanted to be present at Kill Devils Hills on December 17, 1953, to observe the planned fiftieth anniversary celebration of the first flights. Sadly, Bill Tate was unable to fulfill his wish. He died six months short of the golden anniversary of flight at the age of eighty-four.

Notes

Chapter 1

1. Tom D. Crouch, *A Dream of Wings: Americans and the Airplane, 1875–1905* (New York: W. W. Norton, 1981; reprint ed., Washington, D.C.: Smithsonian Institution Press, 1988); Crouch, "Taking to the Air: Modern Aviation Got Its Lift from Vacuum Cleaners and Vortices," *Science 84*, November 1984, pp. 79–81; Charles Harvard Gibbs-Smith, *Aviation: An Historical Survey from Its Origins to the End of World War II*, 2nd ed. (London: Her Majesty's Stationery Office, 1970).

2. Monte A. Calvert, *The Mechanical Engineer in America, 1830–1910: Professional Cultures in Conflict* (Baltimore: Johns Hopkins Univeristy Press, 1967); Edwin T. Layton, "Mirror-Image Twins: The Communities of Science and Technology in 19th-Century America," *Technology and Culture* 12 (October 1971):562–80; Layton, *The Revolt of the Engineers: Social Responsibility and the American Engineering Profession* (Cleveland: Case Western Reserve University Press, 1971).

3. Quoted in Fred C. Kelly, *The Wright Brothers* (New York: Harcourt Brace, 1943), p. 28.

4. For details concerning the Wrights' education, see Tom D. Crouch, *The Bishop's Boys: A Life of Wilbur and Orville Wright* (New York: W. W. Norton, 1989), pp. 57–58, 65, 75, 93–95; Kelly, *The Wright Brothers*, pp. 23–27; and Arthur G. Renstrom, *Wilbur and Orville Wright: A Chronology Commemorating the Hundredth Anniversary of the Birth of Orville Wright, August 19, 1871* (Washington, D.C.: Library of Congress, 1975), p. 5.

5. Crouch, *A Dream of Wings*.

6. Eugene S. Ferguson, "The Mind's Eye: Nonverbal Thought in Technology," *Science*, 26 August, 1977, pp. 827–36; Brooke Hindle, *Emulation and Invention* (New York: New York University Press, 1981); Thomas Parke Hughes, *Elmer Sperry: Inventor and Engineer* (Baltimore: Johns Hopkins University Press, 1971).

7. Hindle, *Emulation and Invention*, pp. 85–142.

8. Charles Harvard Gibbs-Smith, *The Invention of the Aeroplane: 1799–1909* (New York: Taplinger, 1965); Gibbs-Smith, *Aviation.*

9. Harry Combs, *Kill Devil Hill: Discovering the Secret of the Wright Brothers* (Englewood, Colo.: TernStyle Press, 1979); Fred Howard, *Wilbur and Orville: A Biography of the Wright Brothers* (New York: Knopf, 1987); and Kelly, *The Wright Brothers,* are examples, but virtually every book or article on the Wrights states this.

10. Quoted in Charles J. Bauer, "Ed Sines: Pal of the Wrights," *Popular Aviation* (June 1938):40; and in Crouch, *The Bishop's Boys,* pp. 94–96.

11. James Means, "Wheeling and Flying," *The Aeronautical Annual* (1896):24–25.

12. David A. Hounshell, *From the American System to Mass Production, 1800–1932* (Baltimore: Johns Hopkins University Press, 1984), pp. 189–215.

13. Ibid., p. 192.

14. Tom D. Crouch, "How the Bicycle Took Wing," *American Heritage of Invention and Technology* (Summer 1986):13.

15. Ibid., pp. 13–14.

16. Ibid., pp. 14–15.

17. Combs, *Kill Devil Hill*; Howard, *Wilbur and Orville*; and Kelly, *The Wright Brothers,* are examples, but virtually every book or article on the Wrights treats this.

18. Wilbur Wright, deposition of 3 April 1912, in Marvin W. McFarland, ed., *The Papers of Wilbur and Orville Wright,* 2 vols. (New York: McGraw-Hill, 1953), p. v.

19. Crouch, *The Bishop's Boys,* p. 50.

20. Quoted in Howard, *Wilbur and Orville,* p. 7; and in John Evangelist Walsh, *One Day at Kitty Hawk: The Untold Story of the Wright Brothers and the Airplane* (New York: Thomas Y. Crowell, 1975), p. 253.

21. Crouch, *The Bishop's Boys,* pp. 102–3.

22. McFarland, ed., *Papers,* p. 3, note 3.

23. Howard, *Wilbur and Orville,* pp. 7–8; Kelly, *The Wright Brothers,* p. 26.

24. For a detailed analysis of how the Wright brothers' family life influenced their self-confidence, conditioned their interaction with others, and shaped how they regarded the outside world, see "Book One: Family" and "Book Three: The World" in Crouch, *The Bishop's Boys.*

25. O. Wright to Katharine Wright, 18 October 1900, *Papers,* pp. 37–40.

26. Crouch, *A Dream of Wings.*

27. Ibid.

Chapter 2

1. Charles Harvard Gibbs-Smith, *Aviation: An Historical Survey from Its Origins to the End of World War II,* 2nd ed. (London: Her Majesty's Stationery Office, 1970).

2. Quoted in John D. Anderson, "The Historical Development of Aerodynamics Prior to 1810, and Its Application to Flying Machines," paper presented at the annual meeting of the Society for the History of Technology, Raleigh, N.C., 31 October 1987, p. 38.

3. Tom D. Crouch, *A Dream of Wings: Americans and the Airplane, 1875–1905* (New York: W. W. Norton, 1981; reprint ed., Washington, D.C.: Smithsonian Institution Press, 1988); Crouch, "Engineers and the Airplane," in Richard P. Hallion, ed., *The Wright Brothers: Heirs of Prometheus* (Washington, D.C.: Smithsonian Institution Press, 1978).

4. Charles Harvard Gibbs-Smith, *Sir George Cayley's Aeronautics, 1796–1855* (London: Her Majesty's Stationery Office, 1962); J. Laurence Pritchard, *Sir George Cayley: The Inventor of the Aeroplane* (London: Max Parrish, 1961).

5. George Cayley, "On Aerial Navigation," Part 1, *Nicholson's Journal of Natural Philosophy, Chemistry and the Arts* 24 (November 1809):164–74; Part 2, *Nicholson's Journal* 25 (February 1810):81–87; Part 3, *Nicholson's Journal* 25 (March 1810):161–69. All three parts reprinted in Gibbs-Smith, *Sir George Cayley's Aeronautics*, Appendix I, pp. 213–37.

6. Gibbs-Smith, *Sir George Cayley's Aeronautics*; Pritchard, *Sir George Cayley*.

7. M. J. B. Davy, *Henson and Stringfellow: Their Work in Aeronautics* (London: His Majesty's Stationery Office, 1931); Harald Penrose, *An Ancient Air: A Biography of John Stringfellow of Chard* (Washington, D.C.: Smithsonian Institution Press, 1989).

8. W. H. G. Armytage, *A Social History of Engineering* (New York: Pitman, 1961); Monte Calvert, *The Mechanical Engineer in America, 1830–1910: Professional Cultures in Conflict* (Baltimore: Johns Hopkins University Press, 1967); Edwin Layton, "Mirror-Image Twins: The Communities of Science and Technology in 19th-Century America," *Technology and Culture* 12 (October 1971); Layton, *The Revolt of the Engineers: Social Responsibility and the American Engineering Profession* (Cleveland: Case Western Reserve University Press, 1971).

9. Crouch, *A Dream of Wings*; Crouch, "Engineers and the Airplane."

10. Ibid.

11. Hiram Maxim, *The Cosmopolitan*, June 1892; quoted in Valerie Moolman, *The Road to Kitty Hawk* (Alexandria, Va.: Time-Life Books, 1980).

12. Gibbs-Smith, *Aviation*, pp. 61–63; Hiram S. Maxim, *Artificial and Natural Flight* (London: Whittaker, 1909).

13. Charles Harvard Gibbs-Smith, *Clément Ader: His Flight Claims and His Place in History* (London: Her Majesty's Stationery Office, 1968).

14. Ibid., p. 9.

15. Gibbs-Smith, *Sir George Cayley's Aeronautics*; Pritchard, *Sir George Cayley*.

16. Crouch, *A Dream of Wings*, pp. 255–305; Samuel P. Langley and Charles M.

Manly, *Langley Memoir on Mechanical Flight* (Washington, D.C.: Smithsonian Institution, 1911), pp. 164–281.

17. Crouch, "Engineers and the Airplane," p. 13.

18. Gibbs-Smith, *Aviation*, pp. 43–44; Alphonse Pénaud, "Aeroplane Automoteur; Equilire Automatique," *L'Aeronaute* 5 (1872):2–9; Pénaud, "Laws Relating to Planes Gliding in the Air," *Eleventh Annual Report of the Aeronautical Society of Great Britain* (1876):45–49.

19. Pritchard, *Sir George Cayley*, p. 206.

20. Gibbs-Smith, *Sir George Cayley's Aeronautics*; Pritchard, *Sir George Cayley*.

21. The discussion on Lilienthal is drawn from Crouch, *A Dream of Wings*, pp. 157–74; Otto Lilienthal, *Birdflight as the Basis of Aviation*, A. W. Isenthal, trans. (London: Longmans Green, 1911); Werner Schwipps, *Lilienthal: Die Biographie des ersten Fliegers* (München: Aviatic Verlag, 1979); Schwipps, *Lilienthal und die Amerikaner* (München: Deutsches Museum, 1985).

22. Otto Lilienthal, "The Best Shapes for Wings," *The Aeronautical Annual* (1897):95–97.

23. Otto Lilienthal, "At Rhinow," *The Aeronautical Annual* (1897):92–94; Lilienthal, "The Best Shapes for Wings," *The Aeronautical Annual* (1897):95–97; Lilienthal, *Birdflight as the Basis of Aviation*; Lilienthal, "The Flying Man," *McClure's Magazine*, September 1894, pp. 1–10; Lilienthal, "Our Teachers in Sailing Flight," *The Aeronautical Annual* (1897):84–91; Lilienthal, "Practical Experiments for the Development of Human Flight," *The Aeronautical Annual* (1896):7–22. Lilienthal,

24. R. W. Wood, "Lilienthal's Last Flights," *Boston Transcript*, 16 August 1896.

25. Crouch, "Engineers and the Airplane," p. 14.

26. Philip Jarrett, *Another Icarus: Percy Pilcher and the Quest for Flight* (Washington, D.C.: Smithsonian Institution Press, 1987).

Chapter 3

1. Tom D. Crouch, *The Bishop's Boys: A Life of Wilbur and Orville Wright* (New York: W. W. Norton, 1989), pp. 56–57; Fred C. Kelly, *The Wright Brothers* (New York: Harcourt Brace, 1943), pp. 8–9; Otto Lilienthal, *Birdflight as the Basis of Aviation*, A. W. Isenthal, trans. (London: Longmans Green, 1911), p. xi; Arthur G. Renstrom, *Wilbur and Orville Wright: A Chronology Commemorating the Hundredth Anniversary of the Birth of Orville Wright, August 19, 1871* (Washington, D.C.: Library of Congress, 1975), p. 4; Orville and Wilbur Wright, "The Wright Brothers' Aeroplane," *Century Magazine*, September 1908, pp. 641–42.

2. John F. Kasson, *Civilizing the Machine: Technology and Republican Values in America, 1776–1900* (New York: Grossman, 1976).

3. Tom D. Crouch, *A Dream of Wings: Americans and the Airplane, 1875–1905*

(New York: W. W. Norton, 1981; reprint ed., Washington, D.C.: Smithsonian Institution Press, 1988).

4. W. Wright to Milton Wright, 12 September 1894, in Fred C. Kelly, ed., *Miracle at Kitty Hawk: The Letters of Wilbur and Orville Wright* (New York: Farrar, Straus and Young, 1951), pp. 8–10.

5. Fred Howard, *Wilbur and Orville: A Biography of the Wright Brothers* (New York: Knopf, 1987) pp. 13–14; Kelly, *The Wright Brothers*, pp. 45–46; Orville Wright *How We Invented the Airplane*, Fred C. Kelly, ed. (New York: David McKay, 1953).

6. They read Jules Marey, *Animal Mechanism: A Treatise on Aerial Locomotion* (1890), but little else. See Wilbur Wright, "Some Aeronautical Experiments," 18 September 1901, in Marvin W. McFarland, ed., *The Papers of Wilbur and Orville Wright*, 2 vols. (New York: McGraw-Hill, 1953), p. 103.

7. *The Evening Item*, 17 July 1890, p. 4; *The Evening Item*, 26 July 1890, p. 3; microfilm edition, vol. 1, F167, Ohio Historical Society.

8. Otto Lilienthal, "The Flying Man," *McClure's Magazine*, September 1894, pp. 1–10.

9. McFarland, ed., *Papers*, pp. 6–7, note 9; Wilbur Wright, deposition of 15 February 1912, *The Aeronautical Journal* 20 (July-September 1916):115.

10. Howard, *Wilbur and Orville*, pp. 13–14; Kelly, *The Wright Brothers*, pp. 45–46; McFarland, ed., *Papers*, pp. 6–7, note 9; Wilbur Wright, deposition of 15 February 1912, p. 115.

11. Probably James Bell Pettigrew, *Animal Locomotion, or Walking, Swimming, and Flying, with a Dissertation on Aeronautics* (1874).

12. "Orville Wright on the Problem of Flight," deposition of 13 January 1920, excerpted in *Papers*, pp. 3–4.

13. W. Wright to the Smithsonian Institution, 30 May 1899, *Papers*, pp. 4–5.

14. Ibid.

15. Crouch, *A Dream of Wings*, pp. 20–41, 61–77, 175–202.

16. James Howard Means, *James Means and the Problem of Manflight* (Washington, D.C.: Smithsonian Institution, 1964); James Means, ed., *The Aeronautical Annual 1895–97* (Boston).

17. Howard, *Wilbur and Orville*, p. 31.

18. Crouch, *A Dream of Wings*, p. 228; Kelly, *The Wright Brothers*, pp. 47–48.

19. Wilbur Wright, "Some Aeronautical Experiments," p. 99.

20. Crouch, *A Dream of Wings*, pp. 216–20.

21. Lynwood Bryant, "The Beginnings of the Internal-Combustion Engine," in Melvin Kranzberg and Carroll W. Pursell, eds., *Technology in Western Civilization* (New York: Oxford University Press, 1967), Vol. 1, pp. 648–64; Samuel P. Langley and Charles M. Manly, *Langley Memoir on Mechanical Flight* (Washington, D.C.: Smithsonian Institution, 1911); C. R. Roseberry, *Glenn Curtiss: Pioneer of Flight* (Garden City, N.Y.: Doubleday, 1972); Howard S. Wolko, *In the Cause of Flight* (Washington, D.C.: Smithsonian Institution Press, 1981), pp. 50–63.

22. Wright Cycle Co. to the Daimler Mfg. Co., 3 December 1902, *Papers*, p. 287.

23. Crouch, *A Dream of Wings*, pp. 20–41, 61–77, 175–222; Charles Harvard Gibbs-Smith, *Aviation: An Historical Survey from Its Origins to World War II*, 2nd ed. (London: Her Majesty's Stationery Office, 1970), pp. 53–54.; Lilienthal, *Birdflight as the Basis of Aviation*; N. H. Randers-Pehrson, *Pioneer Wind Tunnels* (Washington, D.C.: Smithsonian Institution, 1935).

24. Wilbur Wright, "Some Aeronautical Experiments," pp. 99–118.

25. Ibid., p. 100.

26. Charles Harvard Gibbs-Smith, *The Rebirth of European Aviation, 1902–1908: A Study of the Influence of the Wright Brothers* (London: Her Majesty's Stationery Office, 1974), pp. 12–13.

27. Crouch, *A Dream of Wings*, pp. 177–78, 192; Howard, *Wilbur and Orville*, p. 19.

28. Ibid.; Wilbur Wright, "Some Aeronautical Experiments," p. 100.

29. Octave Chanute, "Recent Experiments in Gliding Flight," *The Aeronautical Annual* (1897):31; Wilbur Wright, "Some Aeronautical Experiments," p. 101.

30. Wilbur Wright, "Some Aeronautical Experiments," p. 100.

31. Ibid., p. 103.

32. Quoted in Kelly, *The Wright Brothers*, p. 298.

33. Howard, *Wilbur and Orville*, p. 33; Wilbur Wright, deposition of 15 February 1912, pp. 115–24.

34. W. Wright to Octave Chanute, 13 May 1900, *Papers*, pp. 15–19.

35. O. Wright to J. Horace Lytle, 27 December 1941, *Papers*, pp. 1168–69.

36. Wilbur Wright, deposition of 15 February 1912, p. 118.

37. Crouch, *A Dream of Wings*, p. 230.

38. Accession file, Gallaudet kite, National Air and Space Museum Registrar's Office, Smithsonian Institution, Washington, D.C.; "Diary, 1898," Gallaudet Family Papers, Manuscript Division, Library of Congress, Washington, D.C.; E. F. Gallaudet biographical file, National Air and Space Museum Library. The 1898 Gallaudet wing-warping kite is in the collection of the National Air and Space Museum.

39. Kelly, *The Wright Brothers*, p. 49.

40. "Orville Wright on the Wright Experiments of 1899," deposition of 13 January, 1920, excerpted in *Papers*, pp. 5–12.

41. Octave Chanute, *Progress in Flying Machines* (New York, 1894; reprint ed., Long Beach, Calif.: Lorenz and Herweg, 1976), pp. 227–31; Chanute, "Recent Experiments in Gliding Flight," pp. 30–53; Augustus M. Herring, "Recent Advances toward a Solution of the Problem of the Century," *The Aeronautical Annual* (1897):54–74; Charles Lamson, "Work on the Great Diamond," *The Aeronautical Annual* (1896):133–37; Otto Lilienthal, "The Flying Man," pp. 1–10; Lilienthal, "Practical Experiments for the Development of Human Flight," *The Aeronautical Annual* (1896):7–22; J. B. Millet, "Some Experiences with Hargrave Kites," *The Aeronautical Annual* (1896):127–32.

42. Chanute, "Recent Experiments in Gliding Flight," pp. 30–53; Herring, "Recent Advances toward a Solution of the Problem of the Century," pp. 55–74. Herring felt that Chanute had not accurately credited him with his contribution to the success of the glider and insisted that his own article be published with Chanute's.

43. Carl W. Condit, "Buildings and Constructions," in Kranzberg and Pursell, eds., Vol. 1, pp. 383–84; Crouch, *A Dream of Wings*, pp. 190–94.

44. Gibbs-Smith, *The Rebirth of European Aviation*, pp. 29–31.

45. Milton Wright's diary, 7 July 1899, *Papers*, p. 8.

46. "Orville Wright on the Wright Experiments of 1899," pp. 5–12.

47. Milton Wright's diary, 22 July 1899, quoted in *Papers*, p. 8, note 3.

48. Crouch, *The Bishop's Boys*, pp. 162–64.

49. The physical description of the 1899 kite is drawn from "Orville Wright on the Wright Experiments of 1899," pp. 5–12; and W. Wright to Octave Chanute, 10 August 1900, *Papers*, p. 22.

50. Chanute, *Progress in Flying Machines*; Lilienthal, *Birdflight as the Basis of Aviation*; J. Laurence Pritchard, "The Dawn of Aerodynamics," *The Journal of the Royal Aeronautical Society* 61 (March 1957):163–65.

51. "Orville Wright on the Wright Experiments of 1899," pp. 5–12.

52. Interview with Fred E. C. Culick, California Institute of Technology, Pasadena, Calif. July 1988; interview with Ken Kellett, Virginia Beach, Va., June 1988.

Chapter 4

1. Wilbur Wright, "Some Aeronautical Experiments," 18 September 1901, in Marvin W. McFarland, ed., *The Papers of Wilbur and Orville Wright*, 2 vols. (New York: McGraw-Hill, 1953), p. 109.

2. O. Wright to Griffith Brewer, 30 June 1938, quoted in *Papers*, p. 42, note 8; W. Wright to Octave Chanute, 1 July 1901, *Papers*, pp. 63–64.

3. Wilbur Wright, "Some Aeronautical Experiments," p. 101.

4. Ibid., p. 102.

5. Tom D. Crouch, *A Dream of Wings: Americans and the Airplane, 1875–1905* (New York: W. W. Norton, 1981; reprint ed., Washington, D.C.: Smithsonian Institution Press, 1988), p. 35; N. H. Randers-Pehrson, *Pioneer Wind Tunnels* (Washington, D.C.: Smithsonian Institution, 1935).

6. Wilbur Wright, "Some Aeronautical Experiments," pp. 109–11.

7. O. Wright to Griffith Brewer, 30 June 1938, p. 42, note 8.

8. Wilbur Wright, "Some Aeronautical Experiments," p. 104.

9. Maxim had both a forward and a rear stabilizing surface on his 1894 craft, but of course it failed to fly.

10. O. Wright to Alexander Klemin, 11 April 1924, quoted in *Papers*, p. 44, note 1.

11. W. Wright to Milton Wright, 23 September, 1900, *Papers*, pp. 25–27.
12. Wilbur Wright, "Some Aeronautical Experiments," p. 104.
13. W. Wright to Octave Chanute, 3 December 1900, *Papers*, pp. 49–50.
14. Octave Chanute to W. Wright, 29 November 1900, *Papers*, pp. 46–47.
15. W. Wright to Octave Chanute, 16 November 1900, *Papers*, pp. 40–44; W. Wright to Octave Chanute, 26 November 1900, *Papers*, pp. 45–46.
16. John D. Anderson, "The Historical Development of Aerodynamics Prior to 1810, and Its Application to Flying Machines," paper presented at the annual meeting of the Society for the History of Technology, Raleigh, N. C., 31 October 1987, pp. 18–23.
17. Material on Smeaton and his work has been drawn from Anderson, "The Historical Development of Aerodynamics Prior to 1810, and Its Application to Flying Machines," pp. 27–28; Fred E. C. Culick, ed., *Guggenheim Aeronautical Laboratory at the California Institute of Technology: The First Fifty Years* (San Francisco: San Francisco Press, 1983), p. 6; *Dictionary of Scientific Biography* x.v. "Smeaton, John," by Harold Dorn; J. Laurence Pritchard, "The Dawn of Aerodynamics," *The Journal of the Royal Aeronautical Society* 61 (March 1957):155–56.
18. John Smeaton, "An Experimental Enquiry Concerning the Natural Powers of Water and Wind to Turn Mills and Other Machines Depending on Circular Motion," *Philosophical Transactions* 51 (London 1759).
19. In modern terms, this is a misnomer. By definition, a coefficient is an experimentally determined value, whereas a constant is a number that results from measurable physical properties. It is now known that the constant of proportionality for air is equal to the density of air divided by two, a directly measured quantity. In Smeaton's time, however, this was unknown, and the figure was experimentally obtained. Thus, in the eighteenth and nineteenth century, it was proper to call the Smeaton value a coefficient.
20. Culick, *Guggenheim Aeronautical Laboratory at the California Institute of Technology*, p. 6.
21. The lift and drag equations and Lilienthal's table of coefficients appeared in Octave Chanute, "Sailing Flight," *The Aeronautical Annual* (1897):115–16; see also Otto Lilienthal, *Birdflight as the Basis of Aviation*, A. W. Isenthal, trans. (London: Longmans Green, 1911), plate 6.
22. W. Wright to Octave Chanute, 10 August 1900, *Papers*, p. 22.

Chapter 5

1. W. Wright to Octave Chanute, 13 May 1900, in Marvin W. McFarland, ed., *The Papers of Wilbur and Orville Wright*, 2 vols. (New York: McGraw-Hill, 1953), pp. 15–19.
2. Ibid., Octave Chanute to W. Wright, 17 May 1900, *Papers*, pp. 19–21.
3. Ibid.

4. Willis L. Moore, Chief of the National Weather Bureau, to Wright Cycle Co., 4 December 1899, in Fred C. Kelly, ed., *Miracle at Kitty Hawk: The Letters of Wilbur and Orville Wright* (New York: Farrar, Straus and Young, 1951), p. 24.

5. W. Wright to Milton Wright, 3 September 1900, quoted in *Papers*, p. 23, note 6.

6. Harry Combs, *Kill Devil Hill: Discovering the Secret of the Wright Brothers* (Englewood, Colo.: TernStyle Press, 1979), p. 81; Fred Howard, *Wilbur and Orville: A Biography of the Wright Brothers* (New York: Knopf, 1987), p. 44.

7. Joseph J. Dosher, Kitty Hawk weather station, to Wilbur Wright, 16 August 1900, *Miracle at Kitty Hawk*, p. 25; William J. Tate to Wilbur Wright, 18 August 1900, *Miracle at Kitty Hawk*, pp. 25–26.

8. Katharine Wright to Milton Wright, 5 September 1900; Fragmentary Memorandum by Wilbur Wright, 13 September 1900, *Papers*, pp. 23–25.

9. Fragmentary Memorandum by Wilbur Wright, pp. 23–25.

10. Ibid.

11. William J. Tate to Wilbur Wright, 18 August 1900, pp. 25–26.

12. Fragmentary Memorandum by Wilbur Wright, pp. 23–25.

13. Ibid.

14. Ibid.

15. Howard, *Wilbur and Orville*, p. 46.

16. Fragmentary Memorandum by Wilbur Wright, pp. 23–25.

17. Quoted in Tom D. Crouch, *A Dream of Wings: Americans and the Airplane, 1875–1905* (New York: W. W. Norton, 1981; reprint ed., Washington, D.C.: Smithsonian Institution Press, 1988), p. 238.

18. Howard, *Wilbur and Orville*, p. 46.

19. Katharine Wright to Milton Wright, 26 September 1900, *Papers*, pp. 27–28.

20. O. Wright to Katharine Wright, 18 October 1900, *Papers*, pp. 37–40.

21. Ibid.

22. O. Wright to Katharine Wright, 14 October 1900, *Papers*, pp. 28–34.

23. O. Wright to Katharine Wright, 18 October 1900, pp. 37–40.

24. Tom D. Crouch, *The Bishop's Boys: A Life of Wilbur and Orville Wright* (New York: W. W. Norton, 1989), p. 191.

25. O. Wright to Katharine Wright, 28 July 1901, *Papers*, pp. 71–76.

26. O. Wright to Katharine Wright, 14 October 1900, pp. 28–34; O. Wright to Katharine Wright, 18 October 1900, pp. 37–40.

27. O. Wright to Katharine Wright, 14 October 1900, pp. 28–34.

28. The technical description of the 1900 glider is drawn from Wilbur Wright's Notebook A, September–October 1900, *Papers*, pp. 34–37; W. Wright to Octave Chanute, 16 November 1900, *Papers*, pp. 40–44; W. Wright to Octave Chanute, 26 November 1900, *Papers*, pp. 45–46.

29. W. Wright to Octave Chanute, 16 November 1900, pp. 40–44.

30. Ibid.

31. Ibid.
32. Otto Lilienthal, "Practical Experiments for the Development of Human Flight," *The Aeronautical Annual* (1896):8–9.
33. W. Wright to Octave Chanute, 13 May 1900, pp. 15–19.
34. Wilbur Wright, "Some Aeronautical Experiments," 18 September 1901, *Papers*, p. 103.
35. W. Wright to Octave Chanute, 13 May 1900, pp. 15–19.
36. O. Wright to Katharine Wright, 14 October 1900, pp. 28–34.
37. Ibid.
38. Ibid.
39. Wilbur Wright's Notebook A, September–October 1900, pp. 34–37.
40. O. Wright to Katharine Wright, 18 October 1900, pp. 37–40.
41. Combs, *Kill Devil Hill*, p. 82; Crouch, *A Dream of Wings*, p. 236.
42. W. Wright to Octave Chanute, 16 November 1900, pp. 40–44.
43. Ibid.
44. Ibid.
45. Wilbur Wright, "Some Aeronautical Experiments," pp. 106–7.
46. Luis Marden, "She Wore the World's First Wings," *Outer Banks Magazine*, 1984, pp. 23–29; McFarland, ed., "Aeroplanes and Motors," Appendix 5, *Papers*, p. 1184; Rupert E. West, "When the Wrights Gave Wings to the World," *U.S. Air Services*, December 1927, pp. 21–22.
47. Wilbur Wright, "Some Aeronautical Experiments," p. 107.
48. The term *drag* in its modern aerodynamic sense did not come into common usage until after the Wrights' experimental work. They worked in terms of *total resistance*, which included not only the parasitic drag of the airframe, but several other components. One of them the Wrights called *drift*, which they identified not as a horizontal resistance, but as a loss of altitude they expressed as a downward force.
49. Wilbur Wright, "Some Aeronautical Experiments," p. 105.
50. Crouch, *A Dream of Wings*, pp. 238–39.
51. Orville Wright, deposition of 13 January 1920, quoted in McFarland, ed., "1901 Wind Tunnel," Appendix 2, *Papers*, p. 547.
52. W. Wright to Octave Chanute, 12 May 1901, *Papers*, p. 54.
53. McFarland, ed., "Aeroplanes and Motors," pp. 1184–85.
54. Charles E. Taylor, "My Story of the Wright Brothers," *Collier's Weekly*, 26 December 1948, pp. 27, 68–70.
55. W. Wright to Octave Chanute, 29 June 1901, *Papers*, pp. 57–58; W. Wright to Octave Chanute, 1 July 1901, *Papers*, pp. 63–64.
56. O. Wright to Katharine Wright, 28 July 1901, pp. 71–76.
57. Wilbur Wright's Diary A, 27 July 1901, *Papers*, p. 71; Arthur G. Renstrom, *Wilbur and Orville Wright: A Chronology Commemorating the Hundredth Anniversary of the Birth of Orville Wright, August 19, 1971* (Washington, D.C.: Library of Congress, 1975), p. 128.
58. Renstrom, *Wilbur and Orville Wright*, p. 128; O Wright to Katharine Wright,

28 July 1901, pp. 71–76; O. Wright to Alexander Klemin, 11 April, 1924, quoted in *Papers*, p. 44, note 1; Wilbur Wright's Diary A, 27 July 1901, p. 71.

59. Wilbur Wright's Diary A, 29 July 1901, *Papers*, p. 76.

60. Wilbur Wright, "Some Aeronautical Experiments," p. 112.

61. Ibid., pp. 110–11.

62. Wilbur Wright's Diary A, 7 August 1901, *Papers*, pp. 79–81; Wilbur Wright, "Some Aeronautical Experiments," pp. 110–11.

63. Wilbur Wright's Diary A, 7 August 1900, and 30 July 1901, *Papers*, pp. 77–78, 79–81; Chanute-Huffaker Diary, 31 July 1901, and 2 August 1901, *Papers*, p. 79.

64. Katharine Wright to Milton Wright, 26 August 1901, *Papers*, p. 84; Crouch, *A Dream of Wings*, p. 242.

65. W. Wright to George A. Spratt, 21 September 1901, *Papers*, pp. 118–19; W. Wright to George A. Spratt, 16 September 1902, *Papers*, pp. 253–54.

66. Renstrom, *Wilbur and Orville Wright*, p. 128.

67. Chanute-Huffaker Diary, 9 August 1901, *Papers*, p. 81.

68. W. Wright to Octave Chanute, 22 August 1901, *Papers*, pp. 83–84.

69. Chanute-Huffaker Diary, 9 August 1901, and 11 August 1901, *Papers*, p. 81.

70. Renstrom, *Wilbur and Orville Wright*, p. 129; W. Wright to Octave Chanute, 22 August 1901, pp. 83–84.

71. Wilbur Wright to the Aéro-Club de France, speech given 5 November 1908, Paris, transcript in *Papers*, pp. 934–35.

72. Fred C. Kelly, *The Wright Brothers* (New York: Harcourt Brace, 1943), p. 72.

Chapter 6

1. Katharine Wright to Milton Wright, 3 September 1901, in Marvin W. McFarland, ed., *The Papers of Wilbur and Orville Wright* (New York: McGraw-Hill, 1953), p. 92.

2. Ibid.; W. Wright to George A. Spratt, 21 September 1901, *Papers*, pp. 118–19.

3. Orville Wright's Notebook I, September–October 1902, Wright Papers, Manuscript Division, Library of Congress, Washington, D.C.; see also McFarland, ed., *Papers*, pp. 254–55, note 2.

4. Wilbur Wright, "Some Aeronautical Experiments," 18 September 1901, *Papers*, p. 116.

5. W. Wright to Octave Chanute, 2 September 1901, *Papers*, p. 92; Katharine Wright to Milton Wright, 3 September 1901, p. 92; Katharine Wright to Milton Wright, 11 September 1901, *Papers*, p. 95.

6. Katharine Wright to Milton Wright, 25 September 1901, quoted in *Papers*, p. 99, note 2.

7. Ivonette Wright Miller, *Wright Reminiscences* (Dayton, Oh.: Ivonette Wright Miller, 1978), p. 64.

8. Katharine Wright to Milton Wright, 25 September 1901, p. 99, note 2.

9. Wilbur Wright, "Some Aeronautical Experiments," pp. 99–118.

10. W. Wright to Octave Chanute, 26 September 1901, *Papers*, pp. 120–22.

11. The table appeared in Octave Chanute, "Sailing Flight," *The Aeronautical Annual* (1897):116.

12. McFarland, ed., "1901 Wind Tunnel," Appendix 2, *Papers*, pp. 573–74; W. Wright to Octave Chanute, 6 October 1901, *Papers*, pp. 123–28; Octave Chanute to W. Wright, 10 October 1901, *Papers*, pp. 128–31; Octave Chanute to W. Wright, 10 November 1901, *Papers*, pp. 148–50.

13. McFarland, ed., "1901 Wind Tunnel," p. 548; W. Wright to Octave Chanute, 26 September 1901, pp. 120–22.

14. W. Wright to Octave Chanute, 6 October 1901, pp. 123–24.

15. Ibid.

16. McFarland, ed., "1901 Wind Tunnel," p. 548; W. Wright to Octave Chanute, 6 October 1901, pp. 123–24. Samples of the wallpaper are in the collection of the Franklin Institute, Philadelphia, Pa.

17. W. Wright to Octave Chanute, 6 October 1901, pp. 126–27.

18. W. Wright to Octave Chanute, 16 October 1901, *Papers*, pp. 131–37.

19. Ibid.; W. Wright to Octave Chanute, 24 October 1901, *Papers*, pp. 140–43.

20. W. Wright to Octave Chanute, 16 October 1901, pp. 131–37.

21. W. Wright to Octave Chanute, 6 October 1901, pp. 123–28.

22. W. Wright to Octave Chanute, 2 November 1901, *Papers*, pp. 144–48.

23. For a brief description of these early wind tunnels, see N. H. Randers-Pehrson, *Pioneer Wind Tunnels* (Washington, D.C.: Smithsonian Institution, 1935).

24. For a full description of the Wright brothers' wind tunnel experiments, see George W. Lewis, "Some Modern Methods of Research in the Problems of Flight," *Journal of the Royal Aeronautical Society* (October 1939):771–78; McFarland, ed., "1901 Wind Tunnel," pp. 547–93; W. Wright to Octave Chanute, 16 October 1901, pp. 131–37; W. Wright to Octave Chanute, 22 November 1901, *Papers*, pp. 159–64; W. Wright to Octave Chanute, 1 December 1901, *Papers*, pp. 168–71; W. Wright to Octave Chanute, 19 January 1902, *Papers*, pp. 204–5; W. Wright to Octave Chanute, 7 February 1902, *Papers*, pp. 210–13.

25. McFarland, ed., "1901 Wind Tunnel," pp. 548–49; W. Wright to Octave Chanute, 16 October 1901, pp. 131–37; W. Wright to Octave Chanute, 19 January 1902, pp. 204–5.

26. W. Wright to Octave Chanute, 19 January 1902, pp. 204–5.

27. W. Wright to Octave Chanute, 16 October 1901, pp. 131–37, note 8.

28. W. Wright to Octave Chanute, 23 December 1901, *Papers*, pp. 184–87.

29. W. Wright to Octave Chanute, 16 October 1901, pp. 131–37.

30. W. Wright to Octave Chanute, 24 October 1901, pp. 140–43.

31. Ibid.; W. Wright to George A. Spratt, 15 December 1901, *Papers*, pp. 181–82; W. Wright to Octave Chanute, 19 January 1902, pp. 204–5. If the area of the test surface were larger or smaller than the total area of the four resistance

strips, the obtained C_L would have to be multiplied by an appropriate correction factor. The total area of the four strips was eight square inches. Most of the model wings tested were six square inches in area. This meant that most of the C_Ls had to be multiplied by 6/8 before being entered into the table.

32. W. Wright to George A. Spratt, 15 December 1901, pp. 181–82.

33. Harry Combs, *Kill Devil Hill: Discovering the Secret of the Wright Brothers* (Englewood, Colo.: TernStyle Press, 1979), pp. 28–29; Fred C. Kelly, *The Wright Brothers* (New York: Harcourt Brace, 1943), pp. 24–25.

34. O. Wright to George A. Spratt, 7 June 1903, *Papers*, pp. 310–15.

35. W. Wright to Octave Chanute, 16 October 1901, pp. 131–37; W. Wright to Octave Chanute, 24 October 1901, pp. 140–43.

36. W. Wright to George A. Spratt, 16 October 1909, *Papers*, pp. 967–68.

37. Ibid.

38. W. Wright to Octave Chanute, 7 February 1902, pp. 210–15.

39. See Chapter 5, note 48, for the distinction between *drift* and *drag*.

40. McFarland, ed., "1901 Wind Tunnel," p. 549.

41. W. Wright to Octave Chanute, 22 November 1901, pp. 159–64.

42. Octave Chanute to W. Wright, 18 November 1901, *Papers*, pp. 156–59.

43. McFarland, ed., "1901 Wind Tunnel," p. 549.

44. W. Wright to George A. Spratt, 23 January 1902, *Papers*, pp. 205–9.

45. W. Wright to Octave Chanute, 23 December 1901, pp. 184–87; W. Wright to Octave Chanute, 10 January 1902, *Papers*, pp. 201–3; McFarland, ed., "1901 Wind Tunnel," pp. 556–72.

46. W. Wright to Octave Chanute, 19 January 1902, pp. 204–5.

47. Orville and Wilbur Wright, "The Wright Brothers' Aeroplane," *Century Magazine*, September 1908, p. 647; W. Wright to Octave Chanute, 1 December 1901, pp. 168–71; W. Wright to Octave Chanute, 15 December 1901, *Papers*, pp. 173–81.

48. W. Wright to Octave Chanute, 1 December 1901, pp. 168–71.

49. McFarland, ed., "1901 Wind Tunnel," p. 550; W. Wright to Octave Chanute, 22 November 1901, pp. 159–64; Wilbur Wright's Notebook H, January 1903, *Papers*, p. 297; W. Wright to Octave Chanute, 4 February 1903, *Papers*, pp. 297–98; O. Wright to George A. Spratt, 7 June 1903, pp. 310–15. There is evidence of a second tunnel built in late 1902 in which the tests on struts may have been done. This tunnel was to be used for further airfoil tests; however, the Wrights apparently never followed up on this. See McFarland, ed., "1901 Wind Tunnel," pp. 550–51; W. Wright to Octave Chanute, 12 November 1902, *Papers*, pp. 282–83; O. Wright to George A. Spratt, 7 June 1903, pp. 310–15.

50. Katharine Wright to Milton Wright, 7 December 1901, *Papers*, p. 171.

51. W. Wright to Octave Chanute, 23 December 1901, pp. 184–87.

52. W. Wright to Octave Chanute, 15 December 1901, pp. 173–81.

53. Octave Chanute to W. Wright, 19 December 1901, *Papers*, pp. 183–84.

54. W. Wright to Octave Chanute, 23 December 1901, pp. 184–87.

Chapter 7

1. W. Wright to Octave Chanute, 6 October 1901, in Marvin W. McFarland, ed., *The Papers of Wilbur and Orville Wright* (New York: McGraw-Hill, 1953), pp. 123–28; W. Wright to Octave Chanute, 16 October 1901, *Papers*, pp. 131–37; W. Wright to Octave Chanute, 1 December 1901, *Papers*, pp. 168–71.
2. W. Wright to Octave Chanute, 1 December 1901, pp. 168–71.
3. W. Wright to Octave Chanute, 15 December 1901, *Papers*, pp. 173–81.
4. W. Wright to Octave Chanute, 1 December 1901, pp. 168–71.
5. W. Wright to Octave Chanute, 24 November 1901, *Papers*, pp. 163–64.
6. Ibid.
7. Ibid.
8. W. Wright to Octave Chanute, 2 November 1901, *Papers*, pp. 144–48.
9. McFarland, ed., "Aeroplanes and Motors," Appendix 5, *Papers*, p. 1187.
10. W. Wright to Octave Chanute, 31 August 1903, *Papers*, pp. 351–52.
11. W. Wright to Octave Chanute, 15 December 1901, pp. 173–81. This letter includes a diagram of surface #12.
12. Orville Wright's Diary B, 16 September 1902, *Papers*, pp. 252–53; W. Wright to George Spratt, 16 September 1902, *Papers*, pp. 253–54.
13. Orville Wright, deposition of 2 February 1921, quoted in McFarland, ed., "1901 Wind Tunnel," Appendix 2, *Papers*, p. 551.
14. W. Wright to Octave Chanute, 7 February 1902, *Papers*, pp. 210–13.
15. W. Wright to the Smithsonian Institution, 30 May 1899, *Papers*, pp. 4–5.
16. W. Wright to Octave Chanute, 29 May 1902, *Papers*, pp. 234–35.
17. The Wrights actually were experiencing a phenomenon known as *adverse yaw*, in which the aircraft drifts sideways in the opposite direction of the intended turn. It is not a true control reversal because the aircraft is acting only in the yaw axis, and not in roll. However, the response felt by the pilot is similar. In the Wrights' day, the term *adverse yaw* had not yet come into use.
18. W. Wright to Octave Chanute, 7 February 1902, pp. 210–13.
19. Octave Chanute to W. Wright, 4 March 1902, *Papers*, p. 223.
20. Octave Chanute to W. Wright, 5 May 1902, *Papers*, pp. 232–33.
21. W. Wright to Octave Chanute, 29 May 1902, pp. 234–35.
22. W. Wright to Octave Chanute, 2 June 1902, *Papers*, pp. 235–36.
23. W. Wright to Octave Chanute, 9 July 1902, *Papers*, pp. 237–38.
24. Ibid.
25. Ibid.

Chapter 8

1. Tom D. Crouch, *The Bishop's Boys: A Life of Wilbur and Orville Wright* (New York: W. W. Norton, 1989), pp. 43, 215–18; Fred C. Kelly, ed., *Miracle at Kitty Hawk: The Letters of Wilbur and Orville Wright* (New York: Farrar, Straus and Young, 1951), pp. 65–66.

2. W. Wright to Octave Chanute, 16 May 1902, in Marvin W. McFarland, ed., *The Papers of Wilbur and Orville Wright* (New York: McGraw-Hill, 1953), p. 233.

3. Katharine Wright to Milton Wright, 20 August 1902, *Papers*, pp. 243–44; W. Wright to Octave Chanute, 17 July 1902, *Papers*, p. 238.

4. Katharine Wright to Milton Wright, 20 August 1902, pp. 243–44.

5. W. Wright to Octave Chanute, 28 May 1905, *Papers*, pp. 493–94.

6. See Crouch, *The Bishop's Boys*, for a thorough treatment of the Wrights' personality traits and conditioning experiences.

7. Katharine Wright to Milton Wright, 20 August 1902, pp. 243–44.

8. Ibid.

9. Orville Wright's Diary B, 27–28 August 1902, *Papers*, p. 245; W. Wright to Milton Wright, 31 August 1902, *Miracle at Kitty Hawk*, pp. 70–71.

10. Ibid.; W. Wright to Octave Chanute, 2 September 1902, *Papers*, p. 246.

11. W. Wright to Octave Chanute, 2 September 1902, p. 246.

12. Orville Wright's Diary B, 3–5 September 1902, *Papers*, pp. 246–47; W. Wright to Milton Wright, 31 August 1902, pp. 70–71; W. Wright to Octave Chanute, 2 September 1902, p. 246.

13. W. Wright to George Spratt, 16 September 1902, *Papers*, pp. 253–54.

14. Orville Wright's Diary B, 6 September 1902, *Papers*, p. 248; W. Wright to George A. Spratt, 16 September 1902, pp. 253–54.

15. W. Wright to Katharine Wright, 31 August 1902, *Miracle at Kitty Hawk*, pp. 71–72.

16. W. Wright to George A. Spratt, 16 September 1902, pp. 253–54.

17. Ibid.

18. Ibid.

19. Orville Wright's Diary B, 8 September 1902, *Papers*, p. 249.

20. W. Wright to Octave Chanute, 12 September 1902, *Papers*, pp. 250–51.

21. Ibid.

22. Wilbur Wright, "Experiments and Observations in Soaring Flight," *Journal of the Western Society of Engineers* (December 1903), reproduced in full in *Papers*, pp. 318–35 (quotation, p. 320).

23. McFarland, ed., "Aeroplanes and Motors," Appendix 5, *Papers*, pp. 1185–87; Orville Wright's Notebook C, 21 October 1902, *Papers*, p. 278; Wilbur Wright, "Experiments and Observations in Soaring Flight," p. 320.

24. Wilbur Wright, "Experiments and Observations in Soaring Flight," p. 319.

25. Orville Wright's Diary B, 19 September 1902, *Papers*, pp. 254–55.

26. Orville Wright's Diary B, 20 September 1902, *Papers*, pp. 256–57; Wilbur Wright, "Experiments and Observations in Soaring Flight," p. 321.

27. Arthur G. Renstrom, *Wilbur and Orville Wright: A Chronology Commemorating the Hundredth Anniversary of the Birth of Orville Wright, August 19, 1871* (Washington, D.C.: Library of Congress, 1975), p. 130; Wilbur Wright, "Experiments and Observations in Soaring Flight," p. 322.

28. W. Wright to Octave Chanute, 21 September 1902, *Papers*, pp. 257–58.

29. Orville Wright's Diary B, 20 September 1902, pp. 256–57.
30. Wilbur Wright, "Experiments and Observations in Soaring Flight," pp. 321–22.
31. Orville Wright's Diary B, 22 September 1902, *Papers*, p. 258.
32. Renstrom, *Wilbur and Orville Wright*, p. 130; Orville Wright's Diary B, 23 September 1902, *Papers*, pp. 258–60.
33. Wilbur Wright, "Experiments and Observations in Soaring Flight," p. 323.
34. W. Wright to Octave Chanute, 23 September 1902, *Papers*, pp. 260–61.
35. Orville Wright's Diary B, 23 September 1902, pp. 258–60.
36. Wilbur Wright, "Experiments and Observations in Soaring Flight," p. 323.
37. Numerous interviews with Tom D. Crouch, National Museum of American History, Smithsonian Institution, Washington, D.C.; and Rick and Sue Young, Richmond, Va.
38. Wilbur Wright, "Experiments and Observations in Soaring Flight," p. 323.
39. Orville Wright's Diary B, 26 September 1902, *Papers*, p. 262.
40. Renstrom, *Wilbur and Orville*, pp. 131–32; Orville Wright's Diary B, 27 September 1902, *Papers*, pp. 262–63; Orville Wright's Diary B and Notebook C, 29 September–2 October 1902, *Papers*, pp. 264–68.
41. W. Wright to Milton Wright, 2 October 1902, *Miracle at Kitty Hawk*, pp. 79–80.
42. Wilbur Wright, "Experiments and Observations in Soaring Flight," p. 323.
43. Fred C. Kelly, *The Wright Brothers* (New York: Harcourt Brace, 1943) pp. 80–81.
44. Fred Howard, *Wilbur and Orville: A Biography of the Wright Brothers* (New York: Knopf, 1987), p. 88; Kelly, *The Wright Brothers*, pp. 80–81.
45. In particular, Orville Wright, deposition of 13 January 1920, excerpted in *Papers*, pp. 469–71, note 5; and Wilbur Wright, deposition of 15 February 1912, *The Aeronautical Journal* 20 (July-September 1916):121–22.
46. Kelly, *The Wright Brothers*, pp. 80–81.
47. Howard, *Wilbur and Orville*, p. 89; Wilbur Wright, deposition of 15 February 1912, pp. 121–22.
48. Orville Wright's Diary B, 3 October 1902, *Papers*, pp. 268–69.
49. Orville Wright's Diary B, 4–6 October 1902, *Papers*, pp. 270–71.
50. Wilbur Wright, "Experiments and Observations in Soaring Flight," p. 324.
51. Orville Wright's Diary B, 10 October 1902, *Papers*, pp. 272–73.
52. Wilbur Wright, "Experiments and Observations in Soaring Flight," p. 325.
53. Ibid.
54. Orville Wright's Diary B, 10 October 1902, pp. 272–73; O. Wright to Katharine Wright, 23 October 1902, *Papers*, pp. 279–80.
55. Orville Wright's Diary B, 24 September and 5–6 October 1902, *Papers*, pp. 261–62, 270–71.
56. Orville Wright's Diary B, 6 October 1902, pp. 270–71.
57. Orville Wright's Diary B, 11 October 1902, *Papers*, p. 273.
58. Orville Wright's Diary B, 14 October 1902, *Papers*, p. 275.

59. Orville Wright's Diary B, 13–14 October 1902, *Papers*, pp. 274–75.

60. Octave Chanute to W. Wright, 16 October 1902, *Papers*, p. 276; Octave Chanute to Hermann Moedebeck, 21 October 1902, *Correspondence of Octave Chanute*, typewritten transcriptions, 10 vols., National air and Space Museum Library, Smithsonian Institution, Washington, D.C.; Octave Chanute, "Aerial Navigation in the United States," *L'Aérophile* (August 1903), reproduced in full in *Papers*, pp. 659–73 (quotation, p. 664).

61. O. Wright to Katharine Wright, 23 October 1902, *Papers*, pp. 279–80.

62. Orville Wright's Diary B, 13 October 1902, p. 274; O. Wright to Katharine Wright, 23 October 1902, pp. 279–80.

63. Renstrom, *Wilbur and Orville*, pp. 134–35; O. Wright to Katharine Wright, 23 October 1902, pp. 279–80; W. Wright to Octave Chanute, 3 November 1902, *Papers*, p. 281; Wilbur Wright, "Experiments and Observations in Soaring Flight," p. 325.

64. O. Wright to Katharine Wright, 23 October 1902, pp. 279–80. Lilienthal had made glides of one thousand feet, but of course his aircraft did not have the effective control of the Wrights' glider.

65. Wilbur Wright, "Experiments and Observations in Soaring Flight," p. 324.

66. W. Wright to Octave Chanute, 3 November 1902, p. 281.

67. O. Wright to George A. Spratt, 7 June 1903, *Papers*, pp. 310–15; O. Wright to Katharine Wright, 26 September 1903, *Papers*, pp. 356–57; W. Wright to Octave Chanute, 3 November 1902, p. 281; W. Wright to Octave Chanute, 29 March 1903, *Papers*, pp. 302–3.

Chapter 9

1. The Wright 1902 glider differed in that the wing-warping roll control and the movable vertical rudder were coupled, making it, along with the elevator, a two-control airplane for the pilot. Nevertheless, it was controllable in all three axes, which of course is the fundamental principle of control underlying all successful airplanes. The Wrights did eventually separate the wing warping and the rudder on their third powered machine in 1905.

2. Octave Chanute to W. Wright, 9 December 1902, in Marvin W. McFarland, ed., *The Papers of Wilbur and Orville Wright* (New York: McGraw-Hill, 1953), p. 290; W. Wright to Octave Chanute, 11 December 1902, *Papers*, pp. 290–91.

3. *United States Aeronautical Patents; Specifications of Patents Granted by the United States Patent Office, 1844–1906*, 3 vols. (Washington, D.C.), in National Air and Space Museum Library, Smithsonian Institution, Washington, D.C.

4. Tom D. Crouch, *The Bishop's Boys: A Life of Wilbur and Orville Wright* (New York: W. W. Norton, 1989), pp. 246, 276; Fred Howard, *Wilbur and Orville: A Biography of the Wright Brothers* (New York: Knopf, 1987), pp. 149–50; Rodney K. Worrel, "The Wright Brothers' Pioneer Patent," *American Bar Association Journal* (October 1979):1512–1518. The Wrights' basic airplane pat-

ent, U.S. Patent Office number 821,393, simply titled "Flying Machine," was granted on 22 May 1906.

5. Samuel P. Langley to Octave Chanute, 7 December 1902, quoted in *Papers*, p. 290, note 4.

6. W. Wright to Octave Chanute, 11 December 1902, pp. 290–91.

7. W. Wright to Octave Chanute, 24 July 1903, *Papers*, pp. 346–47.

8. Octave Chanute to W. Wright, 27 July 1903, *Papers*, p. 348; Tom D. Crouch, *A Dream of Wings: Americans and the Airplane, 1875–1905* (New York: W. W. Norton, 1981; reprinted., Washington, D.C.: Smithsonian Institution Press, 1988), p. 197; Howard, *Wilbur and Orville*, pp. 95–101.

9. W. Wright to Octave Chanute, 2 August 1903, *Papers*, p. 349.

10. W. Wright to Octave Chanute, 11 December 1902, pp. 290–91.

11. The analysis of the Wright Flyer is adapted from R. L. Bisplinghoff, "The Structural Engineering Practice of the Wright Brothers," *Aeronautica* (Fall-Winter 1956); Howard S. Wolko, "Structural Design of the 1903 Wright Flyer," in Wolko, ed., *The Wright Flyer: An Engineering Perspective* (Washington, D.C.: Smithsonian Institution Press, 1987), pp. 97–106; O. Wright to George A. Spratt, 7 June 1903, *Papers*, pp. 310–315; O. Wright to Charles E. Taylor, 23 November 1903, *Papers*, pp. 385–87; W. Wright to George A. Spratt, 29 December 1902, *Papers*, pp. 292–93; Wilbur Wright's Notebook H, 6 March 1903, *Papers*, p. 606.

12. The Langley engine was actually built by Charles M. Manly and Stephen M. Balzer. Tom D. Crouch, *A Dream of Wings*, pp. 259–64, 269–73, 278–81; Samuel P. Langley and Charles M. Manly, *Langley Memoir on Mechanical Flight* (Washington, D.C.: Smithsonian Institution, 1911); Hiram S. Maxim, *Artificial and Natural Flight* (London: Whittaker, 1909).

13. Lynwood Bryant, "The Beginnings of the Internal-Combustion Engine," in Melvin Kranzberg and Carroll W. Pursell, eds., *Technology in Western Civilization* (New York: Oxford University Press, 1967), Vol. 1, pp. 648–64; Howard S. Wolko, *In the Cause of Flight* (Washington, D.C.: Smithsonian Institution Press, 1981), pp. 50–63.

14. Wright Cycle Co. to the Daimler Mfg. Co., 3 December 1902, *Papers*, pp. 286–87.

15. Charles E. Taylor, "My Story of the Wright Brothers," *Colliers Weekly*, 26 December 1948, p. 27.

16. Sources on the design and details of the Wright brothers' engine include: M. P. Baker, "The Wright Brothers as Aeronautical Engineers," *Annual Report of the Smithsonian Institution* (Washington, D.C.: Smitsonian Institution, 1950), pp. 217–20; Leonard S. Hobbs, *The Wright Brothers' Engines and Their Design* (Washington, D.C.: Smithsonian Institution Press, 1971); Harvey Lippincott, "Propulsion Systems of the Wright Brothers," in Wolko, ed., *The Wright Flyer*, pp. 79–95; McFarland, ed., *Papers*, p. 298, note 8; McFarland, ed., "Aeroplanes and Motors," Appendix 5, *Papers*, pp. 1210–14; Taylor, "My Story of the Wright Brothers," pp. 27, 68–70; O. Wright to George A. Spratt,

7 June 1903, *Papers*, pp. 310–15; O. Wright to George A. Spratt, 28 June 1903, quoted in *Papers*, p. 307, note 2.

17. Milton Wright's Diary, 3 February 1903, *Papers*, p. 298.

18. Details of development of the propellers and the transmission system are from the following sources: Lippincott, "Propulsion Systems of the Wright Brothers," pp. 79–82; McFarland, ed., "The Wright Propellers," Appendix 3, *Papers*, pp. 594–640; Taylor, "My Story of the Wright Brothers," p. 68; Orville Wright, "How We Made the First Flight," *Flying*, December 1913, pp. 10–11; Orville and Wilbur Wright, "The Wright Brothers' Aeroplane," *Century Magazine*, September 1908, pp. 647–49.

19. Orville and Wilbur Wright, "The Wright Brothers' Aeroplane," p. 648; W. Wright to Octave Chanute, 18 June 1903, *Papers*, pp. 316–18.

20. W. Wright to George A. Spratt, 29 December 1902, pp. 292–93.

21. Orville and Wilbur Wright, "The Wright Brothers' Aeroplane," p. 648.

22. Orville Wright, "How We Made the First Flight," p. 11.

23. Orville and Wilbur Wright, "The Wright Brothers' Aeroplane," p. 647.

24. See Wilbur Wright's Notebook H and J, Orville Wright's Notebook K., Wilbur and Orville Wright's Notebook O, and Orville Wright's notes of 1916–17, McFarland, ed., "The Wright Propellers," p. 594.

25. Orville and Wilbur Wright, "The Wright Brothers' Aeroplane," p. 648.

26. McFarland, ed., "The Wright Propellers," pp. 597–634.

27. O. Wright to George A. Spratt, 7 June 1903, pp. 310–15.

28. Orville Wright, "How We Made the First Flight," p. 11; McFarland, ed., "The Wright Propellers," pp. 634–36.

29. McFarland, ed., "The Wright Propellers," p. 636.

30. The wing ribs on the 1903 Flyer currently have thin metal strips joining the section of the ribs behind the rear spar to the section ahead of the spar. These metal strips have been shown on most of the drawings made of the Flyer since it left the Wrights' possession. Inspection of the ribs during the 1985 restoration of the airplane at the National Air and Space Museum make it all but certain that the strips were added during one of the previous restorations and were *not* part of the original construction. They were most likely added when the Flyer was first repaired and reassembled by Orville in 1916 for its first public exhibition. Since nearly all the ribs were broken at the rear spar after the airplane's last flight in 1903, it appears that it was easier to simply rejoin them with the metal strips rather than to replace the wood. Orville never specifically states that this is what was done. However, based on an examination of the actual airplane, and on the Wrights' description in 1903 of how they made the ribs, this would seem to be the most plausible explanation for the presence of the metal strips. The strips bear no relation to the wing warping, as they are located behind the point where the wing flexes.

31. McFarland, ed., "Aeroplanes and Motors," pp. 1187–89; O. Wright to George A. Spratt, 7 June 1903, pp. 310–15; O. Wright to Milton Wright, 15 October 1903, quoted in *Papers*, p. 363, note 5.

32. O. Wright to George A. Spratt, 7 June 1903, pp. 310–15.
33. George W. Lewis, "Some Modern Methods of Research in the Problems of Flight," *Journal of the Royal Aeronautical Society* (October 1939):771–77.
34. Wilbur Wright's Notebook H, 1903 January, *Papers*, p. 297; W. Wright to Octave Chanute, 4 February 1903, *Papers*, pp. 297–98.
35. O. Wright to George A. Spratt, 7 June 1903, pp. 310–15.
36. Wolko, "Structural Design of the Wright Flyer," pp. 104–5.
37. Harry Combs, *Kill Devil Hill: Discovering the Secret of the Wright Brothers* (Englewood, Colo.: TernStyle Press, 1979), p. 213; and from inspection of the Flyer in the National Air and Space Museum, Smithsonian Institution, Washington, D.C.
38. The best and most detailed are Combs, *Kill Devil Hill*; Crouch, *The Bishop's Boys*; Howard, *Wilbur and Orville*; and Kelly, *The Wright Brothers*.
39. O. Wright to Katharine Wright, 26 September 1903, *Papers*, pp. 356–57; W. Wright to Katharine Wright, 18 October 1903, *Papers*, pp. 365–67.
40. W. Wright to Katharine Wright, 18 October 1903, pp. 366–67.
41. Ibid.
42. O. Wright to Charles E. Taylor, 20 October 1903. *Papers*, pp. 369–70.
43. Orville Wright's Diary D, 18–19 November 1903, *Papers*, p. 383.
44. O. Wright to Milton and Katharine Wright, 15 November 1903, *Papers*, pp. 380–82.
45. Orville Wright's Diary D, 15 November 1903, *Papers*, p. 380.
46. O. Wright to Charles E. Taylor, 23 November 1903, pp. 385–87.
47. Ibid.
48. Ibid.
49. Ibid.; W. Wright to George A. Spratt, 2 December 1903, *Papers*, pp. 389–90.
50. O. Wright to Charles E. Taylor, 23 November 1903, pp. 385–87.
51. Milton Wright's Diary, 9 December 1903, p. 391; Orville Wright's Diary D, 28 November and 11 December 1903, *Papers*, pp. 388, 391; W. Wright to George A. Spratt, 2 December 1903, pp. 389–90.
52. Orville Wright's Diary D, 14 December 1903, *Papers*, pp. 391–92; Orville Wright, "How We Made the First Flight"; Orville and Wilbur Wright, "The Wright Brothers' Aeroplane"; W. Wright to Milton and Katharine Wright, 14 December 1903, *Papers*, pp. 392–93; W. Wright to Octave Chanute, 28 December 1903, *Papers*, pp. 401–3.
53. Ibid.
54. O. Wright to Milton Wright, 15 December 1903, in Fred C. Kelly, ed., *Miracle at Kitty Hawk: The Letters of Wilbur and Orville Wright* (New York: Farrar, Straus and Young, 1951), p. 114.
55. The account of the events of December 17 is drawn from Orville Wright's Diary D, 17 December 1903, *Papers*, pp. 394–97; Orville Wright, "How We Made the First Flight"; Orville and Wilbur Wright, "The Wright Brothers' Aer-

oplane"; and W. Wright to Octave Chanute, 28 December 1903, *Papers*, pp. 401–3.

56. William O. Saunders, "Then We Quit Laughing," *Collier's Weekly*, 17 September 1927, p. 24.
57. Orville Wright, "How We Made the First Flight," p. 36.
58. O. Wright to Milton Wright, 17 December 1903, *Papers*, p. 397 and plate 71.

Chapter 10

1. Statement by the Wright brothers to the Associated Press, 5 January 1904, in Marvin W. McFarland, ed., *The Papers of Wilbur and Orville Wright* (New York: McGraw-Hill, 1953), pp. 409–11.
2. F. E. C. Culick and Henry R. Jex, "Aerodynamics, Stability, and Control of the 1903 Wright Flyer," in Howard S. Wolko, ed., *The Wright Flyer: An Engineering Perspective* (Washington, D.C.: Smithsonian Institution Press, 1987), pp. 19–43; Frederick J. Hooven, "Longitudinal Dynamics of the Wright Brothers' Early Flyers: A Study in Computer Simulation of Flight," in Wolko, ed., *The Wright Flyer*, pp. 45–77.
3. Arthur G. Renstrom, *Wilbur and Orville Wright: A Chronology Commemorating the Hundredth Anniversary of the Birth of Orville Wright, August 19, 1871* (Washington, D.C.: Library of Congress, 1975), pp. 143, 149–50; Wilbur Wright's Diary E, 15–20 September 1904, *Papers*, pp. 454–55, 456; Wilbur Wright's Diary F, 5 October 1905, *Papers*, p. 514.

Bibliography

Manuscripts

The majority of primary materials relating to Wilbur and Orville Wright are held in two repositories: the Manuscript Division of the Library of Congress, Washington, D.C.; and the Wright State University Archives, Dayton, Ohio. Most of the correspondence, notebooks, and diaries focusing on the invention of the airplane are in the Library of Congress. The Wright State collection is made up largely of material concerning family history and legal documents pertaining to the patenting and sale of the airplane. For a directory to this collection, see Patrick A. Nolan and John Zamonski, *The Wright Brothers Collection: A Guide to the Technical, Business and Legal, Genealogical, Photographic, and Other Archives at Wright State University* (New York: Garland, 1977).

The core of the material in the Library of Congress collection has been published in Fred C. Kelly, ed., *Miracle at Kitty Hawk: The Letters of Wilbur and Orville Wright* (New York: Farrar, Straus and Young, 1951); and Marvin W. McFarland, ed., *The Papers of Wilbur and Orville Wright*, 2 vols. (New York: McGraw-Hill, 1953). Citations in the text are largely to these works to afford the reader the opportunity to take advantage of the extensive explanatory footnotes and commentary in these compilations of the Wrights' personal papers.

The other major manuscript collection used in the preparation of this study is the *Correspondence of Octave Chanute, 1888–1910*. The originals are in the Manuscript Division of the Library of Congress; however, typewritten transcripts are available in the National Air and Space Museum Library, Smithsonian Institution, Washington, D.C., under this title.

Reference Works

Andrews, A. S. *The Andrews, Clapp, Stokes, Wright, Van Cleve Genealogies.* Fort Lauderdale: privately printed, 1984.

Renstrom, Arthur G. *Wilbur and Orville Wright: A Bibliography Commemorating the Hundredth Anniversary of the Birth of Wilbur Wright, April 16, 1867.* Washington, D.C.: Library of Congress, 1968.

————. *Wilbur and Orville Wright: A Chronology Commemorating the Hundredth Anniversary of the Birth of Orville Wright, August 19, 1871.* Washington, D.C.: Library of Congress, 1975.

————. *Wilbur and Orville Wright: Pictorial Materials, a Documentary Guide.* Washington, D.C.: Library of Congress, 1982.

Other Published Sources

Beck, Mabel. "The First Airplane After 1903." *U.S. Air Services*, December 1954, pp. 9–10.

Brewer, Griffith. "The Life and Work of Wilbur Wright," and "Wilbur Wright." *The Aeronautical Journal* 20 (July–September 1916):68–84, 128–35.

Brunsman, August E., and Brunsman, Charlotte K. " Wright & Wright, Printers: The 'Other' Career of Wilbur and Orville." *Printing History* 10, no. 1 (1988): 1–19.

Calvert, Monte A. *The Mechanical Engineer in America, 1830–1910: Professional Cultures in Conflict.* Baltimore: Johns Hopkins University Press, 1967.

Cayley, Elizabeth, and Fairlie, Gerard. *The Life of a Genius.* London: Hodder and Stoughton, 1965.

Chanute, Octave. "Experiments in Flying." *McClure's Magazine*, June 1900, pp. 127–33.

————. "Gliding Experiments." *Journal of the Western Society of Engineers* (November 1897):593–628.

————. *Progress in Flying Machines.* New York, 1894; reprint ed., Long Beach, Calif.: Lorenz & Herweg, 1976.

Combs, Harry. *Kill Devil Hill: Discovering the Secret of the Wright Brothers.* Englewood, Colo.: TernStyle Press, 1979.

Conover, Charlotte Reeve. *The Story of Dayton.* Dayton, Oh.: The Greater Dayton Association, 1917.

Crouch, Tom D. *The Bishop's Boys: A Life of Wilbur and Orville Wright.* New York: W. W. Norton, 1989.

————. "Capable of Flight: The Feud between the Wright Brothers & the Smithsonian." *American Heritage of Invention and Technology* (Spring 1987):-34–46.

————. *A Dream of Wings: Americans and the Airplane, 1875–1905.* New York: W. W. Norton, 1981; reprint ed., Washington, D.C.: Smithsonian Institution Press, 1988.

————. "How the Bicycle Took Wing." *American Heritage of Invention and Technology* (Summer 1986):10–16.

————. "The 1905 Wright Flyer: A Machine of Practical Utility." *Timeline* (August–September 1985):24–37.

Davy, M. J. B. *Henson and Stringfellow: Their Work in Aeronautics.* London: His Majesty's Stationery Office, 1931.

Ferguson, Eugene S. "The Mind's Eye: Nonverbal Thought in Technology." *Science*, 26 August 1977, pp. 827–36.

Fetters, Paul H. *Trials and Triumphs: A History of the Church of the United Brethren in Christ*. Huntington, Ind.: Church of the United Brethren in Christ, Department of Church Services, 1984.

Fisk, Fred C. "The Wright Brothers' Bicycles." *The Wheelmen*, November 1980, pp. 2–15.

Fitzgerald, Catharine, and Young, Rosamond. *Twelve Seconds to the Moon: A Story of the Wright Brothers*. Dayton: The Journal Herald, 1978.

Freudenthal, Elsbeth E. *Flight into History: The Wright Brothers and the Air Age*. Norman, Okla.: University of Oklahoma Press, 1949.

Frost, Robert, "A Trip to Currituck, Elizabeth City, and Kitty Hawk." *North Carolina Folklore* 16 (May 1968):3–9.

Gibbs-Smith, Charles Harvard. *The Aeroplane: An Historical Survey from Its Origins to the End of World War II*. 2nd. ed. London: Her Majesty's Stationery Office, 1970.

———. *Clément Ader: His Flight-Claims and His Place in History*. London: Her Majesty's Stationery Office, 1968.

———. *The Invention of the Aeroplane, 1799–1909*. New York: Taplinger, 1965.

———. *The Rebirth of European Aviation, 1902–1908: A Study of the Wright Brothers' Influence*. London: Her Majesty's Stationery Office, 1974.

———. *Sir George Cayley's Aeronautics, 1796–1855*. London: Her Majesty's Stationery Office, 1962.

Gollin, Alfred. *No Longer an Island: Britain and the Wright Brothers, 1902–1909*. Stanford, Calif.: Stanford University Press, 1984.

Gruber, Howard. *Darwin on Man: A Psychological Study of Scientific Creativity*. New York: E. P. Dutton, 1974.

Hallion, Richard P., ed. *The Wright Brothers: Heirs of Prometheus*. Washington, D.C.: Smithsonian Institution Press, 1978.

Harris, Sherwood. *The First to Fly: Aviation's Pioneer Days*. New York: Simon and Schuster, 1970.

Hart, Clive. *The Dream of Flight: Aeronautics from Classical Times to the Renaissance*. New York: Winchester Press, 1972.

———. *The Prehistory of Flight*. Berkeley and Los Angeles: University of California Press, 1985.

Hart, Ivor B. *The Mechanical Investigations of Leonardo da Vinci*. London: Chapman and Hall, 1925.

Hindle, Brooke. *Emulation and Invention*. New York: New York University Press, 1981.

Hobbs, Leonard S. *The Wright Brothers' Engines and Their Design*. Washington, D.C.: Smithsonian Institution Press, 1971.

Hounshell, David A. *From the American System to Mass Production, 1800–1932*. Baltimore: Johns Hopkins University Press, 1984.

Howard, Fred. *Wilbur and Orville: A Biography of the Wright Brothers.* New York: Knopf, 1987.

Jarrett, Philip. *Another Icarus: Percy Pilcher and the Quest for Flight.* Washington, D.C.: Smithsonian Institution Press, 1987.

Kasson, John F. *Civilizing the Machine: Technology and Republican Values in America, 1776–1900.* New York: Grossman, 1976.

Kelly, Fred C. *The Wright Brothers.* New York: Harcourt Brace, 1943.

Koontz, Paul R., and Roush, Walter Edwin. *The Bishops: Church of the United Brethren in Christ.* 2 vols. Dayton, Oh.: Otterbein Press, 1950.

Langley, Samuel P. *Experiments in Aerodynamics.* Washington, D.C.: Smithsonian Institution, 1891.

———. *Langley Memoir on Mechanical Flight.* Washington, D.C.: Smithsonian Institution, 1911.

Layton, Edwin. "Mirror-Image Twins: The Communities of Science and Technology in 19th-Century America." *Technology and Culture* 12 (October 1971): 562–80.

———. *The Revolt of the Engineers: Social Responsibility and the Engineering Profession.* Cleveland: Case Western Reserve University Press, 1971.

Lilienthal, Otto. *Birdflight as the Basis of Aviation.* A. W. Isenthal, trans. New York: Longmans Green, 1911.

Loening, Grover C. *Our Wings Grow Faster.* New York: Doubleday Doran, 1935.

Maxim, Hiram S. *Artificial and Natural Flight.* London: Whittaker, 1909.

McMahon, John R. *The Wright Brothers: Fathers of Flight.* Boston: Little Brown, 1930.

Means, James, ed. *The Aeronautical Annual.* Boston, 1895–1897.

Means, James Howard. *James Means and the Problem of Manflight.* Washington, D.C.: Smithsonian Institution, 1964.

Miller, Ivonette Wright. *Wright Reminiscences.* Dayton, Oh.: Ivonette Wright Miller, 1978.

Moolman, Valerie. *The Road to Kitty Hawk.* Alexandria, Va.: Time-Life Books, 1980.

Penrose, Harald. *An Ancient Air: A Biography of John Stringfellow of Chard.* Washington, D.C.: Smithsonian Institution Press, 1989.

Pritchard, J. Laurence. *Sir George Cayley: The Inventor of the Aeroplane.* London: Max Parrish, 1961.

Pye, David. *The Nature of Design.* New York: Reinhold, 1964.

Root, Amos I. "Our Homes." *Gleanings in Bee Culture* (1 January, 1905):36–39.

Roseberry, C. R. *Glenn Curtiss: Pioneer of Flight.* Garden City, N.Y.: Doubleday, 1972.

Schwipps, Werner. *Lilienthal: Die Biographie des ersten Fliegers.* München: Aviatic Verlag, 1979.

———. *Lilienthal und die Amerikaner.* München: Deutsches Museum, 1985.

Smith, Robert. *A Social History of the Bicycle.* New York: American Heritage, 1972.

Sullivan, Mark. *Our Times: The United States, 1900–1925.* 5 vols. New York: Scribner's, 1927.

Tate, William. "I Was Host to the Wright Brothers at Kitty Hawk." *U.S. Air Services,* December 1943, pp. 29–30.

———. "With the Wrights at Kitty Hawk." *Aeronautic Review* (December 1928):188–92.

Taylor, Charles E. "My Story of the Wright Brothers." *Collier's Weekly,* 25 December 1948, pp. 27, 68–70.

Voisin, Gabriel. *Men, Women and 10,000 Kites.* London: Putnam, 1963.

Walsh, John Evangelist. *One Day at Kitty Hawk: The Untold Story of the Wright Brothers and the Airplane.* New York: Crowell, 1975.

Wolko, Howard S. *In the Cause of Flight.* Washington, D.C.: Smithsonian Institution Press, 1981.

———, ed. *The Wright Flyer: An Engineering Perspective.* Washington, D.C.: Smithsonian Institution Press, 1987.

Worrel, Rodney K. "The Wright Brothers' Pioneer Patent." *American Bar Association Journal* (October 1979):1512–18.

Wright, Orville. *How We Invented the Airplane.* Fred C. Kelly, ed. New York: David Mackay, 1953.

———. "How We Made the First Flight." *Flying,* December 1913, pp. 10–12, 35–36.

———. "The Wright Brothers' Aeroplane." *Century Magazine,* September 1908, pp. 641–50.

Wright, Wilbur. "Angle of Incidence." *The Aeronautical Journal* (July 1901): 47–49.

———. "Experiments and Observation in Soaring Flight." *Journal of the Western Society of Engineers* (August 1903):400–17.

———. "Octave Chanute's Work in Aviation." *Aeronautics* (January 1911):4.

———. "Some Aeronautical Experiments." *Journal of the Western Society of Engineers* (December 1901):489–510.

———. "What Clément Ader Did." *Aero Club of America Bulletin,* May 1912, pp. 17–19.

———. "What Mouillard Did." *Aero Club of America Bulletin,* April 1912, pp. 2–4.

Index

Ader, Clément, 27–28, 37

Aerial Steam Carriage (1842), 24

Aerodynamics, 19, 47–49, 59, 63–69, 76–80, 100–101, 119–40; bicycle test apparatus and, 121, 123–24, 128; center of pressure in, 63–69, 81, 109–10, 194; lift-to-drag ratio and, 150–52; Wright 1902 glider and, 150–53; Wright 1903 powered airplane and, 187–89

Aeronautical Annual, 44, 55, 58, 78, 117

Aeronautical research and engineers, 16, 20, 25–26

Aeronautical Society of Great Britain, 20

Aspect ratio, 140, 143; forward elevator (canard) of Wright 1902 glider and, 167; Wright 1902 glider performance and, 153–54

Bell, Alexander Graham, xii, 40

Bicycles, 114–15, 140, 158; aeronautics and, 7, 9–10, 50–52, 75, 81, 95–96, 196–98; airfoil test apparatus and, 121–24, 128; industry, 7–9, 40; propulsion and, 196–98; wind tunnel balances and, 128; Wright brothers' involvement with, 7–9, 11, 40–41; Wright brothers' shop, 8–9, 15,

54, 58, 86, 163, 191, 223–24

Birds and bird flight, 21, 33, 59

Browning, John, 126

Canard (forward elevator), 68–74, 81, 104, 106–8, 114, 173, 214–15, 217, 245; advantages of, 71–74; favorable stall characteristics of, 71–73, 106–7; Wright 1900 glider and, 94, 98–100; Wright 1902 glider and, 166–70; Wright 1903 powered airplane and, 200, 209–10, 212–14

Carnegie, Andrew, 141

Carrillon Park, 222

Cayley, Sir George, 21–25, 28–29, 32, 36–37, 46, 55, 76, 78, 119; 1804 glider, 23, 28; *Boy Carrier* glider, 23, 31; *Coachman Carrier* glider, 23, 31; modern conception of airplane and, 22–23; "silver disk," 22–23; whirling arm and, 21–22, 76, 119

Chanute, Octave, 25, 45–50, 52, 55–59, 67, 70, 75, 102, 105–6, 111–14, 120, 134, 141, 156, 158–59, 184, 202, 234–35; clearinghouse of aeronautical information, 42–44; death of, 228; disagreements with Wrights, 185–86, 227–28; dissemination of Wright brothers' ideas to Europe, 185–86, 227; gliders and, 43,

Photo Credits

The authors and publishers wish to thank the following for giving permission to reprint material in their collections.

National Air and Space Museum, Washington, D.C.:

Figures 1 (SI A43268), 2 (SI 86–9864), 3 (SI A4441–B), 5 (SI A43204–B), 7 (SI A45975), 8 (SI A45975–A), 9 (SI A18481–C), 10 (SI A212–A), 11, 12 (SI 73–9000), 13 (SI A18853), 14 (SI A19627), 16 (SI 39013), 17 (SI A627–B), 18 (SI A21147–B), 20 (SI A30907–H2), 27 (SI 84–12140), 29 (SI 84–12143), 31 (SI 73–1859), 33 (SI 10456AC), 34 (SI A41898–E), 35 (SI A2708–G), 36 (SI 41899–B), 38, 39 (SI 41899–C), 40, 41 (SI A41898–D), 43 (SI A4189), 44 (SI A38722), 45 (SI 10461AC), 46 (SI 10457AC), 47 (SI A43395–A), 49 (SI A4943), 50 (SI A38626–F), 51 (SI 38388–A), 52 (SI 85–2519, frame 26a), 53 (SI 84–11865), 54 (SI A38618), 55, 56 (SI 73–859), 57 (SI A38618–A), 58 (SI A26767–B), 59 (SI 73–861), 60 (SI A42710), 61 (SI 84–2385), and 62 (SI A317–B).

Wright State University, Dayton, Ohio:

Figures 4, 28, 30, and 32.

Library of Congress, Washington, D.C.:

Figures 19, 24, 25, 26, and 37.

Smithsonian Institution Press, Washington, D.C.:

Figures 21, 22, 23, 42, and 48.